"When I first laid eyes on what was inside the plain, brown wrapper, I was stunned. I simply had no idea that for more than half my life my name had been on file in Washington as a dangerous radical, a disloyal American, a national security risk, a subversive 'too clever' to be caught holding a membership in the Communist Party."

THE FILE
PENN KIMBALL

The File is the unnerving account of what happened to an ordinary citizen caught in the government's security apparatus. In 1945 Penn Kimball passed the Foreign Service exams and was offered a post in Saigon. Eager for a career in journalism, he asked for a postponement. Yet all along—without his knowledge—he had been under investigation by the FBI. Sparked by a remark that Kimball's prewar job with a liberal tabloid "might indicate his sympathies," a series of inept and mistaken investigations had determined that this Eagle Scout and Rhodes Scholar was a national security risk.

For the next thirty years the file continued its malign growth, fed by the FBI's investigation into the *New York Times* in the '50s and the CIA's mysterious entry into the case in the '60s. Professor Kimball reflects on his actual life in journalism and public affairs—in contrast to the "life" in the file—as he teases apart the puzzles of this dual existence: Who were the informants? What were their motives? What secrets still hide beneath the censor's strokes? The answer to the CIA's use of The File ends the book on a note that should be hilarious—if it were fiction.

The security system first tested on Kimball thirty years ago—and still untouched by due process—is even now gathering names. What happened to Kimball can happen to anybody. It may have happened to you.

Penn Kimball is distinguished as a writer on politics and as an active participant in public affairs. He has held positions on *Time*, *Collier's*, and the *New York Times* and served as executive secretary to Sen. William Benton and as campaign aide to Gov. W. Averell Harriman. Kimball lives in New York City, where he has been a professor at the Columbia Graduate School of Journalism for twenty-five years.

THE FILE

ALSO BY PENN KIMBALL:

Bobby Kennedy and the New Politics
The Disconnected

THE FILE

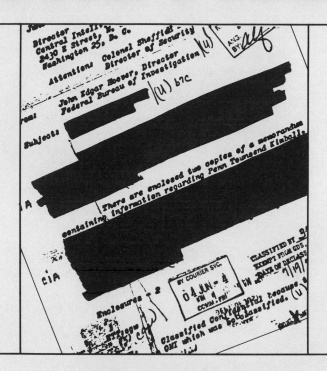

PENN KIMBALL

HARCOURT BRACE JOVANOVICH, PUBLISHERS

San Diego   New York   London

HBJ

Copyright © 1983 by Penn Kimball

Requests for permission to make copies of any
part of the work should be mailed to: Permissions,
Harcourt Brace Jovanovich, Publishers, 757 Third Avenue,
New York, N.Y. 10017.

Library of Congress Cataloging in Publication Data
Kimball, Penn.
The file.
1. Kimball, Penn. 2. Journalists—United States—
Biography. 3. Government information—United States.
I. Title.
PN4874.K54A33   1983   070′.92′4   [B]   83–12574
ISBN 0–15–130952–3

Designed by Kate Nichols
Printed in the United States of America

First edition

For Janet

AUTHOR'S NOTE

OVER THE YEARS when this book was being thought about and finally completed many persons lent a helping hand. My friend, Arthur Zegart, recognized the possibilities at the very outset, suggested the title and projected the enthusiasm which is lifeblood to an author. He led me to Barbara Wasserman, who kindly went over an early draft, gave me professional encouragement and offered valuable writing suggestions. My colleague James R. Boylan likewise gave a tentative manuscript an early read and came up with the basic approach for organizing the extensive material. John F. Cooney contributed valuable research necessary to my understanding of the legal and historical context. My longtime friend and neighbor, William D. Patterson, was instrumental in helping me to find a publisher. And I cannot fail to mention my students, past and present, who never cease to help me appreciate the value of constancy amid the winds of change.

To my editor, Sara Stein, there is no adequate expression of my thanks. She believed in the book that was trying to escape from my original manuscript and deftly helped to shape and discipline it. Her queries and suggestions triggered new ideas and released emotions I had been searching for without realizing it. She is a wonderful example of how a good professional editor can sustain and liberate an author in a mutual undertaking.

To repeat what is obvious in the book itself, my daughter, Lisa Carlson, and my wife, Janet Fraser Kimball, were sources of continual and loving support. Janet, to whom *The File* is dedicated, did not live to share with me the thrill of seeing it all come to final fruition. But she is still everywhere in it, just as she was so much a lasting presence in all of the moments of our years together.

Chilmark, Mass.

CONTENTS

PART ONE

1. A PLAIN BROWN WRAPPER 3
2. A CURIOUS COLLECTION OF COINCIDENCES 16
3. GROWING UP 28
4. THE MAKING OF AN IVY LEAGUE RADICAL 44
5. GRINDING THROUGH THE SECURITY MILL 63
6. THE RED HERRING 79
7. CONFIDENTIALLY SPEAKING 98
8. HOME FROM THE WAR 118
9. THE FINAL WEIGHTS GO ON THE SCALE 135
10. THE CASE IS CLOSED 163

PART TWO

11. TRIAL BY POSTAL SERVICE 191
12. INTERLUDE 218
13. THE LIBERAL COLUMNIST 239
14. THE *TIME* SUPERVISOR 254
15. THE *TIME* RESEARCHER 264
16. THE *TIME* WRITER 274

CONTENTS

17. AFTERMATH 288
18. A VISIT FROM THE COMPANY 314
19. THE PLOT THICKENS 332
20. THE FUTURE IS NOW 339

Index 347

PART ONE

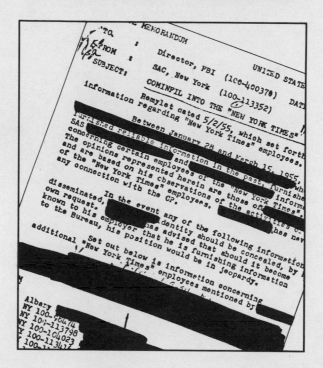

1

A PLAIN BROWN WRAPPER

A FEW WEEKS out of the Marine Corps, in which I had served in the South Pacific during three and one-half years of active duty in World War II, I took and passed the written examination for the United States Foreign Service. It was the autumn of 1945. I had just turned 30. That seemingly laudable accomplishment by a returning veteran turned out to have grave consequences for my future standing as a reputable American. Just how serious I myself did not discover until more than 30 years later when I exercised my rights under the newly passed Freedom of Information and Privacy acts.

My flirtation with a prospective postwar job in the Foreign Service never amounted to much because I chose instead to resume a career as a journalist. It was sufficient, however, for the Office of Security in the State Department to start a file under my name. That file has been maintained and circulated within the government until now, although I was past 60 before I had more than an inkling about its extraordinary contents. Through the years, however, I had this feeling that something the government might have done was affecting my life. I never was quite sure what was going on. I am still trying to get the full answer.

The story of my file comes direct from original materials—minus those parts which the government has refused to release to me after years of appeals and a mountain of correspondence. The information I have been allowed to have, however, speaks for itself. The nub of the story is that the State Department in an official memorandum, classified Secret, declared me in 1946 to be a "dangerous national security risk" of doubtful loyalty to the United States Government and American institutions. That alarming verdict was reached in proceedings *in camera* with specific instructions not to tell me anything about it. Had I known what the charges were or who had made them I might have been able to defend my character and reputation then and there. But the documents that ultimately came into my possession warned that no one was to talk to me personally, nor to let on to me that I was being investigated. In the event that I should make inquiry, the official directive to those government employees handling my case was—lie.

An advantage enjoyed by me in telling this tale is that I have no embarrassing secrets to explain away. I never had any trouble with the law. I rarely sign petitions. I never joined anything that could remotely be classified as subversive. I was never called before any investigating committees nor forced to exercise any rights not to testify. I am not now, or ever was, or ever thought about being a member of the Communist Party. Or the Socialist Party. Or the Veterans of Foreign Wars. Or Americans for Democratic Action. Or the Republican Party. I joined the Democratic Party on my 21st birthday in 1936 and have stayed there.

There is a classical purity to the case against me in my file. It is 100 percent hearsay. The web spun by the United States Government depends on the thinnest of threads, but it might as well be steel wire.

My file also has the advantage of dealing principally with a tidy period of time. The original security investigations all took place during seven months in one year—from March through September, 1946. The entire process by which I was ultimately classified as a national security risk lasted just a little longer, until November of that year. This was because skeptics inside the State Department questioned the evidence. I received security clearance the first time around. Then a second and a third investigation was ordered by the Office of Security to plug up the holes. There still remained plenty of room for doubt, but the process wore the protesters down. The then Assistant Secretary of State, Donald Russell, put his final imprimatur on my case on November 12, 1946. From that day to this, my status as a national security risk has been available to government officials.

The whole file of unsubstantiated allegations has been circulated every time I have applied for a passport or a Fulbright Fellowship or have been considered for a federal post. It cropped up again in June, 1959, when for reasons unknown to me, J. Edgar Hoover himself forwarded copies of the FBI reports in my file to the director of security for the Central Intelligence Agency. I had just been appointed professor at the Graduate School of Journalism at Columbia University, a post I still hold. At Hoover's request, the New York FBI office updated my file, including "information furnished confidentially" by an informant on the staff of *The New York Times*, where I had worked for several years in the early 1950s. The CIA has refused to release Hoover's letter of transmittal, in which everything except my own name and his has been censored, on the ground of national security.

I didn't even find out about the State Department's activities nor the serious nature of the charges against me by the Office of Security nor their effect on my life until February, 1978—31 years and 3 months after Assistant Secretary of State Russell's decision. It was then that I finally obtained my State Department file.

I had read in the newspapers about the passage of new amendments effective in 1975 opening up somewhat the privileges of citizens under the Freedom of Information and Privacy acts. This came about as part of the reaction in Congress toward the Watergate exposures as well as revelations that United States intelligence agencies had themselves engaged in questionable, even illegal, practices.

The idea that a citizen has the right to know what is going on inside his own government is appealing. Even more appealing is the idea that a citizen is entitled to know about government actions involving him personally. A window on such things was opened slightly by Congress, although government agencies have been lobbying intensely since to slam the window shut again.

Having no reason to believe my own file would be all that rewarding, I did nothing at first about trying to exercise the new privileges for citizens to obtain copies of documents indexed under their own name in government files. Then I began to read accounts of the bizarre contents of some of these file drawers. I was finally moved to write to the Secretary of State for my own file while I was spending my summer vacation on Martha's Vineyard in 1977.

Knowing little about such matters, I obtained a couple of pamphlets issued by the American Civil Liberties Union that explained the standard procedures for obtaining information in the government's possession. One dealt with access to the broad fund of information in government records; a second focused on access to personal records on file in federal agencies. The Freedom of Information Act and Privacy Act, as their titles suggest, cover these two categories, but the guidelines and exceptions vary. Some materials withheld under the Privacy Act are available under the FOIA, so it is prudent to invoke both.

One has to apply separately to each agency where there might be information of interest. Furthermore, one agency won't release information in its file obtained from another agency without the latter's permission. Then if one is seeking the full file from which bits and pieces turn up in another agency's records, one has to apply all over again to the source. A movable feast.

I chose to write to the State Department first, because of a strange go-around I had experienced in 1948, two years after my flirtation with a position in the Foreign Service. The incident bobbed up again in my memory when I heard that government files were being opened for inspection. Partly out of curiosity and partly because I was out of a job, I had written to Washington in 1948 to inquire about the status of my eligibility for appointment to the Foreign Service. That inquiry had produced an evasive answer. I tried for more information, but in those days the bureaucracy was not compelled to account to outsiders. Occupied with other problems, and with no burning desire to take up a life of overseas diplomacy, I dropped the matter. At long last, I now had a belated opportunity to satisfy my curiosity.

I soon found out one's rights under the new legislation were not fulfilled easily—nor quickly. I did not receive my first batch of documents through the mail until seven months after requesting them, and then only after extensive prodding. I didn't manage to get everything by any means from my files released by the end of that year, or the next, or the year after that. It takes stamina, I can tell you, to outlast the file-and-forget artists working for the United States Government.

The first batch of stuff arrived in a plain brown wrapper, just as competing forms of pornography. Each set of copies of the original documents, ranging from a single paragraph to 10 single-spaced pages, in the State Department file was numbered—from 1 through 99, in reverse chronological order for some reason. The documents included examination scores, application forms, internal memoranda, committee recommendations, security alerts. There was correspondence with the Federal Bureau of Investigation, Office of Naval Investigative Services and the Central Intelligence Agency, letters addressed to me (sent and not sent), comments by State Department officials working in the Office of the Foreign Service and the Office of Security and for the Assistant Secretary of State for Administration, as well as original reports from special agents sent out into the field, summaries prepared from their findings and official rulings once classified Top Secret, Secret and Confidential. And the log from the file room registering the names and dates when persons from within the government had signed out my papers. Still, not quite the works.

Selected parts of the copies had been blotted out by thick, black strokes. It was no use holding these expurgated portions up to a strong light or putting them under a magnifying glass. In some respects the government can be devilishly efficient. The names and other identifying material for informants—particularly those quoted as saying something negative about me—were thus concealed. Background information from intelligence agencies was blacked out, too, along with the names of others mentioned in a derogatory way. Sometimes several lines in the middles of my copies of the reports from security agents would be eliminated without a clue as to the reason. Or whole pages, as in the memorandum originated by J. Edgar Hoover.

Sometimes the gaps in the documents were white space, as if they had been covered over with another piece of paper before being placed on the copying machines. But black strokes were far more popular, though they must be a tedious way to earn a living.

I was billed at 10 cents a page for every piece of paper copied from my file.

When I laid eyes on what was inside the plain, brown wrapper, I was stunned. I simply had no idea that for more than half my life my name had been on file in Washington as a dangerous radical, a disloyal American, a national security risk, a subversive "too clever" to be caught holding a membership card in the Communist Party.

The reports struck me at first as pathetically inept. I shared the contents of my file for a while as after-dinner entertainment for my friends, particularly those who had rebuked me for my plebeian habit of watching TV sportscasts or for my hawkish views in the early days of the Vietnam War. We all had a good laugh together. Incredible, they said. Funny. Not so funny. Outrageous.

It takes a while to sense the full bouquet of a government security file. The scent grows on the consciousness. It is full of little oddities that escape notice on first reading. One of the insidious consequences is that one keeps going over the pages, over and over, picking up a clue here, a nuance there. The thing becomes an obsession, driving other interests out of the mind. After years, I am still poring over the pages, still writing letters to Washington about the file, still searching for information about confidential informants, reliving my life. Writing a book.

THE DOGGED DETERMINATION of the State Department to protect my country from me was rooted chiefly in charges that as a young newspaperman in the fledgling American Newspaper Guild, CIO, my interests and associations were judged to be insufficiently anti-Communist by the government's selected informants. I had two jobs after leaving university and before joining the Marine Corps right after Pearl Harbor—one in Washington, D.C., with *United States News*, published by conservative columnist David Lawrence; the other in New York with the newspaper *PM*, a feisty, liberal tabloid that boasted its opposition to "people who push other people around." My first postwar job fresh from nearly four years in uniform was with *Time* magazine. As an admirer of Heywood Broun since my college days, I became an active member of the news employees' union founded by Broun on all three of those widely differing publications. I continued membership in the Newspaper Guild until *The New York Times* promoted me to "management" status in 1954, when, under the terms of its Guild contract, I automatically received an honorary withdrawal card. And so matters have stood on that score for nearly 30 years.

As one government informant conceded, during my early years in the Guild I was "too young and unimportant" to be noticed during the union debates on issues which came to be regarded as litmus-paper tests of who might be called a "Red." When I worked for *PM*, I was once seen drinking beer in the company of alleged Communists. ("Both men agreed that it would take a real expert to determine if it was the Communists' beer or the Communistic politics that interested him.") Another informant reported to a government investigator that I had been overheard in the corridors of *Time* to say something favorable about Tito. The very day in 1978 that I received in the mail the part of my file containing that damning piece of intelligence so incriminating to my reputation back in 1946, Tito was wining and dining with Jimmy Carter in the White House.

No one would offer any evidence or accuse me of being a Communist Party member myself. As the chief special agent of the Department of State concluded, according to my file, "the applicant has not followed blindly, as he is too smart to blunder and his effectiveness is much greater than a Communist member because of his winning personality and superior ability." While I blush modestly at the sight of such compliments in the official record, I am not unaware of their purpose: to set me up for the kill.

The disparity between the picture of me sketched out in my government security file and my own firsthand knowledge of what really happened is enormous. There is a familiar parlor game in which a message is whispered from person to person to measure how much the meaning can change from the first person in the chain to the last. A government security check goes through a similar transformation, but the consequences at the end are far less amusing.

The information in the file was gathered by the FBI and special investigators within the State Department's own security arm. The quality of their reporting is so shoddy as to make one fear for the safety of the nation. Their reports consist almost exclusively of hearsay gathered from informants whose identity the government continues to refuse to disclose to me, even though many of them must be dead by now. Some of the scuttlebutt goes back 50 years, to anonymous sources in my old hometown in Connecticut. I was an Eagle Scout there, sang in the church choir and left in my teens to go away to prep school at Lawrenceville. No matter. Some of the FBI stuff assembled from local crackpots is really very funny—except that it hurts to laugh when I read my file now knowing that I am still on the books in Washington as a possible political traitor to my country.

Government investigating agents as a type appear to be persons with limited horizons turned loose on a task that would tax a careful scholar, and the language in their reports often reads more like catechism than a judicious account of all the evidence. The names of these special agents share a certain uniformity—McCorry, Whalen, Heald, McCarthy, Clare. They might have once made up the backfield at Fordham. These young chaps all had a way with words, a talent they exercised mostly through paraphrase, with a direct quote sprinkled in from time to time where it seemed to confirm the investigator's thesis. The documents do not reveal the techniques the investigators used to assemble their interview data; the investigations preceded the era of tape recorders. But some of the language betrays a filter, as when a Washington journalist was reported by the FBI to have described me as a fellow member of "the writing gentry." Not even the correspondent for *The Times* of London would be likely to use such language.

The targets of investigative journalism these days complain that reporters rely too much on negatives which merely document their preconceptions. Perhaps fate meant to prepare me to be a better teacher of more sensitive reporters, for my file is rich in lessons.

The frame of reference for those sent out to investigate me was laid down in advance in terms that fell considerably short of objectivity—"to conduct a more thorough investigation with a view of bringing out information concerning communistic sympathies or any other subversive information that may be found." The result was that their technique relied heavily upon the leading question.

In one document a special agent from the State Department revealed his exasperation after a long interview with a prominent working newsman in Washington. "At the time the undersigned asked [Name blacked out] the following question: 'Would it be proper to say that Kimball, during the period of unrest at *PM* and while he was apparently associated with the radical or Communist element, teetered for a while as far as his political beliefs and loyalties were concerned?' " The source, quite to the contrary, had just told the investigator that "a *PM* employee who did not associate with persons of radical or communistic views would of necessity have had to be a hermit . . . I know Mr. Kimball was inquisitive by nature and I know that his thinking in some instances, especially regarding Labor, was of a liberal type. His natural inquisitiveness and his desire to learn more of the ideologies advanced by the radical group may have led him at times to share the light with them when in reality he was only doing so so as to be able to form his own opinions."

The confidential source then demurred at the special agent's characterization of me as teetering on the brink of subversion, but the source's own words disappear in the file. Enter the paraphrase. "In answer to this question," the special agent noted, "[name blacked out] stated that he believed the undersigned had properly summed up Mr. Kimball's activities, but that in doing so he had leaned a little too far to the Left."

Having tilted his question to improve upon the actual words of the witness, the investigator thereupon substituted his own version of the answer. In the process, the pronoun "he" was left dangling. Who "had leaned a little far to the Left"? Kimball, or the special agent in his capsule account of the interview? A hasty reader of the government file could easily be misled by such language.

The manipulation of meaning was not always so accidental. The bureaucrats in the State Department's Office of Security, applying their talents at the next level of abstraction, summaries prepared for their superiors, usually chose only those parts of the field reports that suited their purpose. A former FBI agent with whom I had grown up in New Britain, Connecticut, was interviewed by an ex-colleague out of the New Haven office, Special Agent Edward Whalen. Whalen reported that the informant "advised that he has known the applicant since childhood. . . . He added that if the applicant is suspected of being communistic, that there was nothing to it as far as is known to the informant. This individual added that in his own opinion the applicant is no more communistic than the informant." Not a word of this clean bill of health from a former FBI agent was included in any of the summaries passed from hand to hand during the long summer of 1946 when the State Department was judging my loyalty.

The names of informants who were critical of me were blacked out in documents released to me and their identity was kept confidential even though the record shows that few explicitly asked for anonymity. The ground rules were understood by all parties. The accusers were guaranteed not to face the risk of being confronted by the accused. The work the investigators put into their task of locating witnesses may not be fully represented in my file. They may have tried and failed to reach some; maybe others they contacted declined to be interviewed. But one thing is clear: Friendly witnesses encountered by investigators specifically under instructions to be on the lookout for communistic sympathies or any other subversive information that could be found were like small fish to be cast back disgustedly into the water. Their names were not censored.

In these cynical times I am pleased to report that the evidence in my file shows that my friends who were interviewed all stood by me, without exception. Friends or even close colleagues, however, were avoided by the investigators. When a source admitted by chance to the interviewer that he or she was a friend of mine, it was immediately noted in the record, as if to discount the charitable view. Their remarks, like those of my boyhood friend from New Britain, were expurgated from summaries of my case prepared by security officials. As noted in their instructions, the government investigators focused exclusively on the negative.

Confidential informants, as a class, turned out to be people who clearly never knew me very well. Their quoted remarks were the comments of those watching from afar. No intimate details, no hard facts, lots of general opinion.

It gives me a queasy feeling, I must confess, to read some of the things persons out of my past were prepared to say about me to the government investigators. Guessing at the identity of one or two, I can recollect instances where they might have been piqued over disagreements which may have transpired between us at the office. The incidents, as I recall, were comparatively trivial, certainly not offenses grave enough to warrant expatriation. Something deeper was driving these accusers. The confidential informants in my file all described themselves as partisans of an "anti-Communist" faction within the New York Guild which, in 1946 at least, was in a voting minority among the broad cross-section of nearly 4,000 working journalists and office support staff who belonged to the Guild locals that had signed contracts with eight daily newspapers, three wire services and two news magazines in the city. Minority status must have added to the vehemence of their views.

What makes their nonsense so scary even today is that most of the informants still being protected by the government were colleagues of mine in the working press. That says something, I'm afraid, about the state of the First Amendment. Even though the government won't officially disclose informants' identities, a trained journalist is able once in a while to reconstruct who might have said what, when and why, and in addition, the bureaucracy is sufficiently inefficient, thank heaven, to fail sometimes to blot out every last mention of a protected source. One or two who have thus escaped anonymity have since prominently proclaimed in the popular press their devotion to the cause of civil liberties. The investigative system that still mocks those liberties was remarkably efficient even way back then.

It strikes me as significant that a Guild pamphlet circulated in *PM*'s city room in Brooklyn in 1941 was in the hands of the FBI in Washington within hours; and that a member of *Time*'s Washington Bureau volunteered in 1946 to make "discreet inquiry" about a fellow *Time* writer on behalf of a government agent, and that a member of the staff of *The New York Times* in 1955 begged the FBI not to disclose to his employers that he was giving the bureau the names of 14 "Communists" on the paper, including the *Times*' Sunday editor, who at the time had served honorably in that post for 32 years. It's all in my file.

I should not have been surprised, I suppose, to learn from my file that these vigilantes worked closely with government investigators sent to the field. These informant/journalists were hampered by no qualms about objectivity. What surprised me the most, however, was their lack of compassion. They betrayed me to the Feds without turning a hair. I had always thought of reporters as sentimentalists at heart. Not these professional anti-Communist folks.

My accusers never seemed to waver from the conviction that their suspicions were inspired by pure patriotism. My file is an allegory of human tendencies that I fear may always be with us. That makes it all the more prudent, perhaps, to sound the alert as we pass through the age of the Moral Majority.

If they could do that to a stout fellow like you, my friends say, we are all at risk. Even though I personally managed to survive the experience to go on as a reporter, editor, teacher and staff assistant to two Governors and a United States Senator, I feel ill served. I did not enjoy the discovery in my 60s that I had been stamped disloyal for most of my life.

Beyond my personal gripe, a principle is at stake. A citizen should be entitled to due process to defend himself against a charge like that. Judging from the official procedures in my case, the human rights of an ordinary citizen dealing with the United States Government were and remain in appalling shape.

By the end of 1982 and now a senior citizen, I had spent better than five years in unsuccessful appeals under the Carter and Reagan administrations to set the record straight. The State Department under the Carter Administration refused to give me the personal hearing I never was granted in the first place. ("The Department has neither the capabilities nor the apparatus, due to the time factor involved in this case, to convene a hearing of this nature and is unable to comply with your request.") It refused to disclose the identity of those who, three decades ago, supplied them with derogatory information about me. ("There is a strong reason to believe these sources would not have provided derogatory information to representatives of the Office of Security without expressed or implied assurance that their identities would be held in confidence. . . . The principle of confidentiality in the context of governmental investigations is a time-honored principle and its application must be possible to assure the free flow of relevant information from the public.")

No fewer than three governmental agencies have denied me full access to the information kept on file under my name. ("The Privacy

Policy and Appeals Board has upheld the Office of Security's decision to continue to withhold information which pertains to other individuals. . . . CIA information continues to be classified and is being withheld pursuant to exemptions. . . . Excisions have been made from FBI documents in order to protect information which is exempt from disclosure.") Under both the Carter and Reagan administrations, the State Department has refused to embargo my file even though no official report in it is less than 20 years old and more than 95 percent of its contents are more than 35 years out of date. The State Department has also refused to correct the record, although I have spelled out to the department the chapter and verse of the errors therein. ("The Office of Security has agreed to include your letters as an integral part of your security file. . . . The inclusion of those letters will inform all file reviewers of your accomplishments, and will serve as a refutation of statements contained in your file.") Not bloody likely. My word alongside the official pronouncements of the United States Government? Who is prepared to read the minds or predict the reactions of the "file reviewers" until the end of time?

The consequences of the file are more or less behind me at age 68, as far as my own life is concerned, though I might be pardoned for wanting to clear my reputation for the benefit of my family. And my case is as nothing compared to those whose careers were wrecked in the madness of the McCarthy era, still four years in the future at the time my file was assembled and my loyalty judged lacking. But the government investigative process goes on. As yet another national administration worries about the infiltration of organizations such as Nuclear Freeze, how much have things changed from the McCarthy era? How will the individual citizen fare if this government should desire to compile a dossier on his activities? What does the future hold—as government officials amass more and more data?

Disturbed by such questions, I decided to write down for others to see the anatomy of my own file. It is a story requiring some patience on the part of the reader. Not a blockbuster. More like water dripping in some dark cave. Funny at times, with a certain black humor. Incredible at times, but you had better believe it.

2

A CURIOUS COLLECTION
OF COINCIDENCES

MY GETTING MIXED UP in this whole loyalty check business was a succession of flukes.

I was serving in July, 1945, as executive officer of a Marine radar outfit in training in South Carolina for the anticipated assault on mainland Japan. I had returned to the States a few months previously after a bout with dengue fever on Guam. My commanding officer called me in to his hut one morning; he was holding a circular from Marine Corps headquarters announcing that special examinations were being scheduled by the United States Foreign Service for military personnel on active duty against the day when the State Department would need to replenish its postwar ranks. In its inimitable way, HQ requested that each command look for at least one "volunteer" to take the exam. That turned out to be me.

Nothing came of it at the time, because the commanding general at Cherry Point, North Carolina, knowing I was about to be shipped out overseas again, disapproved my CO's nomination on the grounds that "the applicant is in a critical specialty and his services cannot be spared in the foreseeable future."

That was that, until the papers reached the Marine Corps director of personnel in Washington on August 6, 1945, the very day that the first atomic bomb was dropped on Hiroshima. Unknown to me until the papers turned up in my file, the Marine Corps speedily overruled the general and ordered that my name be placed on a list designated to take the written examinations to be administered by the College Entrance Examination Board in November.

I was discharged quickly after V-J Day on the basis of a point system under which I was credited for nearly four years of service and four combat stars in the South Pacific. I was out of uniform and looking for a job when the notice finally caught up with me that I had been chosen to take the Foreign Service exams. Although I had not cracked a book on any of the exam subjects since college and the exams were only a few days away, I decided to take a shot. Nothing to lose. How was I to guess the consequences?

After two days of exams in the Federal Building on New York City's Christopher Street—the first examination papers I had seen in over six years (including translations from both French and German), I was not very optimistic about the results. The question seemed to become moot, when *Time* magazine the next month offered me a job as a writer for its National Affairs section at a salary twice the going rate for junior members of the Foreign Service. The unexpected death of my widowed mother, moreover, left me with personal obligations that would have made it difficult to take off abroad again so soon after my long hitch in the service. I had already turned down an offer from my old boss, David Lawrence, to be a foreign correspondent for *U.S. News and World Report*.

I joined the staff of *Time* in January, 1946. I shared an office with Ed Cerf, an old friend who had been on the *Daily Princetonian* with me and who also had just been mustered out of the Marines. That winter, returning veterans like us felt we had it made.

To my astonishment the State Department notified me in March that I had passed the written exams for the Foreign Service and should present myself in Washington in April to take the orals. (Document 79). I thought, what the hell, I might as well finish the course. As far as I was aware, I would go on some kind of Civil Service list for the next few years if accepted, while the Foreign Service was being gradually restaffed to carry on the postwar responsibilities of expanding U.S. power. It might look good on my resume if I should ever seek a post overseas as foreign correspondent for *Time*; or perhaps I might marry a rich wife and be able to afford a hobby like diplomacy.

On April 10, 1946, I found myself in a room in the old ginger-bread State Department Building across the street from the White House, carrying on conversation in French and answering questions I can no longer remember.

(As noted in the official instructions, the Foreign Service Oral Examination was "designed to test such qualities as appearance; manner; diction; readiness; clarity and precision in oral expression; forcefulness; earnestness; effectiveness of personality; initiative; imagination; resourcefulness; and general adaptability for the Foreign Service. The degree of proficiency in any modern foreign language or languages will be taken into consideration in estimating adaptability to the Service." A test for paragons who were expected to exhibit their correct breeding while being looked over.)

I do remember what happened next.

The candidates assembled in an anteroom outside the offices where the oral examiners from the Foreign Service talked over their impressions of us. I was loose; it didn't really mean that much to me. Finally, a gray-haired old gentleman (Dr. Edson, says my file) came out of the chamber, called my name and ushered me through the slatted doors of his high-ceilinged office.

"Congratulations, Mr. Kimball," he said, extending his hand. "We will be sending your name up to the Hill in the near future for appointment as vice consul to Saigon."

I must confess I had barely heard of Saigon and had only the faintest inkling where Indo-China, as Vietnam was then known, lay on the map. Perhaps I should have taken the appointment, but my immediate instinct was to say "whoa!". I hadn't been prepared by any information in the circular to expect such a sudden posting. I had a lot of personal business to clean up. I couldn't leave my job without proper notice. Document 75 records that I was personally informed that I had "successfully passed the examinations." Write a formal letter requesting a postponement, I was advised, receiving a rather dyspeptic look from the senior diplomatic officer.

I rushed back to New York and wrote out same on *Time* stationery. The letter is in my file as Document 73. Though that was the last

I heard of the matter for a long, long time, unbeknownst to me, the cogs of bureaucracy continued to turn, grinding me up into mincemeat.

The file records that when the State Department was informed that I had passed the November written exams for the Foreign Service, that automatically triggered a check of my background and of the five character references I had supplied on my application before being invited to take part in the orals. By the time I wrote the postponement letter the State Department had already checked out my background: boyhood, education, military service, employment (Documents 83 through 90).

In my old hometown of New Britain, Connecticut, Mr. Richard L. White, president, Landers, Frary & Clark, and my father's one-time business associate, stated that "he has known the applicant since he was a small child; that his father was president of the company until his death in 1940, and that he had the pleasure of working with him for over twenty years. He described the Kimball family as a brilliant one, more liberal in their point of view than the average New Englanders, and it is his opinion that they are to be commended for it. [The first part of the sentence is underlined in my file without explanation.] He considers applicant a person of fine character, one who is absolutely loyal, and said he knows of no one he could recommend more strongly for a confidential position with the department."

For the required two references who had to be members of the faculties in institutions in which I had studied, I chose my former housemaster at Lawrenceville and the dean of the college at Princeton, but Special Agent G. V. Hemelt of the State Department's Philadelphia office reported that neither was available. He sent along instead my official transcript from Princeton and spoke to the headmaster at Lawrenceville who had not been there in my time, but allowed he had "heard from others at the school" that "Kimball is considered one of the most distinguished graduates."

Other background gathered officially that winter confirmed that I graduated head boy at Lawrenceville in 1933, 12th in a class of 433 at Princeton in 1937, where also I "was active in football, chairman Daily Princetonian, elected to Phi Beta Kappa, awarded the John G.

Buchanan Prize in Politics and selected a Rhodes Scholar." Police—
no record. Credit agency—no record. Passport division—nothing
derogatory. Committee on Un-American Activities—no record.

The fitness report from my Marine commanding officer rated me
"excellent," adding, "This officer is a man of the highest integrity. He
has an excellent background and has a wide and varied experience.
Since joining this squadron he has shown great initiative in his work
and has amply demonstrated leadership ability in the handling of
officers and men."

My other two references were former bosses of mine on the two
publications I had worked for before the war. My managing editor at
PM, John P. Lewis, was reported to have observed "that applicant
had worked under him for almost two years and, in his opinion, he is
a good worker, conscientious, makes a nice appearance, has poise, a
good personality, and there is no question as to his loyalty." Not a
rave, but you know how managing editors can be about young reporters. The management on *PM* hadn't regarded my character as
questionable. It was the routine interview with my first boss, David
Lawrence of *United States News* in Washington, that raised the red
flag on my file.

My successor as chairman of the *Daily Princetonian*, Frank W.
Rounds Jr., was already working on Lawrence's staff when I came to
Washington after graduating from Oxford in 1939. He introduced
me to Lawrence and, when I got the job, helped me to find an
apartment in the building in which he already lived on New Hampshire Avenue, within walking distance of the office.

David Lawrence had gone to Princeton when Woodrow Wilson
was its president, and Wilson was in the White House when Lawrence arrived in Washington as a cub reporter. The connection had
been invaluable to the young newspaperman, who still called himself
a Wilsonian Democrat years later adrift in the alphabet soup of
Franklin D. Roosevelt's New Deal. He liked young Princetonians
who, like himself, had been college journalists. Rounds and I were
the house tigers on *United States News*, a staid journal of record
which was to switch from newspaper format to a magazine weekly
during our employment there.

Washington in those days was more like a sleepy, Southern
county seat than an international power center. The whole White

House press corps fitted easily into the President's office. We covered what still seemed a small town for all of Lawrence's myriad activities —his own daily column, a weekly newsletter for businessmen, special digests of government regulations and administrative rulings from the burgeoning Washington bureaucracy. Lawrence made a very good living from the system he denounced in his columns by peddling instant reports from congressional hearings and executive regulatory agencies, packaged by his Bureau of National Affairs. The ads in *United States News* came from utilities, railroads and other corporations with whom D. L.—the initials by which Lawrence was known around the office—sympathized in his signed editorials.

Weekly news magazines in those days made their bread and butter from readers too busy to read newspapers or living in provincial communities where coverage of the outside world was poor. *United States News* invented the technique of printing inside dope to look like yellow Western Union telegrams. I was assigned to write a feature called "Washington Whispers," cribbed from reports in the latest edition of the Washington *Star*, and repackaged for the boondocks.

I also covered Capitol Hill under the tutelage of a veteran Alabaman who knew all the committee chairmen by their first names, as well as the brand of bourbon they kept handy for visiting firemen. Frank Rounds and I even went to all the White House press conferences, standing belly up to the desk in the Oval Office where F. D. R. put on his masterful performance taming the Capital Seals, even though I didn't dare ask a question.

It was while working for David Lawrence in Washington in 1939 that I first joined the Guild.

Collective bargaining was in the air of post-Depression America, an idea made legal if not entirely respectable by the Wagner Act of 1935. In Britain and Europe, where I had spent the previous two years, trade unions had long since established a place in the scheme of things, one of the first democratic institutions that Hitler and Mussolini had sought to stamp out. Under the New Deal, the stirrings in the mines, steel mills and auto plants seemed as exciting to us then as other forms of protest that caught the imagination of the young of a subsequent generation.

The leaders of the Washington local of the American Newspaper Guild, CIO, included some of the most highly respected names in the profession; Kenneth Crawford of the United Press was president of the International. A drive was on to sign contracts with the wire service bureaus and the leading dailies in the capital. The men in the back shops—printers, pressmen, plate makers—had long been organized in AFL craft unions. When it came to a crunch, the paychecks of the reporters and editors who created the copy were smaller than the production workers who mechanized their creative effort into paper and ink.

There was no contract of any kind with *United States News*. When Lawrence raised my pay from $25 per week to $27.50, that rated a special audience in his private office for him to bestow his paternal blessing. Although Congress had made the 40-hour week the law of the land in 1938, with time and a half for overtime, Lawrence refused to pay overtime until the Supreme Court would finally rule on the Wages and Hours Act.

United States News was small potatoes among Washington publishing organizations, but offered a challenge to organize from scratch. Merely to take out a union membership while working for a conservative stalwart like David Lawrence was an act of derring-do. Rounds and I signed up for union cards and began to attend the citywide Guild meetings where reporters covering the national labor scene spread the word. One or two others in the shop did the same, but while I was at *United States News*, no one dreamed of confronting D. L. at that stage of our new union's development. Not until I changed jobs and moved to New York did I encounter a situation where my Guild unit could bargain for and win bread-and-butter improvements from my newspaper's management.

When the State Department field checkers called upon David Lawrence, "a reference and a former supervisor of the applicant," he confirmed that I had worked at *United States News* for seven months from October, 1939, to May, 1940—my first job after graduating from Oxford.

Mr. Lawrence also stated that the applicant is a very bright fellow. He has a broad gauge in his views for a fellow of his age and is mentally quite alert. After leaving the United States News the applicant went with the newspaper PM which Mr. Lawrence believes might indicate his sympathies.

David Lawrence's gentle dig at my leaving him for a publication like *PM* was understandable for a person of his conservative bent. (Lawrence once told me that he had put a favorable word about F. D. R. into one of his nationally syndicated columns and immediately was cancelled by 25 clients. He never made that mistake again.)

Mr. Lawrence also stated that the applicant's father was a staid old Connecticut manufacturer and upon his death the applicant could have taken over the business but he preferred not to.

Lawrence had met my father when I invited him down to Washington to go with me to the White House Correspondents dinner. They seemed to get along fine. In D. L.'s world a New England businessman who had sent his son to Princeton was someone he could understand, although I am not sure how my father would have taken the characterization "staid old Connecticut manufacturer." My dad was 58 when the two met, was born in Evanston, Illinois, and voted for F. D. R. in the next election. He composed musical ballads, was an accomplished amateur magician, adored the theater and loved to give parties in our large, Victorian home. So much for the accuracy of quick impressions of government informants.

That I "could have taken over" my father's business was also untrue. Far from owning the business he worked for, my father made his way up from office boy. I never heard him complain about his own lot, but he encouraged my brother and me to stay away from a career in business. My elder brother turned to science, my sister became a theater director and produced her own radio talk show. I took up journalism, but not in preference to taking over my father's business. It was not his to give.

It is the opinion of Mr. Lawrence that the applicant is much more on the "liberal side" than his father could ever have been and his "turning to the left" is probably due to his father's business career.

That little aside about "turning to the left" was to give R. L. Bannerman of the State Department's Office of Controls second thoughts about my clearance. Was that D. L. speaking or a paraphrase by a government agent? It seemed a strange thing for Lawrence to say in view of the final sentence of the field report from the State Department special agent:

> Mr. Lawrence recently offered the applicant a position as foreign correspondent with his organization but the applicant was not keen about accepting it.

If David Lawrence had offered me a job to go overseas for him upon my return from the military, as indeed he did, what was one to make of the old man's comments about my supposed "turning to the left"? We can never know because Mr. Lawrence had departed this world before I ever had a chance to read what he is supposed to have said about me.

The allusion to political ideology didn't escape the State Department Security Office though. In a confidential memo (Document 80) on March 11, 1946, approving my security clearance to the Office of Foreign Service, the chief security officer noted under REMARKS:

> Mr. David Lawrence, a reference and a former supervisor of the applicant, stated that when he left the *United States News* he was employed by the Newspaper *PM*. Mr. Lawrence felt that this might be an indication of the political sympathies of the applicant, and Mr. Lawrence stated that the applicant was much more on the "liberal side" than his father could ever have been.

A neat job of excerpting. Nothing about the "broad gauge in his views for a fellow of his age" or the postwar job offer. That single paragraph of "Remarks" was the sum and substance of anything negative anybody, anywhere, had said about me according to the routine security report passed along to the Office of Foreign Service. But a red flag immediately went onto my file, despite the check mark alongside the word "approved."

There is a certain irony in the fact that my security investigation was triggered by something supposedly thought about me in 1940 by my very first boss, David Lawrence, that most conservative of Princeton gentlemen, and took place while I was toiling for Henry Luce, pillar of the Republican Party, in 1946. What an unlikely pair to harbor me, a threat to the Republic!

The operating arm of the State Department's security and intelligence activities in 1946 was called the Office of Controls—CON as abbreviated on the documents in my file. Pun unintended, I suspect. It was CON which placed the cautionary "Remarks" on my official security clearance of March, 1946, although I was nevertheless cleared to take the oral examinations to complete qualification for the Foreign Service.

CON, on the strength of that lead, and on the very day I passed my orals in April, asked the FBI to check out their files on *PM*. A "blind memorandum," as it is described in my file, came back from the FBI saying they had found my name on a *PM* Newspaper Guild circular in support of members of the United Automobile Workers, CIO, on strike in a West Coast airplane factory six months before Pearl Harbor. "Information available to this office indicates the above-mentioned strike was Communist inspired," wrote Bannerman for the file.

A paragraph of remarks, a blind memorandum, the stuff from which the plots of mystery novels are concocted. The string of coincidences was not over.

On May 23, 1946, my name turned up again on the following internal memorandum within the Federal Bureau of Investigation which I discovered when I wrote away for my file in that agency.

SUBJECT: Penn Townsend Kimball, et al Special inquiry, State Department

You will recall an arrangement whereby the Bureau agreed to check for the State Department applicants for the appointment as foreign service officers. In this regard the State Department advised that although all applications would not be submitted to the Bureau for investigation, that they did desire some specific ones be carefully investigated by the Bureau before appointments were confirmed.

Mr. Roach has received from the State Department a request that the Bureau conduct investigations on seven such applicants, namely on Penn Townsend Kimball, John Quigg Blodgett, Jack Bramson, Joseph John Jova, Edward Barton Bergman, Irving Richard Dickman and Joel Colton. . . .

The State Department is desirous for the Bureau to conduct a more thorough investigation with a view to bringing out information concerning communistic sympathies or any other subversive information that may be found. . . .

Mr. Roach was informed by Mr. Robert Bannerman, Security Officer, State Department, that like requests will be made of the Bureau from time to time, but that the number will never become excessive. You will recall that Mr. Fred Lyon discussed with you the matter of handling such cases as expeditiously as possible, therefore it is suggested that these requests be routed to the Internal Security Section so that investigation may be started immediately.

Four years ahead of Joe McCarthy, State Department Chief Security Officer Bannerman was making special arrangements with the FBI to protect his rear. The seven names sent over by Bannerman to the FBI were not in alphabetical order and I assume I came first by chronological order. Investigation Number One. (Of those on that list, Joseph John Jova, former employee of the United Fruit Company, made it through and on to the rank of Ambassador in Honduras, according to *Who's Who*. Another, John Quigg Blodgett, made it to Saigon eventually as a "pacification planner." Joel Colton, like me, never made it to the Foreign Service. He became director for the humanities at the Rockefeller Foundation and chairman of the History Department at Duke University where I reached him by phone one day. He told me that he had decided to finish his PhD instead of joining the Foreign Service. He had never had the slightest inkling of being investigated by the FBI those many years ago. I don't know what happened to the others on Mr. Bannerman's list.)

A lot worse things happened to more prominent targets than I before the cycle just aborning completed its havoc. One significance of my case, beyond my own indignation, is that the record shows mine was a pilot case for initiating a whole new system of loyalty checks by the administration of Harry S. Truman.

While all this was going on, I continued about my business as a *Time* National Affairs writer back in New York City. For all I knew, my application for the Foreign Service had been approved and marked "hold." Like a guinea pig, I was blissfully unaware that an experiment was taking place, or of my own eventual fate.

3

GROWING UP

WORKING MY WAY through the documents in my file was a little like reading my own obituary, an obituary prepared by my worst enemies. The investigation peeled away each stage of my life like an onion—childhood, first job, *PM*, the war, *Time* magazine. Except that the Penn Kimball that took shape in the documents sent to me from Washington bore little relationship to my own self-image. We all go through that to a certain extent—comparing the self inside our own head to the stranger the world sees. It comes as more of a shock, however, to perceive one's life story as it is filed away in the archives of the security branches of the United States Government.

Although I tried confining my response to an article exposing dangerous antics in the inner recesses of our government, where due process is kept at bay, I was unable to remain impersonal. It is time, I said to myself, to write an autobiography—something to put in the time capsule when the archeologists unearth the bomb craters filled with file cabinets. Something for the grandchildren who might discover to their shame they were descended from a government-graded traitor. Well, something at least for my own hurt ego.

The request to the FBI from the State Department in 1946 for a special field check of me for any possible subversive sympathies meant that my life history up to age 30 was now under formal investigation. The FBI ordered its agents to go to New Britain, Connecticut, where I was born and raised; to Lawrenceville and Princeton; to Washington, D.C., where I held my first job, and to New York City, where I had lived and worked just before and just after World War II. To appreciate the full flavor of a security investigation, it helps to know a little bit about the actual person who is reincarnated in the government's files. Let me tell you a little about my childhood, so that you can compare for yourself my formative years against the version brought back to the State Department by J. Edgar Hoover's G-men.

New Britain was a Connecticut manufacturing city with a population of about 50,000 in 1915 when I was born there. Situated about 10 miles southwest of the capital of Hartford, there seemed no geographical explanation for its existence. It contained no natural resources, was off the main rail route and the original Yankees had built their homes in a swamp. They were, however, smart traders. By the time I came along, New Britain modestly described itself as "The Hardware City of the World."

My father, Arthur, was president of Landers, Frary & Clark, a cutlery firm that he helped to convert to the new products of the age of electricity—stoves, coffeepots, toasters and similar appliances. He had gone to work for the company as an office boy in its Chicago office when he was 16. One of six children, he went to work to help support the family instead of going to high school. Working his way up as a salesman in Iowa, Kansas and the territory west of the Mississippi, he was eventually promoted to the home office in New Britain.

He was an outsider in a community where most of the manufacturing concerns had been handed down from father to son, and practically the only top executive in town who had not graduated from Yale. He used to take me to the Yale Bowl every Saturday, where we would sit on the visitor's side and root for that team whoever it was. Yale football was riding high in those years, so that probably accounts for my sympathy for the underdog which got me into so much trouble at the State Department.

I was named after my grandfather—Penn Townsend Kimball— who came from Salem, Massachusetts, and, according to family legend, moved west to avoid the draft during the Civil War. His name had been handed down from an old Salem clipper captain in the China trade whose portrait used to hang in Salem's Peabody Museum before it was moved to the basement to make way for a relative of one of the trustees. A Salem relative of mine was reputedly Rebecca Nourse, who was hanged as a witch. So you can see it runs in the family.

My mother had gone to normal school—that day's version of a teachers' college—in Chicago, where she met my father at a church social. When it came time to celebrate their wedding anniversary each June, there seemed to be some private banter going on between them beyond the ken of the children. After my father died, my mother confessed that they had secretly eloped and then gone through the church ceremony later which became their official wedding anniversary. The real anniversary they always celebrated on the sly.

I was the youngest of their three children. I can remember my mother bundling me into the family car one day during my adolescence and taking me for a drive around the reservoir to explain to me "the facts of life." She described me as her "little surprise," ten years younger than my brother and six years younger than my sister, both of whom had been born in Chicago. She said she had never regretted the surprise for an instant, which a psychiatrist might say helped my sense of security.

I grew up nonetheless with no other small children at home, and Lexington Street, where I was born, was known as "President's Row," inhabited by the elder statesmen of the Hardware City of the World.

Our two Swedish maids lived on the third floor of our rambling house overlooking Walnut Hill Park. My mother shocked the neighbors by paying the maids slightly over scale, giving them Thursday as well as Sunday afternoon off (we never ate a formal Sunday midday meal) and letting them entertain the other help on the street in our kitchen. The wife of the bank president who lived next door paid my mother a call to explain that such were not the traditions of Lexington Street. My mother dished out lady fingers and lemonade, but paid no attention.

My mother's educational ideas were permissive, years ahead of the vogue and reinforced no doubt by my arrival after the initial energies of parenthood had been expended. I roamed on a loose rein, a fact noted with horror by an FBI informant canvassing my past long after I left town and my parents were no longer living.

My recollection of my boyhood is that I had a wonderful time. "Petey" Kimball (my initials were P. T. and "Penn" is that sort of first name which can produce a black eye in a school playground) became such a legend that every small-boy anecdote which ever came up was usually attributed to me. I had a charge account at Dickenson's Drug Store on Main Street and treated any kid I met to free ice cream sodas. I went to the wading pool in Walnut Hill Park, which was true, and took off all my clothes, which was not true.

I bought papers at the pressroom of the *Herald*, peddled them on downtown streets and was beat up a few times for encroaching on the territory of kids who really needed the income. That was true, and it was also true that my indulgent father would buy up any papers I had left over. He liked the idea of my getting the hang of having to do something for a living, but wanted to spare me the hardships of his own boyhood.

I would go to fires in my little red wagon, hang around the coal stokers at the Russell and Erwin boiler room (my uncle ran the business) and take the trolley to Hartford, 10 miles away. New Britain was small-townish enough and my family prominent enough so that all the cops knew who I was and would bring me home if they found me wandering around at dusk.

My father loved to entertain and I grew up hanging from the bannister on the upstairs landing watching the costume parties—"A Night in Paris" or "Gypsy Cabaret"—going on below. For the latter, my father imported a pair of Hungarian zimbalon players he had heard at the Palm Court of the Biltmore Hotel on a trip to New York. Prohibition was the law of the land, and the bootlegger would come to the back door after dark to deliver bathtub gin or the real stuff "right off the boat." The roaring Twenties.

I seem to remember beaded dresses hanging with fringe, boyish bobs, cigarette holders and ukeleles. My brother and sister would bring their friends home from college and boarding school for foot-ball and Thanksgiving weekends; the young and adult would join their parties together, at least for part of the evening, and I would dart in and out among the dancers, sliding on the waxed floors, balancing my arms like an ice skater.

It is true, as an FBI informant later reported, that I might have impishly drained the remnants of a cocktail. The fact is that I seemed to become more Puritan as I grew older, refusing drinks in speak-easies and lecturing my parents on the carryings-on of their friends. (I never saw my father or mother lose control of their faculties, but I saw their guests sometimes using our front verandah as a refuge of last resort.) Once I picked up a pack of cigarettes in the front living room and lit one up to see what my parents would do. They let me carry on until I turned green and darted for the verandah myself. That cured me for years of the temptation to smoke.

The New England natives were shocked by my parents' child-rearing methods. I went to the public schools while many of their children were sent to a private country-day academy, Mrs. Hale's. The children of immigrant factory workers and of the handful of black families in town went to the public schools; at Mrs. Hale's the lines of caste were preserved. My neighborhood elementary school was used for training teachers from the nearby normal school, and the quality of education had been good enough for my brother to make Phi Beta Kappa in his junior year at Princeton. I learned something from going to school with a cross-section of local society in which I enjoyed a privileged place. That probably had a lot to do with developing my ideas about democracy.

Many of my classmates were smart kids who would never make it to college because their parents couldn't afford to send them. Like my own dad. Many of my classmates who came from across the tracks had better manners than I did. But their clothes were some-times threadbare and they couldn't afford the ice cream sodas I was allowed to charge at Dickenson's. When I stood drinks for the crowd, the soda jerk behind the counter arched an eyebrow. My parents would pay the bill and never mention that things should be otherwise. Nor did any of my schoolmates play this rich kid for a sucker and exploit their opportunity. Thus were the seeds sown of a bleeding-heart liberal.

Another reason for my presence in public school was the fact that my mother was a member of the school board. When women were granted the vote, the Republican party nominated her to run for the post. Besides being a former schoolteacher herself, she had three children to educate and had been an active community worker during the flu epidemic that swept the city during the First World War. Since my father never learned to drive, my mother was the family chauffeur, and with live-in servants at home she had both the mobility and time to involve herself in civic duties. I crawled on the living room floor when the organizing meetings for the League of Women Voters were taking place in our house. My mother was the first woman to be elected to public office in Connecticut, and she took her responsibilities seriously.

I recall that during the pit of the Depression my father was on the committee of local manufacturers trying to keep the city solvent. My mother would come home to dinner on Fridays from school board meetings. The city fathers were planning to cut teachers' salaries. My mother would have none of it. I would sit at the middle of the dinner table listening to the arguments flying back and forth. It was not exactly parliamentary debate; my mother claimed a streak of Irish in her blood and the temper to prove it. My father was of pure English stock; he possessed the stubbornness of a bulldog. I learned something at that table about involvement in public problems and passionate convictions. I was not part of the dialogue; it was more like a good seat in the grandstand.

My mother and father were nominal Republicans, but my mother boasted she voted for Norman Thomas for President. She had been a delegate to the 1920 national Republican convention that nominated Warren G. Harding after the GOP leadership had settled on him in a smoke-filled room. She came home disgusted with party politics. My father had served on a committee with Wendell Willkie to draw up a National Recovery Act code for the electrical industry during one of F. D. R.'s early experiments with business self-regulation. He reported that Willkie was just a frontman for the Southern power companies that preferred high rates to expanding markets for new products such as the electric percolators and toasters manufactured by the company which employed my father. In 1940, without telling his directors, my father voted for F. D. R. over Willkie. My similar position in that same election triggered one of the documents in my file.

The country-club set in New Britain regarded Roosevelt as nothing short of a Communist, not to mention a traitor to his class. My father liked to call himself a "mugwump" and was always good-natured about my politics. My father's eldest brother, on the other hand, never voted anything except the straight Republican ticket. Uncle George was such a party stalwart that he wouldn't have the local paper in the house because the original owner had been a Democrat. My brother, when a chemistry professor at Columbia, signed petitions backing Eisenhower against Stevenson. My sister never registered with any political party.

I am sure many of my parents' friends regarded me as a spoiled brat. I prefer to believe that my free-wheeling boyhood nurtured a spirit of independence. My parents trusted me and I trusted them. Once I went out on Halloween night with a bunch of neighborhood children and tossed a load of rotting tomatoes onto a freshly painted porch. Being somewhat slow of foot, I was the one who was caught by the irate houseowner, an executive at the Stanley Works. He sat me down in his kitchen and bullied me to deliver the names of my accomplices. When I refused, he sent me home with a warning that I would be hearing from the police. Still in tears, I climbed into bed with my parents and confessed all.

When the hardware executive phoned in the morning, I could hear my mother ream him out for threatening young children. She volunteered to pay the cost of repainting the porch, warned him never to call again and hung up. I felt both guilty and proud, but most of all, backed up at home.

Dad was on the road a lot for Landers, Frary & Clark. My mother more than once mentioned the fact that he had been out of town when all three of his children were born. He used to groan about his forthcoming itinerary as "nine nights on the sleeper," but he always returned with a present for the little boy waiting for the huge steam locomotive to come around the bend at the Berlin station.

Despite his lack of formal education, he was a talented man. He composed music in his spare time, and he and my mother had season tickets for the opera in New York City. Whenever a concert artist or famous actor played New Britain—and in those days live entertainment traveled a national circuit—there would be a party for them on Lexington Street. My father would write skits for the annual cabaret at the Shuttle Meadow Country Club and the whole family would play in them. The song-and-dance rehearsals for those shows took place in our living room where we had a huge Steinway grand.

As a young man in Chicago, my father had been in the balcony of the Iroquois Theatre with my grandmother on December 30, 1903, the afternoon of the tragic fire in which 600 persons lost their lives. Whenever we traveled, he always carefully checked for the exits in our hotel. We traveled a lot. Once, when I was about 10, my father gathered the family together and I remember him saying with mock seriousness: "I don't know how much money I will be able to leave you all when I'm gone, but we have a chance to go on a Mediterranean cruise together. Now let's take a vote. Would you rather have an inheritance or go on the cruise?" We all voted for the cruise, and off we went to Gibralter, Algiers, Constantinople, Jerusalem and Cairo.

I climbed the Great Pyramid at Giza in the company of a dragoman who carved my initials on the top. He told my father about it when we descended, hoping for a handsome tip. My father, quite to the contrary, was fit to be tied.

The year my brother graduated from college he took me across the country in a Studebaker roadster, camping out in a pup tent under the stars. I was 13 and my brother taught me to drive on the long, lonely roads crossing the plain in Dakota. We sold the car, and came home on a boat through the Panama Canal. Another year he took me with him on a hiking tour through Switzerland, where we climbed together over the glacier to the top of the Jungfrau. He used to take me to the end of the line on the New York City subway and then see if I could find my way back to the hotel without any help. I suppose he was interested in developing my self-sufficiency, a valuable character trait for the future.

What became of the flavor of all this in the FBI sweep of my old hometown? How much of the real me made it into my file?

THE FBI IN ITS TIME has investigated thousands, perhaps hundreds of thousands of Americans. While J. Edgar Hoover was still alive, the FBI enjoyed a carefully cultivated image of the coolly efficient G-man, uncovering all in peace and war. The image was weakened in recent years when the FBI failed to find Patty Hearst or Jimmy Hoffa's killer. And it was tarnished by revelations that FBI agents posing as Klansmen were involved in the shooting of a civil rights worker and had made a mockery of civil rights with their wiretaps and break-ins. But in civil investigations, at least, the FBI was thought to be like a vacuum cleaner, sweeping up information wherever it was to be found, even though the bureau claimed to take no responsibility for evaluating its reports. Just the facts, Ma'am.

When I obtained my own FBI file I was amazed at the incompetence of its investigations.

At the behest of CON, an FBI agent out of its New Haven office went to New Britain to gumshoe around. The teletype instructions from the director to the branch office in New Haven reiterated the marching orders:

> It is not the intention of the Bureau to repeat the investigation conducted by the State Department; instead it is to supplement that investigation and leads are being sent out for that purpose. The State Department has requested that the investigation proceed along lines to develop particularly any Communist activity or affiliations, together with any subversive activity on the part of this individual.

I had left my hometown at 15 to go away to boarding school. Except for occasional visits to my family, I hadn't seen much of New Britain and it not much of me since boyhood. The FBI was not likely to find too much firsthand information on subversive activity there by me. Still, there were plenty of responsible citizens who could have reported on my boyhood activities, and some who still knew me well during the time of the investigation.

The editor of the local newspaper used to take me fishing. I ate supper at the house of the Congregational minister just down the street when things looked better there than what I figured to get at home that night. Our next door neighbor was head of the savings bank; the father of my best friend was head of the biggest commercial bank. Another local boy who went to college with me came home to practice law and was eventually elected mayor on the Republican ticket. I visited my sister on my days off from *Time*; I saw old friends.

You wouldn't have guessed that any such persons existed from the report of Special Agent Edward R. Whalen of the FBI.

Special Agent Whalen from the New Haven office reported that "the informants of the New Haven Field Division were contacted and were unable to furnish information concerning the applicant." So he was on his own. He checked the Town Hall and found my birth certificate in good order. He checked the police and I had no record there. At New Britain High School, he unearthed a source with some firsthand knowledge of me:

Birth date and attendance at New Britain High School verified. . . . [Name blacked out] recalled that she had the applicant in one of her classes several years ago and recalled that he was a very reliable, fine person. She characterized the applicant as loyal, cooperative and trustworthy and one who had no disciplinary difficulty.

Nothing juicy there. As far as I can tell from any notations in the documents released to me, that was the end of the FBI probe among rank-and-file citizens or local leaders who might have had something positive to offer about my character and reputation. That was the end of talking to sources familiar with my wonderful family and their role in the affairs of the town. As for the idyl of my growing-up years—gone, disappeared, stamped out by the hand of Edward R. Whalen, Special Agent.

The file shows that Whalen settled for four "temporary informants," designated T-1, T-2, T-3 and T-4 in his report from the field. "Temporary symbols are being furnished for the above individuals because of the request in each instance that the identity of the informant be maintained as confidential." From their testimony, my knowledge of events they mentioned and gossip among my sister's circle of friends, I have a pretty good idea who they all were. I believe that T-1 was a former FBI agent, returned home after the war to practice law, and that T-2 was an FBI man on special duty to protect security in the local factories. The two civilian informants, T-3 and T-4 (if my guess as to their identities is correct), were considered by my sister's crowd to be slightly off their rockers.

The information gathered from the field by the FBI was promptly forwarded to Robert L. Bannerman at State, who excerpted those parts he considered pertinent to his summary. My file thus contains the flow chart of my life story as seen through the eyes of Special Agent Whalen's selected sources and then filtered again by the chief of the State Department's Office of Security. Any resemblance to persons living or dead is purely coincidental.

FBI File No. 77-1261, dated June 3, 1946:

T-1, [name blacked out] of New Britain, Connecticut, advised that he had known the applicant since childhood and stated that he is the son of a very wealthy family. . . . The applicant, according to the informant, is highly educated and is very democratic by nature. Informant stated that the applicant expresses liberal ideas and it is the informant's belief that the expression is as much for amusement as for any other reason. He added that if the applicant is suspected of being Communistic, that there was nothing to it as far as is known to the informant. This individual added that in his opinion the applicant is no more Communistic than the informant. He related that he heard the applicant speak on his experience as a Marine Corps correspondent in the Pacific while at the New Britain Club on a recent occasion and there certainly was nothing dangerous or questionable in the applicant's talk on this occasion.

Informant further stated that the applicant was "born with a silver spoon in his mouth" and consequently has exhibited an ultra-democratic nature. He added that the applicant's loyalty to the United States, however, was unquestioned and that he was not a "screw ball" who might become dangerous under influence.

A clean bill of health. But none of it appears in the summaries prepared by Bannerman. Instead the latter's eyes lit on the very last sentence of T-1's interview with his former colleague from the New Haven office of the FBI:

> Informant further stated that if the applicant is or has been a member of the Communist Party, it is a result of his thirst for knowledge.

This last sentence was the one fastened on by Bannerman to the exclusion of everything else when writing his summary. It is hard to tell what T-1, or T-1 as interpreted by Special Agent Whalen, was trying to convey. A hedge? An accusation? A compliment to intellectual curiosity? Or an analysis of a possible defection? The meaning of an FBI report depends on the eye of the beholder.

T-2 reported to Whalen as follows:

> [Name blacked out] advised that in his opinion the applicant is "a rich kid who has always been progressive and for the working people." He stated that the applicant is very superior intellectually and that although he was previously a writer for the newspaper PM, he has entirely broken his connections with that organization. He added that he sees the applicant frequently on the latter's visits to New Britain and that he often checks with the applicant concerning his alleged Leftist tendencies. On these occasions, according to the informant, the applicant laughs and says "After all, I was just a kid at that time." Informant concluded by saying that although the informant is well known to be liberal-minded, he does not in any sense question the applicant's loyalty to the United States.

If my surmise is correct, T-2's parents used to play bridge with my parents. His mother was one of my mother's best friends and his brother dated my sister. I used to see him around playing golf at the country club, and beat him badly once at a dollar a hole; but I never suspected he might have been off his game because he was too distracted checking me out for leftist tendencies. But I couldn't complain about his verdict, which was so uninteresting it received no mention at all in Bannerman's summary for my State Department dossier.

The FBI field reports they went for at State were T-3 and T-4, the confidential informants who volunteered from the citizenry.

T-3 [name blacked out] advised that he had known the applicant for many years and that he was "one of those young fellows who have received too much education and gone Communist or Socialist."

I wondered whether T-3 might not be the old codger, long since departed this troubled world, who wrote me a letter when he heard that as editor of my college paper in 1936 I had written an editorial endorsing Roosevelt for re-election as President. He wondered at that time why I wasn't aware that F. D. R. was a Communist.

Informant stated that both the father and uncle of the applicant were disturbed in past years over the extremely liberal ideas expressed by the applicant. The informant was unable to state exactly what any of the actual ideas or expressions of the applicant may have been and added that it is possible that they could have been uttered merely for the purpose of obtaining a reaction from his relatives.

I will give Special Agent Whalen credit for trying to be fair, and picking up for the second time that I sometimes got a kick out of needling hometown Republicans, including my Uncle George. A dangerous pastime when it came time for a security check. The interview with T-3 ended:

Informant stated that the applicant had worked on the New York newspaper *PM* and has the local reputation in New Britain of being Socialistically inclined. He stated that there is no doubt that the applicant is intelligent and that he had a good war record in the U.S. Marine Corps. The informant stated that he has no knowledge of the applicant's current activities and in fact has no firsthand information concerning the alleged liberalism of the applicant but furnished the above information merely on hearsay evidence.

From this field report on T-3 the State Department gleaned the following, quoted in its entirety from Document 68:

Mr. Kimball has a local reputation in New Britain, Connecticut of being extremely liberal, and inclined toward Socialism. One informant [name blacked out] who has known the subject for many years stated that he was one of these young fellows who have received too much education and gone Communistic or Socialistic.

That brings us to T-4. I am quite certain I recognize him as the person who became notorious in New Britain for reputedly having saved himself from the sinking of the Titanic. He was haunted all his life by the rumor that he had changed into women's clothes in order to be allowed into the lifeboat. His testimony to the FBI rated 20 lines of space in the State Department summation, by far the lion's share of the news from New Britain concerning Penn Townsend Kimball.

T-4 [name blacked out] of New Britain, Connecticut, advised that he has known the applicant's family for years and has been acquainted with the applicant since infancy. . . . This informant stated that the applicant has for several years been possessed of extremely liberal tendencies and that the sister of the applicant also shares some of his feelings, having been educated in them by the applicant to whom she is very close. Informant stated that the applicant was brought up in a family which enjoyed very comfortable circumstances and that very little if any restraint was placed upon any of the children in the family. Informant stated that he has personal knowledge that the applicant was permitted to drink cocktails at a very tender age and likewise conducted himself as he pleased all during childhood and early manhood. . . . The informant was unable to be specific concerning any exact ut-

terances of the applicant but did state that the latter has said
in his presence that the Soviet Union has State Capitalism
and is not a Communist nation today, adding that STALIN has
"sold the Communists down the river." The informant was
unable to state definitely that the applicant has ever openly
advocated Communistic theories or that he has placed himself
in agreement with the economy of the Soviet Union. Informant further related that he is not convinced that the applicant firmly believes all that he puts forth and added that
he possibly enjoys antagonizing people and in starting violent
discussions. He stated that he considers the applicant defiant
if approached in a manner he might consider improper. . . .
The informant considers the applicant to possess a Utopian
idealistic point of view and believes that the "common man
should be taken care of". The informant volunteered the information that he did not believe that the applicant was a
member of the Communist Party, but stated that he might
lean toward the Russian-form of government as being more
in line with the practices that he believes desirable.

The original text of FBI agent Edward R. Whalen's report as
set out above was transformed in the summary of it which appears in a
State Department memorandum, marked SECRET, dated July 12,
1946, Document 68 again.

Another informant stated that applicant has for several years
been possessed of extremely liberal tendencies and that his
sister also shares some of his feelings, having been educated
in them by the applicant. This informant stated he did not
believe the applicant is a member of the Communist Party,
but stated that the applicant might lean toward the Russian
form of Government as being more nearly in line with the
practices he believes desirable. Applicant is reported to have
had a very unrestrained childhood and rearing.

The Secret editing process illustrates how the FBI practice of
writing everything down which was said by its informants lent itself

to the artistry of others. As boiled down by the State Department, T-4 was permitted to say that I was a person of "extremely liberal tendencies" who brainwashed my sister. Although not a member of the Communist Party, I leaned toward the Russian form of Government. What could one expect from one with a very unrestrained childhood and rearing? Gone from the testimony, however, was the crack about drinking cocktails lest it cloud the credibility of the informant. Gone was the FBI agent's observation that the informant was unable to be specific concerning any exact utterances of mine. Gone was my reported criticism of Stalin. Gone was the information from the informant that sometimes I liked to needle those with whom I disagreed; or that he considered me a Utopian idealist with a soft spot for the "common man."

The FBI version of my life and times among those who had known me from infancy in the town of my birth rested principally on the statements made by a single confidential informant. No facts, no for-instances, except that I had brainwashed my sister (who actually did not like political talk at her dinner table and never did register with a political party) and that my mother had raised her children with a minimum of restraint (if she were still alive, she would have skewered Mr. Titanic with a hatpin). There is no mention whatever that two FBI men who had grown up with me had testified unequivocally that there was no question of my loyalty to the United States.

Roger Gleason, the head of the New Haven FBI office who signed my New Britain field check, moved to New Britain after the war to practice law with T-1. He came to be a good friend of mine and his firm acted as my personal lawyer. True to protocol, he never mentioned the investigation and I didn't find out about it until after his death. I forgive him, but, at the risk of being called disloyal, I do not forgive the system set up by the FBI, a system which proved capable of obliterating the truth of, among other things, my own childhood.

4

THE MAKING OF AN
IVY LEAGUE RADICAL

MY COLLEGE YEARS were spent at Princeton and Oxford; the former at least an unlikely spot for a Communist cell. My fellow freshmen at Princeton in 1933 were almost all from families who even in the Depression could afford to send them to Lawrenceville, Hotchkiss, Exeter, Andover, Kent, Choate, Deerfield, Groton, St. Paul's, and other boarding schools along the Eastern Seaboard. The Princeton "type" dressed, thought and behaved conservatively; white tie and tails was *de rigeur* for a prom.

The eating clubs that dominated the social values made life very difficult for "goons" who took too seriously a view of the world outside the Gothic arches and magnolia blossoms of Princeton's rural setting. The college had always been a favorite of Southern gentlemen; there was not a single black and only token Jews. A minimum attendance at Sunday chapel was compulsory and motor cars were forbidden. Freshmen wore black "dinks" on their heads and black ties which could be removed only if the freshman football team beat Yale. Nor were freshmen allowed to set foot on McCosh Walk, the shortest route through the center of the campus, or in Renwicks, the most popular soda shop on Nassau Street. It never occurred to anyone to deviate from the rules.

In such a setting a future journalist didn't have to go very far to earn a reputation for nonconformity. My stint as a college editor was not without youthful protest, but most of it was pretty tame stuff, such as advocating the reform of the selection system for Princeton's eating clubs and the abolition of academic credit for ROTC.

When the *Daily Princetonian* conducted a campus poll during the 1936 election—my senior year—76 percent voted for the Republican candidate, Alf Landon. In the issue announcing the results we ran a front-page editorial endorsing Roosevelt and attached F. D. R. campaign buttons to each copy. That will give you a measure of the thrust of protest at Princeton.

The *Daily Princetonian* made enough money on clothing, movie and cigarette ads to pay its senior board handsome salaries (I made $1,500 for my year as chairman, three times the cost of a full year's tuition). It had a guaranteed circulation, because it was the exclusive source of official notices on class schedules, extracurricular activities and administration regulations. It was the only daily in town, in which could be found the movie listings, sporting events and visiting attractions on campus. And, of course, it covered the news of the tightly knit, isolated college community halfway between New York and Philadelphia.

One went out for the paper during regularly scheduled competitions among freshmen. The freshmen "candidates" would run errands, serve as copyboys, think up story ideas and act as legmen for the sophomores covering their beats. The whole operation was supervised by the undergraduate staff; there were no journalism courses at Princeton and the paper was autonomous from faculty supervision. Upperclassmen held the top policy positions from midyear of their junior year to midyear of their senior year; the theory was that that would leave just enough time to study for final comprehensive exams and get a diploma. Juniors acted as night editors and saw the edition through the local job composing room. Sophomores competed for the spots covering the major athletic teams, the key positions for obtaining a regular byline and future advancement.

But first you had to get on the paper. The freshman candidates would carry around a card on which their superiors would write down points for carrying out chores of varying degrees of difficulty. The points, as I recall, ran into the thousands during a six-week competition and it was difficult to figure out where one stood. The idea was to hang around the office, day and night, volunteer for anything and, if possible, become indispensable to a board member who was generous in calculating the points he wrote down on your card and initialed. The cards would be handed in at the end and the board would meet to pick three or four successful candidates from a field of about a dozen. If you didn't make the paper the first time, you were allowed to try again provided you skipped at least one intervening competition to recover your academic standing. The kicker in the process was that every candidate not only had to amass an impressive quantity of points, but the final decision included a critical assessment of the candidates' "potential."

Potential could mean many things, not excepting whether you were the type who would add to or demean the prestige of the *Daily Princetonian*. In its questionnaire for the graduating class book, seniors always voted chairman of the *Prince* as one of the three undergraduate accomplishments of highest prestige—along with membership in Phi Beta Kappa and winning a "P" in football. Football stars were the only ones sure of being invited to join the best eating clubs (smoothness, family social credentials or important financial connections likewise loomed importantly in the judgment of that peer group). But a place on the *Princetonian* was worth something in the eyes of the college community passing the time before following their fathers into business, banking, Wall Street and the law.

I was a chubby adolescent who wore glasses, got good grades and could claim no social standing sufficient to be invited to coming-out parties in Baltimore, Philadelphia and New York. Perhaps because my "potential" was marginal I did not make it on the first competition. I went back to try again, and doggedly spent so many hours around the office that my card sagged with points. I don't remember any of the stories I wrote, or any other acts of redemption, but this time the board voted me in, in fourth place among four.

The next wave of my *Princetonian* competition was somewhat handicapped by the fact that I was a member of the football squad. This meant long sessions into the late afternoon, several weeks of spring practice and an early return for twice-a-day drills in the fall. It was difficult to hang around the paper as well as keep up with one's studies on such a schedule.

The Princeton football team, coached by H. O. (Fritz) Crisler, who had been recruited from Minnesota and went on to further fame at Michigan, lost only two games my first three years in college and refused an invitation to the Rose Bowl on New Year's Day, 1934, the year Columbia upset Stanford there. We had beaten Columbia, 20–0. I say "we," although I played on the Omelettes, beaten up by the regulars during the week in preparation for each Saturday's opponent. The Omelettes impersonated the plays of the next opponent, ran with the ball for tackling drill and fought off blockers as the Varsity rehearsed its repertoire. There were full-dress scrimmages in midweek under game conditions during which the Omelettes would be thrown into the fray against the athletes competing furiously to make first string. The Omelettes liked to boast that we went toe-to-toe every day with the Princeton team that was beating the best in the East every Saturday.

My passion for football began back in the days when my father and I went to the Yale Bowl and rooted for the visitors. I was heavy enough for the game, but ran to fat and had worn glasses since childhood to beef up the vision in my left eye. In those days football players went both ways, offense and defense. On defense, in the mud, playing in the middle of the line, I was a Rock of Gibralter. Pulling out of the line on offense and running interference for a swift back sweeping the end, well, that was another matter.

I survived the cut on the freshman squad, but never played in a game. I was on the Omelette squad for two years, ate at the training table and, having made the Varsity squad my senior year, suited up for all the games, home and away. The night before Yale, the line coach put his arm around me and said, "Pete, we want you to be ready. We're going to use you tomorrow." When Princeton moved quickly ahead in the first half, I could sense my little-boy dreams about to come true. Things fell apart in the second half and Yale won the game, 26–24. I never left the bench. I went back to the dorm and, age 21, wept.

My career on the *Princetonian*, however, took an unexpected turn when I was elected to the top post of chairman in the middle of my junior year. The full board, editorial and business, seniors, juniors and sophomores, elected the new officers each year.

Distracted by football and mindful of my uncertain start as a freshman candidate, I never thought too seriously about the possibility of making chairman in a full-board election. That turned out to be a tremendous asset when it developed that one of my classmates on the board—whose father and brother before him had held top posts on the paper, who himself was a tall, handsome Texan who had held the coveted post of football editor while I languished on the bench—had been thinking of nothing else. Moreover, he gave the impression that his election was in the bag.

When the full board assembled in Clio Hall for the elections, sure enough the seniors nominated the front-runner for chairman. A minority report recommended Kimball. The Texan and I retired to a pool table in the basement and began a game of billiards while the discussion and voting proceeded upstairs. Neither of us expected to finish a string. As the minutes and finally an hour ticked on, we finished several strings and his game noticeably deteriorated.

When we were finally summoned back upstairs, it was announced that the new chairman was Kimball. I learned later that the margin was one vote after two earlier ties and a recount.

From my point of view that one-vote victory taught me a lesson: there is always a chance for the underdog. And being editor of a college daily unfettered by administrative or faculty control is one of the best ways to learn the true meaning of individual responsibility in the exercise of power. I managed to make Phi Beta Kappa, but my real education at Princeton was acquired while running the paper.

Old grads angry with some editorial indiscretion could write letters to the editor or, as sometimes happened, threaten to eliminate the university from their wills. Censorship, however, had been successfully resisted since the origins of the publication when Woodrow Wilson had been among the first chairmen. We learned through the pain of being allowed to make our own mistakes, an instructional process which left an indelible mark on the character of those lucky enough to experience it. That is not to say our foibles were ignored by the college administration. The system allowed for remonstrations after the fact in hopes that the enlightenment thus acquired from our elders might be the basis of future discretion.

Jawboning at Princeton was carried out by Christian Gauss, dean of the college, whom I later listed as a reference on my application for the Foreign Service. A pleasant, understanding man, Gauss bridged the generation gap with a twinkle in his eye. A summons to his venerable office in historic Nassau Hall meant a lecture more in sorrow than in anger as he patiently suggested the error of our ways. The only time Gauss lost his temper with me I received a note of apology the very next morning saying he never let the sun set on his wrath. Heady stuff for a young lord of the press.

The cause of his distress was an editorial I had written after only 10 days in office as the self-conscious new chairman of the *Princetonian*. The topic was football, which suggests the state of mind of this future national security risk. Football in the 1930s was strictly a college game; professional teams were still in the sandlot stage, and home television was a blessing of the future. Going to a Saturday afternoon college game was the thing to do, for subway alumni who adopted favorites playing at Yankee Stadium, the Polo Grounds and nearby stadiums, as well as old grads. Newspapers brought out extras with the latest scores. Hotels in Boston, New York and Philadelphia held gala dances on the weekend of a big game. For the Yale–Princeton game in the Fall of 1936 the Pennsylvania Railroad ran 33 specials from New Haven, New York, Philadelphia, Washington and Chicago to help carry the crowds to Palmer Stadium.

Rivalries were so intense that Harvard and Princeton severed football relations from the mid-20s to the mid-30s after charges that Princeton linemen had been gouging their losing Cambridge opponents with signet rings. The cover of the Harvard *Lampoon* published just before the break had pictured two pigs wallowing in the mud above the caption: "Come, brother, let us root for Princeton!" The presidents of Yale, Harvard and Princeton had tried to head off a rising tide of "overemphasis" as early as 1922 when the so-called Big Three signed an agreement fixing standards of eligibility and posting limits on how early before the opening of school players could be brought back for preseason practice. Alumni recruiting of promising athletes went on unabated, however, and coaches who had graduated from the Old School gave way to big-time names from the newer football factories in the provinces.

To a young idealist who personally was an amateur of the sport the hypocrisy involved in the insistence upon winning teams was distasteful. Upon assuming the chairmanship of the paper I took up the crusade for sensible intercollegiate athletics, and was almost immediately in trouble. The object of my editorial disapproval was Harvard's director of athletics, William J. Bingham, who in his annual report to Harvard President James B. Conant in February, 1936, proposed that the Big Three ban on early season practice before September 15 be lifted, adding an extra week of permissible football drill before the beginning of classes. The reason given by Bingham for this deviation from de-emphasis was to improve the squad's physical conditioning and thus to cut down on the number of early-season injuries. But the extra time was even more valuable for picking the most promising players and polishing plays. As a newly anointed editor in search of a cause I minced no words:

> Out of Cambridge over the signature of William J. Bingham, Harvard's athletic director, comes a report reaching a new high in equivocation, contradiction and complete surrender to one of the basic principles of "big time" football. . . . The Bingham plan smacks too much of summer training camps and other devices employed by "big time" football squads in the annual campaign for gate receipts under the transparent guise of pseudo-amateurism. Surely it does not require much sincere thought to devise a plan insuring proper physical condition without destroying an ideal which has been a major contribution of the Big Three to intercollegiate sport.

That crack about the sincerity of Harvard's athletic director as much as any other portion of my purple prose earned me my first invitation to the dean's office in Nassau Hall. He reminded me sadly how much energy had been invested in persuading Harvard to return to the Princeton football schedule in 1935 after a lapse of nearly a decade. Questioning the integrity of a Harvard man, he explained, was not up to the standards expected of a Princetonian. He had already received complaints from the academic brass in Cambridge as well as our own alumni.

I shortly received a letter from Henry L. Jones, secretary-treasurer of the Princeton Class of 1908, confirming the dean's arguments and condemning "such an ill-mannered outburst." The letter ended: "Such things are just not done among gentlemen, in or out of college."

It was 1936, the year of my editorial, when Hitler marched into the Rhineland and only a few weeks later when Emperor Haile Selassie fled Ethiopia just ahead of Mussolini's advancing troops; 1936 was also the year of Franco's revolt against Spain's Republican Government. I cannot remember any of these portentous events making the slightest ripple at Princeton. Few undergraduates of that era had ever been abroad by the only means of travel then available —ocean liners. My political science teacher was the author of the definitive biography of Calvin Coolidge. The study of the history of the Great War of 1914–18 was heavily salted with the follies of European leaders and the profits of munitions makers. The Depression was blamed at least in part on the collapse of foreign economies under incompetent regimes. I do remember proving in my departmental graduating thesis in 1937 that it would be physically impossible for a naval engagement ever to take place between the Japanese and American fleets; the work received high honors.

Isolationism is too strong a word to describe the prevailing mood on the Princeton campus in the mid-30s. Skepticism toward the secular world might be more accurate, without the militancy that activated the generation of the '60s. Campus life occupied the center of attention except for party weekends in New York or Philadelphia. During the week, the favorite form of recreation was going to the movies (admission, 35 cents; Errol Flynn starred in "The Charge of the Light Brigade," and the Class of '36 voted Myrna Loy its favorite actress). Princeton was an unlikely locale for ideological fervor or, for that matter, anything else which smacked of political involvement. The editors of the *Princetonian*, having been screened for their "potential," were only slightly removed from the collegiate value system that placed a premium on keeping one's cool.

FBI Special Agent Harry L. McCarthy, assigned out of Newark, New Jersey, ten years later at the request of the State Department to comb my college years for subversive tendencies, couldn't come up with anything at all. Unlike Special Agent Whalen's visit to my old hometown, he established no informant T-3 or T-4 who would blow the whistle, although the FBI routinely blacks out names of all informants in its files. Instead, he made contact with one [name blacked out] who sounded suspiciously like my original reference, Dean Christian Gauss, whom the State Department's investigator had failed to locate the first time around. A second [name blacked out] I could swear was my former housemaster down the road at Lawrenceville whom the State Department had also been unable to find. FBI document 77-2155, dated June 6, 1946:

> [Name blacked out], Princeton University, Princeton, N.J., advises he knew Kimball as editor of Princetonian to be critical of University policy but does not hold this against him as probably some criticism was due the University. Described Kimball as intelligent, capable and a good sound American. States he would have known if Kimball were a Communist while at Princeton University. . . .
>
> [Name blacked out] described him as being very brilliant and very loyal, and stated that an indication of his loyalty was the fact that he was on the Princeton University scrub football team for four years and never earned a letter.

Critical of Princeton's policies, but loyal to the country—no way to have been a Communist in that small society without the dean getting wind of it. All my undergraduate contemporaries, of course, had scattered to the four winds by this time and the professors still around from my time were probably pretty busy with final exams. Still, FBI man McCarthy's investigation was pretty cursory, though he had better luck finding my references than the State Department sleuths on their first go-around.

The investigation illustrated the unevenness of FBI field checks, depending so much on who were chosen to be sought out and whether or not they were easy to find. The FBI's curiosity about higher education took a different turn later in the Senator McCarthy era, and we have only begun to find out the nature and extent of the bureau's infiltration tactics on college campuses all over America during the Vietnam years. But the FBI was too busy chasing bank robbers and bootleggers in the '30s to concern itself with college protesters, and so Special Agent McCarthy somehow overlooked the one episode that might have passed for subversion to a humorless mind.

It had all been on the front pages. The *Princetonian* and the Princeton campus achieved national notoriety in March, 1936, for launching something described by the media as a "youth movement." Its members—how prophetically they knew not—called themselves the Veterans of Future Wars (the initials VFW were borrowed from the veterans' organization formed after our first venture into a foreign war). The movement began innocently enough. Two Princeton seniors went to the movies one evening that March. On the bill was the usual newsreel, the weekly capsule of film clips with commentary which summarized the passing scene for mass audiences before the invention of television. A highlight of the news review from Washington was a celebration of the passage of the Adjusted Service Compensation Act, a bill pushed through Congress over F. D. R.'s veto by the full political force of the veterans' lobby to legalize the payment of a $2 billion bonus to those who had put on a uniform during World War I.

In this deficit age, it may be hard to recapture the impression made on Depression's children by the prospect of the Federal Government shelling out $2 billion at a single clip. To these two young undergraduates the Bonus Bill seemed profligate indeed. Irritated, or slightly cynical in the fashion which flowers near a 21st birthday, they amused themselves over their malts at Viedt's Chocolate Shoppe after the movie by jotting down on a paper napkin their thoughts about a soldier's bonus.

Their doodles opened with a forthright declaration: "War is imminent." The authors of this succinct prophecy were under the impression that they were composing a joke. "Imminent," read against the temper of the times, passed for a preposterous overstatement. In any case, the catchy lead served merely to introduce what was intended to be the cream of the jest:

The Veterans of Future Wars have united to force upon the government and people of the United States the realization that common justice demands that all of us who will be engaged in the coming war deserve, as is customary, an adjusted service compensation, sometimes called a bonus.

We demand that this bonus be $1,000 payable June 1, 1965.

Because it is customary to pay bonuses before they are due, we demand immediate cash payment, plus 6 percent compounded interest for 30 years back from June 1, 1965, to June 1, 1935. All those of military age, that is from 18 to 36, are eligible to receive this bonus.

For the realization of these just demands, we mutually pledge our undivided and supreme efforts.

Soldiers of America, Unite! You have nothing to lose.

The partners in this conspiracy would not have been at home in a candlelit cellar. The one wearing wire-rimmed glasses was a thin, sandy-haired lad with a quiet Alabama drawl. He later taught Shakespeare at the University of Virginia. Although obviously christened to perform historical deeds, Urban Joseph Peters Rushton had occupied himself up to then by writing an occasional column of humor for the *Daily Princetonian*. His roommate and companion came from Louisville, Kentucky, and was also christened to become a future newsmaker, Lewis Jefferson Gorin Jr. The middle name was the decisive factor when the need arose to select a national commander for the VFW. Until that moment, Gorin, who stood 5 feet 6 inches on his toes, had never been a Big Man on Campus.

Succumbing to an impulse, Rushton parted from his roommate and looked in at the office of the *Daily Princetonian* where he found me staring wearily into an uncooperative typewriter and desperate for copy to fill the editorial page. And that is how the fictional existence of the Veterans of Future Wars became the lead editorial in the issue of March 14, 1936.

The circulation of the *Daily Princetonian* was not exactly geared for launching coast-to-coast crusades. I was not aware on that Ides of March that the Future Veterans might serve above and beyond the call of filling an embarrassingly vacant column.

The possibilities of the VFW, however, were not lost upon Robert G. Barnes, a member of the *Princetonian* staff who also worked at space rates for a national wire service (and who later became chief State Department briefing officer for John Foster Dulles).

To give the Veterans of Future Wars some shadow of reality I had written a precede on the editorial page suggesting that the Manifesto—the title was also mine—was the work of a cell already functioning on the campus. When Barnes filed his dispatch over the national wire service, he took a few more liberties. Disregarding the fact that undergraduates had received the pronouncement in the *Princetonian* with customary indifference, Barnes reported that the VFW was far advanced in organization and was already taking Princeton by storm. He needed a name, and I referred him to Rushton, who saw a chance to have some fun at his roommate's expense. Out on the wires went the sly intelligence that Lewis Jefferson Gorin Jr. had been acclaimed national commander by his (imaginary) legions.

Gorin was startled from slumber next morning by a Western Union messenger staggering under the weight of an avalanche of congratulatory telegrams. He awoke a famous man.

Barnes, who recognized a profitable running story when he saw one, immediately acquired the post of VFW director of public relations. He saw to it that the VFW was incorporated under the laws of the State of New Jersey, and that the golden words of the Manifesto were securely copyrighted. Rushton quickly assembled a bona fide executive committee to surround the stunned figure of National Commander Gorin. Ignoring journalistic codes on conflict of interest, I accepted a commission as commander for New England.

Our tongue-in-cheek schemes almost became the victim of a higher order of news priorities. A spring flood in the Ohio Valley temporarily swept the Future Veterans right off the front pages. In the nick of time, the VFW was rescued by adults. James E. Van Zandt, National Commander of the Veterans of Foreign Wars, was asked by a reporter to comment on the namesake organization of young collegians. Van Zandt rose to the occasion: "a bunch of insolent puppies" who deserved to be "ignored and spanked." It was difficult to do both, and Van Zandt chose not to spare the rod. "They're too yellow to go to war," bellowed the rival National Chairman.

That did it.

Once the bonus army had been "denounced" in the headlines by the older generation nothing could stop it. Recruits flocked to march behind the banners of the Veterans of Future Wars on campuses from coast to coast. Catawba and California, Yale and North Dakota State fell in step. The movement spread across the quadrangles of the nation like a raging spring grassfire. Columbia chartered an association of Future War Correspondents. A University of Chicago delegation resolved "to make the world safe for hypocrisy." Within a few weeks, the number of franchises multiplied to a staggering 534. A "March of Time" camera crew descended upon the Princeton campus to record for national release a slightly edited re-enactment of the birth of the national movement. (The film reappears from time to time on early morning television and I can watch myself in my old *Princetonian* office.)

The motives behind these stirrings were as mixed as army chow. To our amazement and amusement, the mail from the Midwest was deadly serious. Iowa held a torchlight parade and burned a military figure in effigy. *Literary Digest* ran an interpretative piece about the VFW as an idealistic revolt against the futility of war. The Veterans of Future Wars was suited perfectly to the contradictions of selective perception.

At Princeton we played it strictly for laughs. Nudged by handouts printed verbatim in the *Daily Princetonian* reporting furious if fictitious activity among future Veterans on the founding campus, an indifferent Princeton student body finally began to live up to its press notices. An overflow rally rocked Alexander Hall with cheers for football end John Paul Jones, another name straight out of central casting. A strapping fellow from steel country, Jones arrived on the platform carrying a live goose under his brawny arm. "Manifest Destiny," he roared, "has laid a golden egg!"

Denounced for disrespect, hailed for impertinence toward the Establishment, the Veterans of Future Wars merely held up a mirror to an America going through the ambivalent twilight between two world wars. *Fortune* magazine waxed ecstatic about "suave, enigmatic" Lewis Jefferson Gorin Jr. An irate Legionnaire encountered by Gorin on the street, however, tried to knock his block off.

The Veterans of Future Wars had traveled a long road from the cozy confines of Viedt's Chocolate Shoppe. A wild stab pricks a sensitive spot and a chain reaction races through the nervous system of a nation. The Veterans of Future Wars touched something unpredictable in adolescent America in 1936. The resultant demonstrations, however motivated, were a forerunner of things to come, no less than the righteous denunciations which were visited upon a subsequent generation. If history has a way of repeating itself, the Veterans of Future Wars marched into history five decades ago to a more lighthearted tune than is heard in these humorless times.

It should be added that the Veterans of Future Wars failed to survive the summer vacation. Gorin and Rushton graduated. The national command scattered to lakeside resorts and vacation jobs. About half the members recruited by Rushton, including the national commander himself, were members of Princeton's Reserve Officer Training Corps for the Field Artillery, a state of affairs which had been glossed over in deference to the antimilitaristic leanings of VFW recruits in the Corn Belt. They spent part of their summer on maneuvers. When the call to arms came, minus a prepaid bonus, the news magazines attached special irony to their discovery that most of the founding contingent of the Veterans of Future Wars indeed ended up in uniform.

When I received Special Agent McCarthy's report, I was puzzled that the whole VFW episode, which reflects both the height of subversion and the degree of its harmlessness among Princeton gentlemen in those days, was not uncovered. Perhaps the oversight is another instance of sloppiness, or maybe the Newark office to which McCarthy reported kept no files of newspaper clips. America was provincial then compared to now; there wasn't even a CIA to watch over me in Europe during my stay there from 1937 to 1939, though I can't say I felt the lack. When the S.S. Statendam cleared the pier from Hoboken, I sailed beyond the jurisdiction of the Newark office of the FBI. As far as the investigators were concerned, I simply disappeared into limbo during these critical years in world politics.

THE TRANSITION FROM Princeton to Oxford at age 21 was greater than merely crossing the Atlantic into foreign lands. It was at Oxford that I first comprehended the meaning of intellectual curiosity and, also, the complexity of truth. By the time I took up my Rhodes Scholarship there, any humor I might have harbored about impending war was bound to be sobered by the conditions in Europe. The choice between war and peace without honor was too close, too real.

The intellectual climate at Oxford in the '30s was a far cry from Princeton. Balliol, where I studied, had the reputation of being the most politically aware of all the Oxford colleges. Balliol men were prominent in the British Establishment: prime ministers, viceroys to India, the Archbishop of Canterbury and editor of *The Times*. A cosmopolitan college, its undergraduates came from all over the Empire—India and Africa as well as Australia and Canada. Attracted by its academic distinction and international reputation, students came to Balliol in my time from China, Japan, the Punjab, Mauritius, Basutoland, Egypt, Greece and Czechoslovakia as well as all the countries of Western Europe, including Hitler's Germany and Mussolini's Italy. Nationalistic shibboleths did not thrive at a place like Balliol. The Junior Common Room, where members of the college gathered for tea and after-dinner coffee, was like the delegates' lounge at the League of Nations, except that the talk was more free and more frank, encompassing the pros and cons of the various isms of our time. Bull sessions continued far into the night before the coal fires which were the only other source of heat.

At Oxford I joined everything—the Oxford Union, the Conservative Club, the Liberal Club, the Labour Club—just to get a seat to listen to the guest speakers. That rather eclectic background might have made me seem a political chameleon to somebody who wanted to make something of it. The truth is I have been one of those down-the-line, New Deal liberals all my life.

The Oxford Union, presided over by officers drawn heavily from Balliol, debated the issues of the day. I was too nervous a public speaker to participate directly in this training school for future members of Parliament, a residue of having forgotten the text of Lincoln's Gettysburg Address on stage in the grade-school auditorium in the midst of Memorial Day exercises. But a young idealist living through the successive crises created by Fascist aggression on the Continent was bound to be deeply concerned about the future. The letters I wrote home from September, 1937, through August, 1939 (saved by my doting parents), were unequivocal expressions of my moralizing commitment to democratic freedoms—even if it meant the risk of war. Sample:

November 11, 1938

Dear Mother and Dad—Armistice Day again in this country where it means so much. Austria and Czechoslovakia have disappeared and as I write this Jews are being beaten, murdered and persecuted in Berlin in one of the greatest pogroms of all time. . . .

I never knew any soldiers who went to the World War, but I think I know what they went for. . . . They saw a moral ideal, a principle of government in their own country threatened by an aggressive, intolerant, illiberal and cruel government which had beaten their own people into a system which they were trying to impose on the world, and were very near succeeding. These men went out to fight, to suffer, to die, because they thought it better to do that than to submit ignobly to a force which threatened the very things that made life worth living. And they won! . . .

We say they died in vain. . . . Are we not perhaps living in vain to throw all that away for an empty peace?

This week the Polish attache at London spoke to us and made some highly complimentary remarks about Hitler in the course of his speech. Talking to him in private later, he admitted that he didn't trust Hitler an inch but just made such statements to give him a few credit marks on his record card in the German Embassy. This is the sort of thing which is necessary at private clubs at universities in England! You can draw your own conclusions as to how things are in the rest of Europe—or America for that matter.

Well I, for one, am not willing to see this sort of thing continue indefinitely and, on this Armistice Day, I feel that there should be others of the same opinion.

Love to all,
Pete

Florid to be sure, but the drift is clear as to where this 23-year-old was coming from. Radical? Subversive? Or a future United States Marine?

Oxford's academic calendar was generous with reading periods which offered ample opportunity for travel while supposedly hitting the books. I did more traveling than formal study. I visited Norway, Sweden, Denmark, Holland, Belgium, Germany, France, Italy, Czechoslovakia, Austria, Hungary and Switzerland as well as the British Isles. I was in Austria during *Anschluss* and in Rome when the Italians invaded Albania, and had just driven through the Sudetenland and Prague at the time of the Munich crisis in the late summer of 1938. My firsthand observations included Hitler and Mussolini in action as well as the last Bastille Day in Paris before the outbreak of war, when Britain and France staged a flyover of their air forces and tanks clanked down the Champs-Elysees.

None of this is in my file.

The gap illustrates the absurdity of the investigative process. What might T-3 and T-4, who had known me as a child, have to offer that was more to the point than classmates and teachers who had known me as I grew to adulthood amid political ferment and outspoken debate? And those who might have been asked the shade of my leanings during those years at Oxford were pretty good competition, I should think, for the anonymous informant who saved himself from the Titanic.

The roster of Rhodes Scholars who shared my years at Oxford and many of whom traveled through Europe with me included Whizzer White, later Mr. Justice Byron R. White; Walt Rostow, later of the White House; broadcast correspondent Howard K. Smith, and James E. King, who spent his entire postwar career with the CIA. John N. Irwin II, my friend and classmate at Lawrenceville and Princeton as well as at Balliol, became an aide to General Douglas MacArthur, served in the Pentagon under President Eisenhower and was appointed Undersecretary of State and Ambassador to France by Richard Nixon.

Of my two best British friends at Balliol one became Queen's counselor and judge, the other managing director of Rolls-Royce. I talked politics in the Balliol Common Room with Edward R. G.

Heath, a future Conservative Party Prime Minister; Roy Jenkins, who became a Labour cabinet member and founder and leader of the Social-Democrat Party, and Denis Healey, a future Chancellor of the Exchequer.

Yet in the same way that anybody who really knew me when I was growing up was excluded from the evidence, my companions who knew me as I was coming to political awareness proved to be of no interest to the FBI sleuths.

The State Department investigators did turn up in Washington one fellow student who had been with me at Balliol, but quickly lost interest when his remarks were favorable. A Foreign Service officer who had known me just before I left for Oxford volunteered to testify in my behalf. He was never called upon. My formative years from 17 to 23, which I think might have been judged crucial to the making of an Ivy League radical, are notable in my files mainly by their absence.

By the summer of 1939, I was in Paris studying French, having been granted permission by the Rhodes trustees to extend my scholarship for a third year at the Ecole Libre des Sciences Politiques, the training school for the French diplomatic service. The entrance examination was in French, and after a summer continuing my studies at the University of Grenoble, I passed and was admitted to read for the diploma in the Diplomatic Section of the Ecole in the term beginning in November, 1939. My scholarship of £400, when converted into French francs under the exchange rates of that day, would be roughly equivalent to the salary of the president of the Bank of France. (The pressed duck with wine at the Tour d'Argent came to roughly $1.50.) I looked forward to a comfortable and exciting year on the Left Bank, though my associates by no stretch of the imagination would be classified as Bohemian.

Alas, it was not to be. The war that the appeasers had been running away from for so long finally intervened, ironically catching me on the wrong side of the Atlantic. I sailed from Le Havre on the *Normandie* in August for a quick visit back home before my third year abroad and to be best man at the September wedding of a close boyhood friend. The *Normandie* weighed anchor on the very day that Stalin and Hitler flabbergasted the world by signing their non-aggression pact. The Germans marched into Poland the week after the ship docked in New York, never to sail again. When Britain declared war on September 1, my scholarship was suspended for the duration, and my visa cancelled. I headed for Washington, looking for work, and found it at *United States News*.

This is where the FBI, having ignored a chunk of my life that was to leave its impression upon my political thinking in all the years to come, picked up the thread of my life.

5

GRINDING THROUGH
THE SECURITY MILL

FBI Special Agent Robert L. Heald, advised that the State Department investigator had already been in touch with David Lawrence of *United States News* during my initial security check in March, didn't bother to go back there. The FBI had its own sources in Washington, D.C.:

> Confidential Informant T-1 advised that in his opinion the applicant is or at least was a "radical" at the time he became a member of the staff of PM. T-1's opinion of a "radical" is a person who has left-wing ideas and who associates with "pinks" and "fellow travelers" and people who make up the subversive element. T-1 further stated that his opinion is based on the fact that applicant took a job with PM Newspaper because he liked its journalistic ideas. T-1 added, however, that Kimball at the time was a young man and just out of college and whose ideas were mostly theoretical. He stated that he may have and probably has changed considerably since that time and that he, T-1, had not seen much of him since then. T-1 concluded by saying, however, that he does not believe that applicant's radical ideas would ever overrule his loyalty or duty to this country.

It seems odd that the FBI should have expended its energy in Washington to gather secondhand opinions on why I had taken a newspaper job in New York. But, as was clear from its investigations of my childhood and college years, the FBI pursued its own devious path.

I think I recognize another anonymous informant who lived in the same apartment house on New Hampshire Avenue and worked for the State Department. Frank Rounds had introduced me to her and we had gone out on a few dates together.

[Name blacked out] stated she remembered the applicant particularly well because she had become rather fond of him and they had many talks together. The applicant lived by himself and at the present there is no one in the apartment house who would know him. [Name blacked out] stated the applicant had an excellent reputation and that he was well liked by the other people in the apartment house. She stated that he had just returned from England and she could remember his saying that he didn't like the English people principally because they didn't like us. She stated that she had never heard him make any remarks that could be considered in any way subversive and that he appeared to be extremely patriotic.

Chief Security Officer Bannerman of State, who had called in the FBI to pin down any derogatory information it could find, managed to boil all the data from Washington into one general observation: "Informants describe Mr. Kimball as a definite liberal or radical, and other informants state that he is a leftist."

The final stop for the FBI after New Britain, Princeton and Washington was New York City, where I had worked for *PM* before the war and was living once again as a new employee of *Time* magazine. The FBI dragnet there swept through the Princeton Club, or rather, fished up one informant. That informant seems more like a manager than a member to me, since he knew exactly the dates I had checked in and out of the club as a resident in 1940 when I had first moved from Washington to New York. On the other hand, I was living there once again in 1946 when the FBI came around and there is no clue to that in the evidence turned up and reported by Special Agent Joseph F. McCorry:

[Name blacked out], Princeton Club, supplied the following information: From June 1 until July 6, 1940, Kimball lived at the club. On the latter date he gave up his residence at the Club, but spent a great deal of time there until he entered the Marine Corps in 1942. When questioned as to the background and character of Kimball, [Name blacked out] described him as a "leftist." When questioned as to just what he meant by that statement, [Name blacked out], who evinced a reluctant attitude, stated he remembered that during the 1940 election campaign between Willkie and Roosevelt, Kimball, who frequented the Club, was overheard to make remarks and comments which indicated to [Name blacked out] that he was a "leftist." [Name blacked out] could not be led into any further remarks or statements along these lines.

McCorry, who failed in the attempt to lead his witness beyond my subversive remarks at the Princeton Club during the Willkie–Roosevelt campaign, didn't reach any of my associates at *PM* either who knew me at the same time. The State Department had during its own investigation dropped by to call on *PM*'s managing editor, who had been one of my references, and he had spoken well of me. Still, there was that matter in the FBI files about my name having appeared on a Newspaper Guild circular during a prewar strike in an aircraft plant in California. When I eventually obtained my full FBI file, I discovered that the FBI had maintained a special file on *PM* going back to memoranda to the staff from Ralph Ingersoll, the founding editor, as of four weeks before publication in May, 1940, plus the list of original personnel, with names, addresses and telephone numbers, mine included, supplied from a "confidential source."

Presumably, McCorry checked out the office files before setting out on the special inquiry requested by State. Nothing there worth following up? One could not accuse this FBI man of excessive initiative. His report, in any event, explored neither my status as a dues-paying member of the newspaper and magazine union nor my reputation as an employee of the paper singled out for special FBI attention. Had there been anything to go on, it seems likely McCorry would have explored further if only to cover himself inside his own agency.

McCorry did visit *Time* magazine, where I had then been working for six months. There he turned up a "Time supervisor" who, though quoted only briefly, became a central figure in the case mustered against me when the FBI report reached the State Department:

> [Line blacked out], Time Inc., was then interviewed. [Name blacked out] advised the writer that he [line blacked out] has only known him since his employment with that magazine. [Name blacked out] stated that Kimball was a very capable writer on foreign affairs, but that he is "very definitely a left winger." When the writer pressed [Name blacked out] to elaborate on the statement, he stated that Kimball is always interested in some sort of social reform and unwaveringly espouses the cause of labor in any dispute regardless of the merits involved in a particular case. [Name blacked out] further elaborated by stating that he would have no qualms at all in assigning Kimball to foreign assignments in some countries, but that he definitely would not trust him in other countries, particularly countries such as France or any other country where there is a growing possibility of Russian dominance.

That was the interview as reported—*in toto*. Note that the whole thing was paraphrased by "the writer" except for the observation that the informant described me as quote very definitely a left winger end quote. And although my full-time occupation at *Time* was in National Affairs, my "supervisor" speaks of me "as a capable writer on foreign affairs."

There was a certain irony in singling out France—where I had been admitted to its diplomatic institute—as a country where I could not be trusted. The "growing possibility of Russian dominance there" in the summer of 1946 is something for historians to argue about, but the cold war was an expression not invented until some years later. *Time* magazine, however, was one of the first to embrace that doctrine, and it is possible that an informant searched out by the FBI would have been out front on that issue.

The interview was exactly what Chief Security Officer Bannerman had been hoping for when he called in the FBI. Reference to it appears over and over in my State Department file. "[Name blacked out] was quoted as having stated that Kimball is 'definitely a left winger', who is 'always vitally interested in some sort of social reform and unwaveringly espouses the cause of labor in any dispute, regardless of the merits of the case' and that he 'definitely would not trust the applicant in any country where there is a growing possibility of Russian dominance.' " Note how McCorry's words in his report are transformed into direct quotes from the source at the hand of Bannerman.

In a memorandum marked SECRET to the Office of Foreign Service (OFS) from R. L. Bannerman, CON, dated July 12, 1946, my security clearance, on the basis of which I had been allowed to take the orals and offered the post of vice consul in Saigon, was officially rescinded. Document 68:

> Reference is made to the case of Penn Townsend Kimball who was born at New Britain, Connecticut, on October 12, 1915, and who has passed the written and oral examinations for the career Foreign Service. His case was originally approved by the Security Committee, but was later submitted to this office by OFS for additional investigation.
>
> The Security Committee originally approved this case on the basis of a CSA [Chief Security Agent, State Department] investigation. It was noted, however, that a reference and former supervisor of the subject stated that after Mr. Kimball left his employment, he accepted a position with the newspaper *PM*. This reference felt that this might be an indication of the political sympathies of the subject.

There follows a few inches of white space on the file copies turned over to me which might be a rehash of the David Lawrence remarks and the blind memorandum from the FBI about the presence of my name on a Guild circular opposing the use of troops during the strike by California aviation production workers, but I can't tell for sure.

The report of the supplementary investigation has now been received, and it contains information of an adverse nature regarding the subject, and leads to the conclusion that his loyalty is questionable.

In view of the above information, which is set forth in more detail in the attached report, the Security Committee has disapproved this case. Mr. Kimball is regarded as a security risk by the Committee because it is of the opinion that his loyalty to the United States is questionable. The Security Committee believes that particular emphasis should be given to the remarks and recommendations of the subject's most recent supervisor, as he has had ample opportunity to observe the subject's attitudes during the past few months.

It is recommended that the subject not be appointed to the career Foreign Service, and it is requested that this office be informed of the action taken in this case.

I was to be informed nothing at all of this. As far as I knew I myself had placed my appointment to the Foreign Service on hold, indefinitely. I had heard nothing to suggest otherwise.

Notified that I had passed my orals and my name would shortly be sent up to the Hill on April 10 (Document 75), I orally expressed my desire for a postponement immediately and was advised to send a written request (Document 76). Accordingly, I wrote a formal request that my appointment "be postponed for some indefinite period within the legal interim of grace" on April 14 (Document 73). On May 7, Selden Chapin, director of the Office of the Foreign Service, wrote to ask for a copy of my birth certificate "to complete the records of the Department." (Document 72.) I complied (Document 71). Only ten days after that seemingly innocuous exchange, the director of the Office of Controls, R. L. Bannerman, was asking the FBI to make a special investigation of me (Document 70).

Within two months my security clearance was revoked (Document 68) after the FBI's visits to New Britain, Princeton, Washington and New York. I was pounding away at my typewriter in the Time–Life Building, without an inkling of my sudden descent from vice consul to Saigon to national security risk.

I innocently wrote a letter on July 26 asking the Board of Examiners of the Foreign Service for official confirmation of the results of my examinations: "It may be that they were sent to me and were misdirected" (Document 65). Scrawled across the bottom of my letter upon its arrival, my file reveals, is a handwritten note: "Hold until August 2, Mr. Russell is considering this case." On August 8, Selden Chapin, the same fellow who had sent for my birth certificate in May, responded to tell me I had received 85 percent on my orals, 77 percent on the written test, for an average grade of 81. "You will be advised shortly regarding your appointment as Foreign Service officer unclassified" (Document 62). I took that to mean confirmation of my request for a place on a list of eligibles for the future. Already the State Department was holding out on me, but I was too preoccupied with my chosen career as a journalist to notice.

The same Mr. Chapin who wrote me the deadpan letter on August 8 had indeed on July 23 forwarded my dossier to Assistant Secretary Russell, along with CON's unfavorable findings. There were two other similar cases in the same batch. Not one, in true Foreign Service fashion, to go out on a limb, Mr. Chapin wrote the Assistant Secretary: "I will be grateful if you will review the files and inform whether these successful candidates should be commissioned as Foreign Service Officers."

An underling in Russell's office, known only as Mr. Klaus in the file, had more guts. On July 25, Mr. Klaus wrote a memorandum to the next man up the line, a Mr. Panuch:

> I have reviewed the three files in these matters submitted by Mr. Chapin to Mr. Russell under memorandum of July 23, 1946. I have reached the following conclusions:
> 1. With reference to Kimball, I cannot concur in the disapproval. The applicant is concededly a person of superior qualifications.

Here there is a gap of about 10 lines of white space marked FBI in the margin. Judging by what follows, it is the full text of McCorry's report of his interview with the "Time supervisor."

The memorandum of Mr. Bannerman of July 12, 1946, omits the complete statement of [Name blacked out] and in my opinion the memorandum is misleading with respect to the statement of this informant. There is no justification in my view for the conclusion "that his [Kimball's] loyalty to this Government is questionable." What reasons for disputes on labor questions Kimball and [Name blacked out] may have had in the short period of their acquaintance is not explained, but a continued support of the position of labor is not equivalent to disloyalty to the United States. Moreover, as against this [Name blacked out] statement, the record shows that David Lawrence, well-known as a newspaper man and publisher on the definitely conservative side, formerly employed Kimball and wants him back now although Kimball is unwilling to work for him. I believe this should be taken as rebuttal on the issue of loyalty of adverse inference from the [phrase blacked out].

I note with respect of Kimball's association on PM some years ago, the investigators made no attempt to find out from the anti-Communist group on the paper or the anti-Communist group of the Newspaper Guild what Kimball's views were. I do not think, however, in view of the lack of emphasis by the investigators on this point, that the case should be sent back for further investigation in this respect unless Mr. Chapin wishes it for his own satisfaction.

Scrawled across the bottom of the covering memo to Donald Russell on the three dossiers from the Office of the Foreign Service is a handwritten note initialed by Panuch. "DR—On Klaus' recommendation in which I concur, I recommend OK for Kimball—additional investigation of [name blacked out] and disapproval of [name blacked out]." As far as Assistant Secretary Russell's staff was concerned my reputation seemed on the verge of rehabilitation.

There follows one of those odd non sequiturs which the workings of the bureaucracy sometimes produce. Donald Russell, on his Assistant Secretary's stationery, addressed a note to Mr. Panuch and Mr. Klaus on July 30: "I have read the recommendation submitted with reference to the induction into the Foreign Service of Penn Townsend Kimball, [two names blacked out]. Mr. Klaus' memorandum appeals to me. I believe that these three cases should be submitted to our Security Committee for its review." On the one hand, Russell seemed to be endorsing Mr. Klaus' recommendation, seconded by Mr. Panuch, that Kimball's commission as a Foreign Service Officer be approved. (No one seemed to notice that I had requested a postponement of such an appointment.) In the next sentence, Russell threw my name back into the security mill. And so by this flick of chance I was soon back in the clutches of CON.

In another scrawl at the bottom of Secretary Russell's ambiguous directive, Mr. Panuch wrote this comment to Mr. Klaus, which may be of historical significance: "Herewith its first case for the Committee." That meant I was to score a double first on the security exams—first for the extra check by the FBI and first for a new review procedure inside State. A new institution, the Appeals Committee on Personnel Security (ACOPS) had apparently just been set up as the State Department adjusted its procedures to a swelling anti-Communist tide in Congress. Charges were coming from the Republican side that the Truman Administration had been harboring radicals left over from wartime agencies and the alliance with the Soviet Union. On July 2, 1946, the House Civil Service Committee appointed a subcommittee to explore the loyalty of federal employees. Congress was principally worried about subversives already on the government payroll, but the State Department was taking no chances. ACOPS received its first case, mine, on July 30, 1946.

The process of security review within the State Department had been conducted up to that time by a five-person Security Committee of which the director of Controls, R. L. Bannerman, was a member and chairman. This committee had been primarily responsible for screening the thousands of wartime employees being transferred to State from the rolls of the emergency war agencies—the Office of Strategic Services, the Office of War Information, the Foreign Economic Administration, and so on. The record shows that of 4,000 such transfers 341 resulted in "disapprovals" because they were (1) aliens, (2) naturalized within the last 15 years or (3) possible security risks. Of the 341 disapproved, two were dismissed under the terms of special authority granted by Congress, on July 5, 1946, to the Secretary of State in his absolute discretion "to terminate the employment of any officer or employee of the Department of State or of the Foreign Service of the United States whenever he shall deem such termination necessary or advisable in the interests of the United States."

That sweeping provision had been attached as a rider to the appropriation bill for State in the 79th Congress by Senator Pat McCarran of Nevada. McCarran was later the author of the Internal Security Act of 1950, passed over Truman's veto, which ordered Communists and officers of Communist front organizations to register their names with the Justice Department. Congress was already on the attack, but a statement submitted by the State Department to the Senate Investigating Committee four years later, after Senator Joseph R. McCarthy's initial allegations, indicates a will to resist.

> The policy of the Department prior to the passage of the McCarran rider was that if there was a reasonable doubt as to an employee's loyalty, his employment was required to be terminated. The McCarran rider freed the hands of the Department in making the policy effective. Basically any reasonable doubt of an employee's loyalty if based on substantial evidence was to be resolved in favor of the Government. After enactment of the McCarran rider the Department did not contemplate that the legislation required or that the people of this country would countenance the use of "Gestapo" methods or harassment or persecution of loyal employees who were American citizens on flimsy evidence or hearsay or innuendo. The Department proceeded to develop appropriate procedures designed to implement fully and properly the authority granted the Department under the McCarran rider. . . .

On July 25, 1946, the previous Screening Committee was

abolished and the Department established a committee of five officers in the Department, designated by Mr. Russell, the Assistant Secretary for Administration, to be known as the Advisory Committee on Personnel Security, hereinafter referred to as ACOPS. The basic responsibility of ACOPS was to report to the Assistant Secretary for Administration findings with respect to security cases. . . . The security officer of the Department, who had previously submitted cases to the Screening Committee of which he was Chairman, now submitted cases to ACOPS. ACOPS refused to assume jurisdiction of cases involving issues of suitability for departmental employment, or mere personnel policy, but confined itself to the exercise of judicial or quasi-judicial discretion and the weighing of security evidence. . . .

It was primarily concerned with risk of penetration of the Department by or in the interest of any foreign government. ACOPS prescribed standards of proof consistent with the requirements of existing loyalty formulations reviewed above and the power contained in the McCarran rider. On questions of proof it required proof "convincing to reasonable men." From time to time, ACOPS formulated additional criteria in the light of experience and developments. In ACOPS' considered view the McCarran rider was subject to procedural limitations. The McCarran rider was not interpreted as permitting reckless discharge or the exercise of arbitrary whims.

On the basis of the foregoing general framework, ACOPS continued from July 25, 1946, to June, 1947, when it was superseded by a Personnel Security Board established by Assistant Secretary Peurifoy under departmental regulation promulgated subsequent to the President's Executive order relating to loyalty. [Truman's loyalty order of March 21, 1947, prescribed a set of Loyalty Boards for the entire executive branch, including State.]

Thus, the staff recommendation to Assistant Secretary Russell of an "OK for Kimball" had preceded by two days the adoption by Congress of the McCarran rider, prompting a reorganization of the whole security review process within the department. For those already on the employment rolls the Secretary's absolute discretion was a definite setback. Under the old rules, based on Civil Service regulations, the accused was entitled to "a notice of the charges and a hearing thereon"; high-ranking employees and veterans had the right of appeal to the Civil Service Commission itself. Applicants for employment, under either system, seemed to enjoy no rights whatsoever except the self-imposed guideline set down for ACOPS that a ruling of disloyalty should be accompanied by proof "convincing to reasonable men." On that slender reed rested my fate.

In the years to come, personnel within the State Department did not fare very well at the hands of ACOPS and its successor, the Loyalty Board, especially the old China hands drummed out of their jobs for "losing" China to the Reds. Had I already been in Saigon, the file shows, I would have rated a personal appearance before the security panel. As an "applicant for employment" I was afforded no such opportunity. And, once again, nobody notified me that I was to be the object of still another confidential security review.

ACOPS itself was a little confused over when and how it was entitled to exercise jurisdiction over charges of disloyalty. When the historic first case was dumped in his lap, Counsel for ACOPS (nameless throughout my file) on August 6 sent it straight back to CON with an advisory that it needed more work.

> 1. This file is being returned to you for additional investigation preliminary to a decision whether the case is adequate for submission to ACOPS, as involving a security risk. The record, in my opinion, does not show Kimball to be a security risk.

That chain of thinking is marvelous to behold: you have investigated Kimball and your findings do not show this fellow to be a security risk; my committee is supposed to review only cases of security risks; please go back and make him a security risk so that the committee can properly decide whether he is or is not.

The order from ACOPS touched off the third round of field checks on me since that day in November, 1945, when I had lightheartedly sat for the Foreign Service examinations. The first round, carried on by State Department personnel in March among the references I had submitted on my application, had resulted in the clearance to take the oral examinations in April, 1946. The comment by David Lawrence on my leaving *United States News* for *PM* before the war, however, had resulted in putting the FBI on my trail. The FBI field check in June—particularly the statement by the *"Time* supervisor"—persuaded the State Department's Security Office to cancel my clearance in July on the ground that I was a national security risk. The staff of the Assistant Secretary for Administration had taken exception to this finding, recommending my appointment as a Foreign Service officer. Assistant Secretary Russell then threw my case to ACOPS for further review. ACOPS, for its part, ordered an additional investigation in August to be carried out by the State Department's own security arm, headed by Chief Security Agent T. J. Fitch, in the Office of Controls, headed by Bannerman.

Counsel for ACOPS, to Security Officer Fitch at CON, was very specific on how he wanted this new investigation handled:

> 2. Additional investigation should be undertaken at the earliest moment by an investigator of superior ability on the following items:
>
> a. Kimball's ideology and sympathy with the Communist Party line and Soviet policies during the crucial periods which are tests in this field. Specifically, the agent should communicate with Mr. Kenneth Crawford, Washington Editor of *Newsweek*, and formerly with *PM*. Mr. Crawford has orally stated that he personally knows Kimball and can vouch for his loyalty, independence of thought, etc. and asserts that he would be a fine Foreign Service Officer.

Nowhere in my file can I find any references to Kenneth Crawford having been interviewed about me up to this date. Could he have "orally stated" his recommendation over the phone in response to a call from Counsel, himself? Such phone calls are not an unknown practice in Washington; they do not always appear on the official records.

Check should be made, through Crawford or otherwise, with anti-Communist former or present members of the *PM* staff closely acquainted with Kimball in New York. In this connection a full explanation should be sought of the Newspaper Guild, *PM* Unit, statement regarding the North American Aviation strike in 1941.

b. Since Kimball rose from Private to Captain in the Marine Corps and was a combat correspondent, associates of his who would be acquainted with his views should be sought out and interviewed.

c. Other associates than the supervisor on *Time* magazine, determined in advance to be anti-Communists, should be interviewed with respect to his present views and activities. In this connection, you may receive some assistance through Mr. Crawford who may be acquainted with members of the *Time* staff.

3. If there are any questions still remaining, please take up with me the matter of interviewing Kimball and obtaining his statement in writing as to doubtful items.

Counsel for ACOPS—the title sounds like a character out of Greek mythology—had been sharp enough to spot the holes in the security-risk arguments made by Bannerman of CON, that well-named division. His attitude seemed sympathetic in that he directed the investigators to contact Kenneth Crawford, who had previously established himself in my corner. Counsel's instruction that somebody finally check out my Marine Corps record seemed a gesture for fair play. And he left open the possibility of speaking directly to me and obtaining my written defense against unsubstantiated accusations.

In truth, the loyalty check procedure was rigged against the suspect. Here was one bureaucrat asking another to reverse himself because of sloppy initial work. No way. CON's whole approach to a new investigation was bound to be a self-fulfilling prophecy. Counsel's instruction to concentrate on those determined in advance to be anti-Communists inevitably led to those who were habitual informants. Why not talk to Communists, if the Government knew who they were, and ask *them* how Kimball felt about "the Communist Party Line and Soviet policies during the crucial periods which are tests in this field"? That might have been more likely to produce data free from preconceptions. If both the Communists and anti-Communists criticized a Foreign Service candidate, that might be exactly the kind of fellow the State Department should be looking for to gather the straight poop.

Of course, that would leave out the whole category of Americans who in 1946 didn't think of themselves as either pro- or anti-Communist or fence-sitters either—just Democrats or Republicans or Independents. Why, according to the records made available to me, didn't anybody want to look at my writings, or more particularly, drafts of my stories before they went through the editing process at *Time*? That could be telling material, especially if the investigators talked to the editors who would certainly know if they had constantly found it necessary to delete a radical slant.

Since Bannerman, as head of the Office of Controls, remained my principal antagonist in the ensuing scenario as portrayed in my file, I am profoundly curious as to what the man might have been like. His name, by coincidence, disappears from the registers in the State Department library the year after he finished my case. (The hand of God? Off to some new secret mission?) All that is recorded is that he graduated from high school in Wisconsin before taking a job as a clerk in the Department of Agriculture. He got a college degree by going nights to George Washington before transferring to the State Department.

Fitch, like his superior in CON, Bannerman, was a Wisconsin boy who had come to Washington for a government job. What was there about Wisconsin in those years to produce these watchdogs of the national security? According to the State Department register, Fitch had started out in life as a railway mail clerk and was a postal-fraud investigator for the Post Office Department before transferring to State.

A memorandum from Bannerman to Fitch, dated August 14, 1946, relayed Counsel for ACOPS' instructions, but with a startling change. Whereas Counsel had concluded: "If there are any questions still remaining, please take up with me the matter of interviewing

Kimball and obtaining his statement in writing as to doubtful items,"
Bannerman wrote, "It has also been requested by Counsel, ACOPS,
that this investigation be undertaken by an investigator of superior
ability, and that the subject not be interviewed during the course of
investigation." Bannerman was not about to alert me that I was
being investigated, nor give me a chance to reply to his anonymous
informants, nor encourage Counsel in any such direction—even if it
meant tinkering a bit with the text of his instructions.

Fitch thereupon assigned two of his men of "superior ability":
Special Agent Elmer R. Hipsley to investigate me in Washington,
and Special Agent Daniel H. Clare Jr. to investigate me in New
York. Fitch's final instruction to Hipsley and Clare gave an air of
urgency to this new round of interviews: "It would be appreciated if
this investigation would be conducted as expeditiously as possible."

No time to waste—on my writings, on associates not vouched for
in advance as anti-Communist, or, most of all, on me. In the end it
took just a few days to dispose of the life it had taken me 30 years to
experience, plus another two months of paperwork to put the finish-
ing touches on my character and reputation within the United States
Government.

6

THE RED HERRING

THE SMALL SMATTERING drawn so far from my State Department file—a few paragraphs from the single-spaced pages of 99 separate documents—begins to convey the idea of what a security investigation is like. One needs to wade in past the ankles, however, to get the full feel of these murky waters.

In all the thousands, the tens of thousands of words in my file— the whole bundle of hearsay, scuttlebutt, guilt by association, guilt by nonassociation—only one specific statement of fact about any concrete action of mine could potentially have been documented by the investigators: while I was employed at *PM* and an officer of the Guild local there, I had defended a strike against North American Aviation.

This single, juicy item had come to the attention of the security officer of the State Department almost as an afterthought. Although I had already been granted security clearance, my file had been flagged by the observation attributed to David Lawrence that my "turning to the left" might be confirmed by the fact that I had left to go to work for the newspaper *PM*. *PM*, it turned out, had been the object of a special file maintained by the Federal Bureau of Investigation since before publication of its first issue. When State Department security sent over a query, the FBI replied that "the indices of the Bureau reflect that a copy of a circular distributed by the PM unit of the Newspaper Guild of New York regarding the strike of the North American Aviation Company indicated that the paper upheld and defended this strike. Among the names appearing on this circular was that of Penn Kimball, member of the Grievance Committee of the Newspaper Guild of New York." Looking further into that labor dispute, the State Department was informed by the Office of Naval Intelligence, it is recorded in the file, "that the above-mentioned strike was Communist inspired as an attempt to slow down the production of war material, and that the President furnished troops to protect the workers."

There it is, the worst of it, the crux of the evidence against me.

In the series of memos prepared in the State Department's Office of Security which dealt with this original intelligence, my participation gradually expanded—from a name appearing on a circular, to a "signer" of the circular, to one "vigorously in favor of the Guild's protests to F. D. R.'s use of troops in the Communist-inspired North American Aviation strike," to a "supporter of a Guild resolution to send a telegram of protest to the President," to one who might have "either signed the telegram or urged its creation." All without a scrap of additional data. If there ever was such a telegram at all, none of the investigators on my case ever found it.

The fact that *PM* might support a strike of production workers trying to form a union and that members of its staff might take exception to government intervention on the side of management was consistent with *PM*'s original editorial charter to cover labor unions as an important new part of the American scene.

My decision to leave Washington for New York in the spring of 1940 was triggered by a story I read in *Editor & Publisher*, the trade magazine of the newspaper business, about the proposed new experimental daily, *PM*. It sounded like the dream paper to a young (24) journalist who had grown up during the New Deal. Its editorial creed was unabashedly on the side of the underdog without being wed to any specific ideology. "We are against people who push other people around." It would accept no advertising, hence be free of the economic pressures I had learned about theoretically in college courses and at first hand working for *United States News*. The prospectus brimmed with innovative ideas, such as organizing the daily flow of the news into separate sections which the reader could readily find, permitting reporters to write their own headlines and editorials to run alongside their stories in the news columns, using color and artists' sketches as well as a generous proportion of photographs to brighten up its pages, which were stapled together for easier handling on the subways, buses and commuter trains of New York City. Ralph Ingersoll, the founding editor, was a former managing editor of *The New Yorker* magazine and as a *Time* executive had been involved in the successful launching of both *Life* and *Fortune*. He had raised nearly a million dollars—in the days when that was a lot of money—from such diverse sources as John Hay Whitney and Lillian Hellman, Chester Bowles and Marshall Field III.

I shot off a letter to New York asking to be considered for a job; that I got it was a fluke. In the National Press Club bar shortly after I sent the letter I found myself one evening involved in a heavy discussion among a group of members gathered around a large, round table after the day's work. I can't remember the topic, but I and a a stranger opposite me ended up alone on the side of right and justice, standing off the rest of the table. Weeks later, I was invited to New York City for a job interview. I knew no one involved, and as I waited in an anteroom for my turn to be looked over, I couldn't imagine how a cub reporter from Washington was going to make the grade. When the screening staff representative, Duncan Aikman, opened his door, you guessed it, he had been the guy at the Press Club that night when we had stood off the table together. Out of thousands of applicants from all over the country, he recommended me for a job on the original staff of *PM*'s National News section (out of a total of 11,062 applicants, *PM* hired only 151). When the offer came through at $40 a week I accepted by telegram. An unpredictable turning point in both my life and my file.

The paper was a tabloid (in confrontation with the *Daily News* and *Mirror*) and sold for a nickel. New York was still a hotly competitive city with more than a half-dozen dailies, including, as well as the two tabloids, outlets for the Hearst and Scripps-Howard chains and Republican organs such as *The Sun* and the *Herald-Tribune*. *PM*'s market position was well to the left on that spectrum, although by today's standards of radical militancy, *PM* was relatively tame. There was no neat label such as "investigative reporting" to categorize what we were trying to do, although we were the first to recognize the potential of consumer news. (One of the paper's first exposés was the common practice of injecting sides of corned beef with water to increase the weight on butchers' scales; 40 years later *The New York Times* was still cautioning readers about "watered meat.") In similar spirit, we were the first New York publication to print the schedules of films in neighborhood movie houses. The paper raised hackles on David Lawrence and Yankee businessmen in my hometown with articles from Washington on tax concessions to business, from the coal fields on mine safety, and in New York City by stories on housing conditions in Harlem and health services in the slums. The paper endorsed Roosevelt, running for a third term against Wendell Willkie. On foreign affairs, it was steadfastly on the side of Bundles-for-Britain.

Ingersoll's prospectus touched the conscience of some of the best newspaper people in town as well as progressives working in the provinces. Writers and photographers from the book and magazine world jumped at the opportunity to transplant their skills to the exciting environment of daily journalism on a crusading experiment in the nation's largest and most glamorous city.

That staff was a fascinating, talented, zany, free-spirited, eclectic bunch. Dashiell Hammett checked copy for style in the inaugural edition; Margaret Bourke-White shot a carload of negatives to illustrate a story on the Hoboken waterfront; and Huntington Hartford, the A&P heir, was a copyboy. Walter Winchell, who pioneered gossip columns on radio and *The Mirror*, moonlighted secretly for us under the pseudonym Paul Revere II, while Dorothy Parker did book reviews, and Heywood Hale Broun, son of the founder of the Newspaper Guild and future TV personality, wrote sports. Lillian Ross, who later earned fame writing profiles for *The New Yorker*, had a job in the morgue, and I. F. Stone commuted between Washington and New York. William Walton, future correspondent for *Life* and Jack Kennedy's close personal friend, worked at the desk next to mine.

PM recognized the trade union movement with special coverage.

The California strike that provided "evidence" for my questionable sympathies to the FBI was the result of a drive by the fledgling United Automobile Workers CIO to organize a fast-growing part of the transportation industry. A few weeks previously the paper had endorsed similar efforts by the Auto Workers to organize the auto plants in Detroit. The paper sent James A. Wechsler and me to Detroit in April to cover a strike at the Ford Motor Company over the issue whether Ford would recognize the union as the collective bargaining agent for its production employees. One of the disputes at the company's huge River Rouge plant, I recall, was that workers were not allowed to leave the assembly line to go to the bathroom. When union members had demonstrated outside the plant gates, they had been set upon and beaten by "goon squads" hired by the personnel department. The workers retaliated by overturning cars parked on streets where the picket lines were patrolling and setting them afire. Both sides were playing for keeps.

The strike ended when the company recognized the Auto Workers for the first time. Henry Ford signed a contract with the union in June. By that time the UAW had moved on to try to establish union locals in the aircraft industry. The North American Aviation strike took place the same month. Pearl Harbor was still six months in the future.

Back in the home office, lesser lights like me mingled with the presently and futurely famous in a converted factory loft adjacent to the Long Island Railroad tracks in Brooklyn. The unusual location, far removed from the news sources in Manhattan, was dictated by Ingersoll's deal to print *PM* on the presses of *The Brooklyn Eagle* during their slack time, thus saving capital to invest in the product. The city room, under the roof and over the hot-lead linotype composing machines on the floor below, was so hot in summer that deskmen stripped to their shorts. Air conditioning was part of the technology of the future. Everyone on the staff except Ingersoll and the managing editor worked cheek by jowl in one vast bullpen. Intimate, friendly, full of *esprit de corps*.

Ingersoll, a tall mustached Yaleman, worked in striped suspenders dictating his editorials. I never saw him touch a typewriter. We would have staff conferences at his Manhattan apartment, where the furniture included a bar and a bank of slot machines from which he would recapture our share of the payroll. The spirit of Democracy at the paper was such in the opening weeks that Ingersoll would gather the entire staff, including the copyboys, around him as he stood on a desk in the city room to conduct a forum on editorial policies. Each news department—city, national, foreign, sports—laid out its own pages and sent them straight down to the composing room without benefit of a central copy desk. As a result, the editions ran later and later so that *PM*'s original name and goal to be an afternoon daily became a fiction. Some of us began reporting to work at 3 a.m. to make sure the paper came out at all.

Ingersoll's liberal principles, which were responsible for *PM*'s special attention to labor disputes, included encouraging the establishment at the outset of a *PM* unit of the New York local of the American Newspaper Guild and announcing that he was prepared to sign a contract binding management to match the top pay scales of other papers in the city. Everybody from the telephone operators to the departmental editors joined the Guild, and meetings began immediately to hammer out the details of a "model" contract with Ingersoll's lawyers. Many on the staff were veterans of bitter battles in other parts of the country with publishers determined to thwart a union including both editorial and service employees. Others, like myself, had joined the union as a form of self-expression in shops where organization had barely begun. Now we were all thrown together on a paper where management said unions were part of conducting good business in a sensible society. Our first unit meetings, held in the back room of a neighborhood beer tavern across the street from the office, were like social mixers where the new staff would meet and greet.

The discussions were focused on the bread-and-butter issues created by the paper's early financial troubles. Ingersoll spent so much money on prepublication promotion that *PM*'s first issue, which sold 200,000 copies on the newsstands, struck many readers as anticlimactic. While the prospectus was geared toward covering the domestic scene, the paper's inauguration coincided with the German breakthrough in France. *PM* started without a foreign staff to speak of, and the Associated Press refused to sell the paper its service. The other tabloids put pressure on newsdealers not to display *PM*. Within weeks after hitting the stands, the paper nearly went broke. Ingersoll began eliminating whole departments. In October, Marshall Field III bought out the other original stockholders for 10 cents on the dollar, threw in $300,000 in new capital and sent in his representatives to reorganize the finances, including a further reduction in staff.

The Guild insisted that management deal with its Grievance Committee, made up of members elected by the local unit, to justify each choice for dismissal after giving each due notice and severance pay to tide him or her over. Quick of tongue and pugnacious in argument (attributes which over the years have not earned me universal admiration), I was a natural for a place on the committee. I took the militant position that even a well-intentioned employer sometimes needed to be prodded to deal fairly with the rank and file, especially in times of economic duress.

Up to this time in my life, it could be said that my political record was pure as the driven snow. The Byzantine wars habitually waged among New York intellectuals were something I had been spared up to then. I first encountered them at citywide meetings of the Newspaper Guild, which usually ran late in auditoriums in Manhattan and were sparsely attended. The citywide meetings were far less parochial than our unit's beer-hall get-togethers. Issues were definitely political; so were the participants. Most Guild members in the city shared *PM*'s militantly liberal position on internal matters, but there was less unity over becoming involved in broader ones. A minority faction huddled together, shaking their heads in disapproval at resolutions which involved the union's taking positions on social issues, whether on endorsing aid to striking bus drivers or opposing United States recognition of the Vichy French. This "conservative" caucus seemed to include a fair proportion of ex-Communists and backslid Socialists publicly purging their systems by bitterly denouncing the "radical" majority, "radical" being almost anyone who didn't share their views.

My efforts on behalf of the Grievance Committee were rewarded by my colleagues when, despite my tender years and inexperience, they elected me chairman of that committee and vice president of the *PM* unit of the New York local of the Guild. That made me part of the "administration" slate in a citywide election in which the incumbents in both the *PM* unit and the New York City local were attacked by the conservative opposition as being soft on Communism, if not actual CP members. Such rhetoric struck me as divisive in the real struggle—better working conditions from reluctant publishers. The individuals who spent most of their energy arguing their political purity, moreover, tended to show less backbone in a tough fight with management over bread-and-butter issues. I do not know why this was so, unless they regarded confrontation against employers as part of a secret conspiracy to wreck the capitalist system. In any event, that side lost the 1940 voting at both *PM* and citywide.

When delegates were being selected in May, 1941, to attend the Guild's national convention, I was picked by the Guild Representative Assembly to be an alternate. Not that I was a big wheel on the Guild local scene—when a couple of original nominees dropped out, my name was substituted in a last-minute shuffle for a place among the remaining alternates. Again an opposition slate was nominated by petition, and again it lost.

Which is not to say the majority and minority were always on the opposite side of every issue. I remember—jogged by a look at microfilm of *The New York Times*—a citywide membership meeting in September, 1940, at the Hotel Capitol on Eighth Avenue which was notable for being the first meeting attended by a newly syndicated columnist and Guild member, Eleanor Roosevelt. Various parliamentary wrangles occupied most of the four and one-half hours, having to do with whether to accept a report by the New York Guild delegation to a recently concluded state CIO convention. That convention was divided between a faction led by Sidney Hillman, head of the Amalgamated Clothing Workers, which wanted to endorse F. D. R. for a third term and a faction led by followers of John L. Lewis, head of the United Mine Workers, who thought the President had gone too far in trying to aid Britain. The New York delegation, which was expected to side with Lewis, had been barred from voting and Hillman's side had won. The voteless delegation came back to New York with a report denouncing Hillman's conduct. The delegation leader charged during the debate at the Hotel Capitol that F. D. R. would "drag us into this war by the heels if he could." Someone in the minority caucus yelled, "That's the Communist opinion." There was also a hot debate over the merits of a draft for military service, which the leadership of the New York Guild opposed. And so it went until members held up their ballots. The motion to accept the delegation report, and by implication to oppose the draft and F. D. R., carried 160 to 74. Being pro-Roosevelt and pro-draft myself, I waved my ballot along with Mrs. Roosevelt's on the losing side of that Guild vote that night, but nobody took any notice. Nobody, at least, who appears in my file.

That is the hazard when security officials jump to firm conclusions from a single scrap of information. None of the concrete data about what I was doing in the Newspaper Guild ever made it into my file, with the single exception of the appearance of my name on the 1941 circular protesting the use of troops to break a strike. That information was placed in my file as if I had been caught red-handed sneaking out of the Kremlin. When State Department Special Agent Daniel H. Clare Jr. was sent to track the incident down five years after its occurrence, he emphasized the incriminating link:

> The strike which precipitated the sending of the telegram was condemned by R. J. Thomas of the United Automobile Workers, CIO, of which the North American Aviation Workers were an affiliate, and it was described as an illegal Communist inspired outbreak.

That must have pleased him, but when Special Agent Clare dug into my personal role in the affair of the circular, of the Guild resolution, of the telegram to the President—whichever it was—the going became harder.

> Mr. William Rogers, Secretary-General, was interviewed after discreet inquiries had established the fact that he had ridden to his office in the national Union on the basis of his anti-Communistic standing. Mr. Rogers stated that he is not in a position to secure [the minutes of the meeting] as they were unquestionably in the possession of the New York News-

paper Guild, and he candidly confessed that there was no one in that local whom he could trust because of its complete Communistic dominance.

Mr. Rogers was questioned concerning Mr. Kimball's participation in the Guild's affairs but said that while he remembered the name he could not recall on what side Mr. Kimball participated. [Three lines blacked out.]

It was learned through contact with [name blacked out], Mr. William Engle of the New York News and Mr. Edward Hunter of the New York Post, that the PM Unit of the local New York Newspaper Guild was solidly behind the resolution which resulted in the aforementioned telegram. However, none of these individuals recalled Mr. Kimball as one of those taking an active part in the promotion of the disloyal resolution. They explained that at the time Mr. Kimball was new to the newspaper business, was a minor figure in it, and that because of his youth and inexperience his voice would carry little weight at that time, even with the Communist element of the Guild. It is known that he was a Vice-President of the PM Unit, but conclusive proof that he either signed the telegram or urged its creation could not be obtained. Mr. Edward Hunter of the New York Post, who has consistently fought the Communists, undertook to engage in a discreet manner in canvassing a number of his friends who have been members of the Guild during the period mentioned, and without indicating the interest of the Department in the matter, ascertain from them whether Mr. Kimball had been active. These informants recalled Mr. Kimball, but could not definitely state that he had openly advocated sending the telegram. The fact that it has been definitely established that the PM Unit of the Newspaper Guild was a proponent of the telegram and that Mr. Kimball was definitely a member of the PM Unit and an officer, it would seem reasonable to suppose that he did participate in the resolution.

Since nobody could be found to place me at the scene of the crime, the investigator concluded it was only "reasonable to suppose" I was guilty. How to build a file!

Aficionados of hearings on television are familiar with the way witnesses try to skirt a perjury rap by answering "I have no recollection. . . ." The night of June 10, 1941, is not exactly etched in fame—or in my memory either. Part of the problem, leaving aside old age, is that I didn't join the Guild to foment revolution. Special Agent Clare reported that the vote on the resolution to send F. D. R. the telegram of protest was carried at a general membership meeting of the New York Guild at Manhattan Center by a vote of 163 to 30, hardly a banner turnout (there were 4,000 members at the time). Severance pay had long since been settled and I was working the 3 a.m.-to-noon lobster trick on the national desk that week in *PM*'s Brooklyn newsroom to the best of my recollection, not a schedule that encouraged a man to attend a late night meeting in Manhattan as well. I know for sure that I wasn't filling out forms in any Western Union office.

To see if I could jog my memory further, I made a trip during the summer of 1982 to the office of Local 3 of the Newspaper Guild, located in the same building on 44th Street just off Times Square as it had been in the summer of 1946 when Special Agent Clare was on the prowl. There I found the minutes of all the general membership meetings going back to 1941 and before, neatly bound and arranged on a shelf, as I presume was the case when government informant Rogers had told Clare they would be impossible for him to see. The North American resolution was the sixth out of nine items on the agenda the night of June 10, 1941, at a meeting which lasted from 9:05 p.m. to 1:00 a.m. Nobody from *PM* is recorded as having participated in the debate. The minutes confirmed that there were 163 in favor and 30 opposed in a vote on a two-paragraph resolution:

Resolved that the Newspaper Guild of New York protests against the use of the United States Army to destroy the right to strike—a threat to the free existence of the entire labor movement in this country and

Resolved that copies of this resolution be sent to the United Automobile Workers in California and President Roosevelt.

The resolution said nothing about a telegram. The substance of the debate was not reported in any detail, but a motion to submit the matter to a referendum was defeated 172 to 37. Nothing in the minutes sounded familiar, but that is really beside the point. If I had indeed been present at the meeting, I am sure I would have voted with the five-to-one majority against the use of troops in a labor dispute. Five minutes' conversation with me would have established that point. But I have never been one to affix my name to petitions; it offends my cantankerous individuality. The FBI indices revealed that my name had never appeared on any other circular of interest to them for the rest of my life.

However, as Clare took pains to point out, it is true that I was an elected officer of the *PM* Guild unit and if the unit was a "proponent of the telegram," as could be determined in some fashion in a sparsely attended debate of the general membership, then someone might have more or less legitimately stuck my name at the end of such a telegram. If there was no telegram, copies of the resolution itself would probably have been signed by officers of the New York Guild. Special Agent Clare, plus his whole squad of discreet canvassers, never could sort out who was where that night, what was sent or who signed it to anyone's satisfaction but his own. In the end, Clare had to concede that "conclusive proof could not be obtained" on any of the allegations.

READING ONE'S OWN FILE over and over again, one's appreciation of the facts begins to merge at some point with the exercise of one's imagination. Having failed to prove the reality of this red herring, what might Clare have done next? What *should* an investigator of superior ability have done?

The Guild resolution of protest to the President was passed on June 10, 1941, 12 days before Hitler invaded the Soviet Union. The date is significant, because the Communist Party, opposed to war prior to Hitler's invasion, changed its mind on the day that Hitler breached the Soviet–German pact. Thus, any activity before Hitler's invasion of the Soviet Union which could be construed as weakening the potential of United States armed intervention on the side of the Western allies became circumstantial evidence, in the view of the anti-Communist watch, of subversive behavior. The investigators must, therefore, have gone to special lengths to implicate me, by virtue of the pre-invasion protest, as a possible peacenick—although that is a word which didn't achieve currency until a much later national crisis. That avenue having failed, they might next have tried other ways to discern my opinions prior to the resolution.

As far as defending the free world was concerned, my own private views were considerably less neutral than the official United States foreign policy line. Clare—or anyone—could easily have found that out, yet my file contains no trace of such an effort.

It is a difficult feat sometimes, I have learned from my students, to get controversial material of bygone times into the proper context of history, especially when a large part of the audience has had no direct experience with the matters at hand. What do you do when no one in the room has ever heard of Dr. Goebbels? I find that today's generation has weak recollection of how reluctantly this country faced up to the threat to liberty posed by Hitler, Mussolini and the military regime in prewar Japan. If it had not been for the sneak attack on Pearl Harbor, I still am not sure that the United States would have soon entered the war on the side of the Western democracies. But when State Department Special Agents Elmer H. Hipsley and Daniel R. Clare Jr. were dispatched by Chief Security Agent Thomas J. Fitch to gather impressions about my political views, a mere five years had passed since the incident of the circular. The drift of my thinking on such matters should not have been difficult to place in context. Certainly my antitotalitarian philosophy should not have been hard to discern; it was there in print, on the record.

Since one of the tasks of the Foreign Service is to monitor outside threats to national security, the period from the outbreak of war in Europe in September, 1939, to our own entry after Pearl Harbor, December 7, 1941, might have suggested itself to Hipsley and Clare as a base period for examining an applicant's capabilities to make such assessments. Indeed, that was part of the Foreign Service oral examination which I had already passed. The record of that time—though not the record in my file—would show that I did my best to raise the alarm before we were attacked.

A script of a radio talk delivered by me over Station WNBC in my hometown of New Britain, on August 30, 1939, the day before Britain declared war on Germany, states:

I don't know whether or not we are finally committed to a gigantic war in Europe. But if it does come, as it seems it will, I hope you will understand the idea and ideals which are in the minds of these Englishmen and their families as they stake all that they have to offer on its result. They are reasons which have no national boundaries, they are common to every man with human instincts.

Age 23. Not one likely to attempt to sabotage the defense effort. When I went to work in Washington that winter the international news was the Soviet invasion of "gallant little Finland." I joined a committee formed to advocate American aid to the Finns and went to fundraisers at the Finnish Embassy with my *United States News* colleague, Frank Rounds. But no investigator ever talked to him.

One of my tasks for *United States News* was to write weekly roundups of the war news. March, 1940: "Neutrality, after barely six months of a slow war, is getting on the nerves of the warring nations." April, 1940: "Last week Herr Hitler was once more on the move. Verdict of Europe's capitals last week appeared to be that Scandinavia was but a preface for grimmer things to come." May, 1940: "When will Americans decide that war abroad seriously begins to touch their vital interests?" Nothing there to excite suspicion.

When I went to work for *PM* in May, 1940, the isolationist voices within the United States were still being heard loud and clear, but Ingersoll and *PM*'s editorial policy had been strongly interventionist on the Allied side from the start. If the editorial policy of the paper's editorials never wavered from its staunch support of the Western Allies, neither did I. The need for collective security among the democracies, lest they be picked off one by one by the dictators, was crystal clear to anyone like myself who had seen it all at firsthand in the Europe of 1937–39. As I viewed it, the United States was morally bound to the side of the free world. In after-work bull sessions at the nearest bar, one of the occupational traits of working newspapermen, I was the resident hawk, another coinage from debates of the future. And as a young reporter on the new newspaper, I enthusiastically accepted every assignment that might help to alert our readers to the risk of noninvolvement.

On *PM* my beat was national affairs, but that included following up stories with a bearing on the paper's strong interventionist stand. In October, 1940, G. Henry-Haye, Ambassador to the United States from the French Vichy government, was staying in New York. A letter from him dated October 27, 1940, is among my souvenirs from this period.

> My attention is called to the article of Penn Kimball published in your number of today concerning the Government of France and its Ambassador to this country. I just want to deny once more and most formally all the lucubrations of your collaborator which are totally false from beginning to end. Allow me to be surprised about the strange manners consisting in insulting a foreign Government and its accredited Representative in your hospitable Country where I have been accustomed to most courteous ways and to a real sense of honor. If you really like to publish the truth, can you afford and will you print that, . . . all the allegations and insinuations of your Mr. Kimball are absolutely contrary to the honest reality. Yours sincerely, G. Henry-Haye, French Ambassador to the United States, de passage Waldorf-Astoria Hotel.

I didn't appreciate being addressed as a "collaborator" myself by an emissary from Vichy and I had to look up "lucubrations" (an overlabored work) in my dictionary. I didn't care much for that either. But "allegations and insinuations" against the Vichy French advanced in the fall of 1940 turned out to be right on the mark. The United States Foreign Service, not me, perhaps should have been indexed by the FBI for its "courteous ways" to the Axis alliance.

When the New York National Guard was called into active service and went to Arkansas in the last full-scale maneuvers before Pearl Harbor (a young colonel named Eisenhower was making his mark), I was sent down by *PM* to cover the local boys in uniform. I wrote back stories criticizing their broomstick artillery and the pitiful state of military preparedness, which could hardly be blamed on the unions. One bylined exclusive in particular might have struck my judges to have been of rather more significance than the appearance of my name as one among many on a union circular.

The war in Europe had been going on for over a year when on the morning of October 3, 1940, a full-page advertisement appeared in *The New York Times* urging America to stop sending aid to Britain. The ad, topped by a line reading PEACE AT HOME OR WAR ABROAD?, urged Americans to "stop our government's sending its planes, guns and ships to belligerents across the sea." It advocated a strong national defense but a strictly isolationist policy to avoid being "dragged into war." The advertisement was inserted by an organization calling itself the America First Committee.

The advertisement listed General Robert E. Wood, chairman of Sears Roebuck, as acting chairman of the America Firsters. The list of committee members read almost as a Who's Who of the Establishment—people such as Henry Ford, Alice Roosevelt Longworth, Chester Bowles, Sterling Morton of Morton's Salt, Jay Hormel of Hormel's Hams and—strangely—Kathryn Lewis, daughter of the head of the CIO whose aviation strike was so soon to be interpreted as "Communist inspired."

I spotted a possible lead to an important story when I saw that the America First ad listed as its national director Robert D. Stuart of Chicago, son of the first vice president of Quaker Oats. Bobby Stuart and I had been classmates at Princeton; he had served as advertising director of the *Daily Princetonian* when I was chairman. I tracked Stuart down by phone and made a date to meet him the next afternoon at the advertising offices of Benton & Bowles where, he told me, he had some brief business to transact.

Late next afternoon I took a seat in the reception room at Benton & Bowles to await Stuart, who was still attending a meeting inside. As I sat there, a familiar, tall, lanky figure came through the front door, spoke to the receptionist and passed in front of me on his way to the inner sanctum. It was Colonel Charles A. Lindbergh, and I had in my lap a *PM* exclusive. The Lone Eagle, America's national hero, had some interest in the America First operation.

Lindbergh reappeared a few minutes later, left the office and shortly afterward Bobby Stuart emerged, apologizing for being late. We adjourned to Peacock Alley at the nearby Waldorf-Astoria where Stuart explained that he had spent the summer working on the America First idea that had hatched at Yale the previous spring. So far, most of his work had been in the Midwest, traditionally isolationist country. But he had raised $2,500 for the *Times* ad, which was to be the first gun in a campaign on the Eastern Seaboard to be directed from a New York office. He said he regretted some of the conservative support he was constrained to solicit and had turned down several offers of help from persons whose anti-Semitism or Fascist motives were blatant. It was his hope, however, that no one person or group would become dominant in the movement.

I told him that I had seen Lindbergh there with my own eyes, and that I intended to write that story for my paper.

Stuart exploded, but the more he carried on, the more information I got. The Colonel had evidently been interested in the ad in *The Times* and had called up Stuart to ask who had been responsible for it. Stuart told him that Chester Bowles had written a memo on which the ad was based. The Colonel said he would like to meet Mr. Bowles, and Stuart had arranged it.

I went back to the *PM* office and wrote the story exactly that way for the next day's edition. While I was at work at my typewriter, Chester Bowles, who was a *PM* stockholder, called in to try to kill the story. Ingersoll refused. The headline on the story was "Isolationist Ad Wins Lindbergh . . . Also, It Makes Strange Bedfellows," such as Henry Ford and the CIO.

Within a month, the Colonel was out in the open and going strong on the America First circuit. I tracked the story up to New Haven, where Lindbergh made a major speech under the auspices of the Yale unit of the America First Committee, chaired by Kingman Brewster Jr., then a student but later to become president of the university.

Lindbergh declared that "our government has deliberately and ineffectively antagonized the great military powers of both Europe and Asia." He said the United States had encouraged England and France to declare a war whose result would be "inevitable failure."

Our policies had left us helpless, Lindbergh argued, against the yellow peril in the Orient.

Brewster, as chairman of the Yale *News* as well as head of its America First chapter, looked over my shoulder as I worked in his news office on the lead I was writing for *PM*: "Col. Charles A. Lindbergh brought to Yale last night his defeatist line of talk favoring appeasement of the totalitarian bullies." More complaints to Ingersoll followed, but he was not a man to back off from his own dictum: call it as you see it. We both thought I was seeing it pretty clearly, but therein lies the irony of this period in our history, and of my file.

Opposition to war in the fall of 1940 was not *prima facie* evidence of pro-Communist leanings. Lindbergh was our greatest national hero, and America First was supported by some of the sturdiest members of the Establishment. By the time of my FBI investigation, any apparent opposition to the war effort had become, in retrospect, a Red brand—but only for some. Bobby Stuart went on to succeed his father as head of Quaker Oats Company and became the Republican national committeeman for Illinois and a delegate to the national convention that picked Nixon for President. Kingman Brewster was named Ambassador to Great Britain 20 years after the war for that country's survival, described by Lindbergh as "doomed to inevitable failure." In the wonderful ways of the Establishment net, Brewster became our official representative to the country he had been urging us to let go down the drain before Pearl Harbor. I don't remember seeing Brewster's old America First connection mentioned in his newspaper profiles at the time of his appointment to the Court of St. James.

During my Marine Corps stint in the South Pacific, I spent some time on a small, jungle-covered rock near the Equator named Green Island. One steaming hot day, jeeps carrying the island's brass swept onto the airstrip. They were all drawn up in parade formation when a Marine transport plane touched down and drew up to a revetment. The Marine officers snapped to salute. Colonel Charles A. Lindbergh, now helping to turn back the peril in the Orient as a technical adviser to the United Aircraft Corporation, descended from the aircraft. Lindbergh was whisked off to the officer's mess as I munched on my Spam, brooding over the strange twists of history.

So much for those whose isolationism I had exposed.

Me? I was declared unfit for the United States Foreign Service.

Any vision of Agents Clare and Hipsley studiously researching my own position on war in the newspaper files of that time amounts to a dream of glory. I suppose that even if the investigators had discovered the unlikelihood that this young hawk was out to sabotage the war effort, logic would not have prevented them from pricking their ears to hearsay alone.

The red herring spotted in the form of the Guild circular nevertheless eluded Clare and Hipsley through the murky waters of their investigation. Without reading my writings, they simply never managed to dig up anything concrete, one way or another, about how I stood on preparing for war. And the "full explanation" of my role in the Guild statement on the North American Aviation strike fell a good deal short of uncovering the smoking pistol sought by Counsel for ACOPS before branding me a security risk.

A lot of taxpayers' money was wasted in the unsuccessful effort to prove my complicity. If Bannerman had not forbidden an interview with me, I am sure I would have obliged him by saying directly that I thought the President had been wrong. I have never thought that in this country that was a hanging offense. As it turned out, the government's security apparatus hung me anyway.

7

CONFIDENTIALLY
SPEAKING

IF YOU HAVE ever been visited by a government agent seeking information about an acquaintance, you will know that there is no mistaking his mission. There is a certain look about a security agent the world over I suspect. The ones I have met in the United States have a personality which recedes into the environment. They are dressed neatly, inconspicuously, and show their pocket credential with deference rather than any air of authority. The members of the FBI and the Secret Service I have seen on the job are hard to tell apart, as if they had all been stamped out from the same piece of plastic. Perhaps Special Agent Daniel H. Clare Jr., working in New York City, was such a one, and his partner, Elmer R. Hipsley, looking into my past in Washington, D.C. I don't know. I haven't been able to find out much about them. But between them, these two mysterious gentlemen turned in 19 pages of single-spaced information about me, gathered in August and September, 1946.

When a government investigator comes to my office, he is usually asking about a former student being considered for government duty. We have made it a rule at the Columbia School of Journalism never to let one look at the files. When an agent asks about politics, I always reply that I do not consider it part of my role as a teacher to inquire into the politics of students. The agents have always accepted the answer, although, in truth, talk about politics is very much a part of my courses in reporting on public affairs. Investigators doing checks on individuals seem content to watch for and wait for—volunteers.

Who would volunteer derogatory information about a fellow citizen to a government agent making a routine security check? A nice question, involving one's responsibility to the public interest measured alongside one's feelings about a fellow human being. A tough choice sometimes, I am sure. A choice one would just as soon not advertise if it went against anyone you were likely to see again.

I learned from my file that the investigators were well aware of this difficulty. A distinction was made between "informants" (complimentary and identified by name) and "confidential informants" (derogatory and anonymous). Inform*ers*—the pros of the business—are either paid for their services in money or are saving their own skin. They don't appear in my file.

Confidential informants who preserve their amateur standing not infrequently have an ax to grind—personal or otherwise. During the nervous 1940s and 1950s political informants were routinely courted by the FBI and other government security agencies. The deal was simple. The informants would spill all they knew or thought they knew about the person under scrutiny in exchange for the promise of perpetual anonymity. The bargain provided a field day, of course, for busybodies, crackpots, ideologues, well-meaning patriots, the genuinely alarmed, the narrowminded, the envious and the scorned. Agents in the field wrote it all down; the evaluations were supposedly left to the higher-ups, who could pick and choose what they judged to be relevant. So it was with Documents 53 and 56 in my security file, the 19 pages of closely packed information requested by ACOPS to determine whether my case was properly before Counsel.

Counsel for ACOPS had specially requested information from that already friendly witness, Kenneth Crawford, former head of *PM*'s Washington Bureau and onetime president of the national Newspaper Guild. He was a highly respected member of *Newsweek*'s staff when Special Agent Hipsley called upon him in his Washington office. According to Counsel for ACOPS, Crawford had already "orally stated" that I was a fine fellow, loyal and true. Under Hipsley's probing, his views were reported to be less unequivocal. Crawford comes across in Hipsley's version of their interview, nevertheless, as a decent fellow trying to be fair.

> When Mr. Kimball first came to work for PM he was a very well educated and extremely liberal young man. In some instances his thinking and liberal beliefs may have seemed to be entirely sympathetic with the Communist Party Line. As I know Kimball to be an independent thinker and consider him to be completely patriotic, I do not think that he ever followed the proposed Communist Party Line in his thinking as a person who stood for Communism. He may have followed the Party Line, and probably did in some instances, as a completely independent thinker who was entirely loyal to his country. . . .
>
> I know Mr. Kimball was inquisitive by nature and I know that his thinking in some instances, especially regarding Labor, was of a liberal type. His natural inquisitiveness and a desire to learn something more of the radical ideologies advanced by the radical group may have led him at times to share the light with them when in reality he was only doing so, so as to be able to form his own opinions. . . . I should also like to point out that a second reason for Kimball's association may most completely be described by the following statement: A *PM* employee who did not associate with persons of radical or Communistic views would have of necessity had to be a hermit. . . . Mr. Crawford further stated that during this period of unrest the word Communist or Red was loosely used and that anyone on the *PM* staff during this period was subject to these titles.
>
> He concluded by stating that the real fight between the conservative and radical elements of the newspaper guild took place after Kimball had left *PM* to go into the Marine Corps. He further stated that he believed Kimball's war record to be a definite beacon which served as proof of his basic patriotism and loyalty. He further stated that Kimball's decision not to

go back to the *PM* staff when they were bound by law to re-employ him, indicates Kimball's present political views and beliefs. Mr. Crawford concluded the interview by stating that he believed Kimball to be a completely loyal young man whose reputation and character were above reproach and who could be placed in a position of trust with complete confidence that he would serve his country honorably and well.

An informant, even a skilled journalist, is always somewhat at the mercy of the inquiring visitor. It was in this interview that Special Agent Hipsley took over when the informant's testimony was not sharp enough for his purposes. The exchange is worth repeating, because it so beautifully illustrates the investigatory process.

The undersigned asked Mr. Crawford the following question: "Mr. Crawford, would it be proper to say that Kimball, during the period of unrest at *PM* and while he apparently associated with the radical or Communistic element, teetered for a while as far as his political beliefs and loyalties were concerned?"

In answer to this question Mr. Crawford stated that he believed the undersigned had properly summed up Mr. Kimball's activities but that in doing so he had leaned a little far to the Left.

Government grammar being in its parlous state, a fast read by a government security officer might well have conjured up the picture that it was Kimball, not Hipsley, who had teetered in the wrong direction.

The government censors definitely teetered on the question of whether Crawford was a confidential informant. His name is blacked out by the government censor in a file document sent to me which repeated Counsel's instructions to interview him a second time and also in Document 53, Hipsley's interview. It appears untouched in others. Since Crawford was described as a known anti-Communist, one bureaucrat apparently treated his name as a confidential informant; another treated him as a friendly witness, entitled to no protection. Quite possibly, of course, the State Department censors just goofed.

But nothing explains why the testimony of someone of national reputation such as Kenneth Crawford carried so little weight with the government evaluators. I had not laid eyes on Crawford for years; I owed him one for a good college try in my behalf. But the record of my case makes it clear that character witnesses in my file such as Ken Crawford were outweighed in the scales by nameless moles working underground.

In Washington Hipsley also found an old colleague from *United States News*, Gordon H. Cole, information officer at the Department of Labor, who said he thought me to be "loyal to this country beyond any question," one whom he would "recommend for a position of trust with the Federal government." No mention in the summary.

Hipsley also turned up Philip M. Kaiser, who vouched for my loyalty. Kaiser, then Executive Assistant to the Secretary of Labor, was later appointed by President Kennedy to be minister to London and Ambassador to Senegal, and was appointed more recently by President Carter to be Ambassador to Hungary and then Austria. Said he:

> I have known Pete Kimball for many years; we went to Oxford together. I consider him a solid citizen of prodigious ability and I would recommend him 100 percent for a position of trust. I consider Kimball a loyal American and feel that we could use about a million like him. My knowledge of Kimball is fairly complete and while we attended Oxford together the conditions there were such that it would have been easy for a person of weak character to fall in with the elements. During my association with Kimball at Oxford I know he maintained a fine sense of proportion and that he evaluated the various isms advocated there which he was confronted with. To my knowledge Pete Kimball has never participated in any un-American activities and I know that he put up a real fight to get into the Marine Corps. Pete Kimball, without his glasses, has very poor sight and the Marine Corps did not want to accept him. After continued persistence, Pete

overcame the opposition and was admitted to the Corps. I also know that after he was in the Corps he was assigned a very soft post in Washington, D.C. and that he again put up a hell of a fight to get a foreign assignment and that he finally was successful and served with honor and distinction overseas.

CON never quoted Kaiser in its summary either. The positive testimony from those who had known me in the days before *PM* at Oxford and the *United States News* was corroborated by Patrick O'Sheel, the only witness who knew me both in the Marine Corps and on my postwar job with Time, Inc. O'Sheel, a *Life* writer at the time he was interviewed by Agent Clare in New York, later became an information officer in Africa and a Foreign Service officer in Eastern Europe. Clare complained that "while in the Service of the United States Marines, Mr. Kimball associated with men who are now scattered through all parts of the country," and did not explain how he had located O'Sheel.

Mr. O'Sheel contended that he had known Mr. Kimball for approximately two years, that he had worked with him as a Public Relations Officer in the Japanese area, and that he had been in a position to observe both his work and his political sympathies at close range. He characterized Mr. Kimball as a man of remarkable talent, unbelievable integrity, excellent character and one who should have an extraordinary future in political affairs. He described him as loyal in every way. Mr. O'Sheel conceded that Mr. Kimball had for years been interested in labor, but he contended that this interest was disassociated from Communism; that it was a type of broad liberalism plus fanatical enthusiasm for the labor movement; that it was a sincere intellectual conviction, but that while it was manifest in his union participation it was never aligned with outright radicalism. Mr. O'Sheel said that he had many discussions with Mr. Kimball while in the Service; that Mr. Kimball had frequently criticized the "stuffier" regulations, pertaining to Marine discipline; that he had gathered around him a group of intellectuals who liked to talk on the broader issues of international relations, but that he could not recall any instance where Mr. Kimball had fomented agitation or had participated in "go home" rallies or "get the Marines out of China" meetings. He contended Mr. Kimball possessed intellectual brilliance with the forthrightness and the courage and vision to make an exceptional foreign service officer. In summarizing his remarks, he stated that he was positive that Mr. Kimball was not a Communist; that his loyalties were not susceptible to Communistic propaganda; and that his basic integrity as well as his remarkably clear perception precluded the possibility that he could ever do anything to the detriment of this country.

In Bannerman's report to Counsel for ACOPS, O'Sheel's "contentions" in my behalf simply disappeared:

The Security Committee has taken note of the request to interrogate former associates of Kimball while serving on active duty in the Marine Corps. In view of the fact that all of his former associates during that period of time have now returned to civilian life and their whereabouts are unknown, it has been impossible to ascertain any factual information regarding his views and activities during that period of time.

A bald lie.

PM was still in business in the summer of 1946, but only a floundering version of the paper I had worked on before the war. Most of the original staff had scattered to the four winds, but many were names well known in the profession and among readers. If he had so desired, Special Agent Clare could have easily found a representative cross-section of character witnesses.

Ingersoll quit in November, 1946, over the issue of accepting advertising, advocated by Field to put the paper in the black. Apparently he didn't fit the description for being interviewed. Nor did my old boss, Kenneth Stewart, by then teaching journalism at New York University. Other former colleagues had also switched jobs.

Bill Walton had gone to *Life*; Wes Price was an editor for *Saturday Evening Post*; Elmer Rosener became a nationally syndicated columnist. Henry Lieberman was at *The New York Times*; Woody Broun, a character actor on Broadway; Tom Meany, publicist for the Brooklyn Dodgers, and Charlotte Adams, food columnist for the *Herald-Tribune*. Hodding Carter was running the Mississippi *Delta-Times*; Sydney Margolis and Albert Deutch were pioneering the new field of consumer journalism, and Lillian Ross was at *The New Yorker*. *PM* alumni were now everywhere: I. F. Stone in Washington, Cecelia Ager in Hollywood, Sam Boal in London, Bob Neville in Hong Kong, and "Barnaby," our comic strip, all over the world.

All, except "Barnaby," probably knew me a good deal better than any [names blacked out] informants, who, I am confident, were none of the above.

> Through sources previously determined to be absolutely reliable, investigation was instigated to locate former or present members of the *PM* staff, whose sentiments were known to be anti-Communist. [Name blacked out] emerged as the individual who most closely filled the required specifications [three lines blacked out] and he has since demonstrated loyalty through his constant opposition to Communist infiltration in the newspaper and labor field.

Some member of the crowd that had lost all the Guild elections while we were together on *PM* got in his licks when the government came calling.

The confidential informant "of known anti-Communist sentiments" who "most closely filled the required specifications" is unknown to me, thanks to the sanctuary still maintained by government authority. But Special Agent Clare seemed glad to find him.

> He discussed Mr. Kimball without mincing any words, [Name blacked out] conceded that while he held the deep conviction in his heart that Mr. Kimball was absolutely loyal to the Communists, he could not prove that he was, nor could he present documentary evidence to that effect. When it was

indicated to [Name blacked out] the type of position Mr. Kimball sought within the Department, he ejaculated, "My God, no! Never!"

He stated that he felt that the appointment of Mr. Kimball to such a position would be fraught with danger and that it would serve Mr. Kimball as a fertile field for the propagation of his Communist sympathies, and that because of Mr. Kimball's undeniable brilliance, smoothness and political acumen, his true sentiments could not be unmasked until a great deal of damage had been done.

[Name blacked out] wanted it made clear that his opinion had been independently arrived at, and was a matter of feeling rather than of proven knowledge.

A reporter's inhibitions not to cloud his facts with his prejudices were clearly not operative in the testimony of this *PM* ex-staffer. The quotations from this old colleague illustrated some of the twists a skillful confidential informant can use to get his message across: (1) the art of the reversed compliment, whereby qualities cited for seeming praise ("undeniable brilliance, smoothness and political acumen") are converted into dangerous debits ("his true sentiments could not be unmasked until a great deal of damage had been done"); (2) the double-edged disclaimer, whereby the informant's confession of a lack of proven knowledge becomes his profession of independent opinion; (3) the in-my-heart-I-know-I'm-right-gambit, made famous two decades later by the followers of Barry Goldwater ("without mincing any words . . . he held the deep conviction in his heart that Mr. Kimball was absolutely loyal to the Communists"), and (4) a snappy tag line to catch the eye of the evaluator ("My God, no! Never!").

When a biased investigator carefully chooses his sources, the result is not likely to be the unvarnished truth. The editorial collaboration between an investigator and his source works especially well when both are trying to prove the same point. Even though the confidential sources in my case were professional journalists, their remarks were continually paraphrased and, it seems clear, rearranged. So it is hard to tell who should be given credit for some of the passages in my file. But the evidence seems clear that my detractors knew exactly what they were doing.

Part of their surety might be attributed to the disease of single-mindedness, a condition causing much difficulty in the politics of current times. The anti-Communists of the '40s were the pro-lifers, if you will, the anti-nukers of those earlier years: single-issue participants in the political process. Fixation upon only one question has had a deleterious effect on the careers of many publicly elected officials who were marked for discard for exhibiting a lack of purity on the only test that counted with an organized minority of selective voters.

An issue touching upon the security of the nation itself in a threatening world order, it has been demonstrated several times in our history, can be the most divisive of all. Those who *know* they are right are equally sure who is wrong. There is no middle ground, no room for fairness and balance. So it must have been among the confidential informants in my file.

The exercise of checking out my political beliefs as of 1940–41 on the basis of recollections of me as of 1946 was in itself perilous. The frame of reference of the two periods was quite different, and conclusions reached in one era about opinions held in an earlier era might be distorted. By the time containment of the Soviet Union reached the top of the national agenda in the postwar years, for example, it was forgotten that before the war the Russian delegates in the League of Nations were almost alone in standing up against the early aggressions of Hitler and Mussolini.

Once the war was under way, the Soviet Union was first a neutral, then our wartime ally, then an uneasy partner in the peace. The initial investigation of me swung into action the same month in 1946 that Winston Churchill made his Iron Curtain speech at Fulton, Missouri.

Many of my contemporaries who flirted with the Communists as an expression of anti-Fascism in the prewar era were hauled before Congressional committees later as postwar subversives. Others who had sincerely felt that the United States should stay out of foreign wars in 1939–40 were charged a decade later with being current fifth-columnists. The years that elapsed between my activities in prewar America and the postwar investigation of my loyalty must have put even "superior" agents such as Hipsley and Clare at a conceptual disadvantage. Indeed, one thing that makes my file pertinent to today's dialogue, I believe, is the example it provides of the unreliability of litmus tests for judging somebody's "Redness." Or, for that matter, "True Blueness."

More careful methods of assessment, however, were of no interest to anti-Communist vigilantes either before or after World War II. Suspicions of Communist penetration into American life were beginning to stir American politicians, especially those from constituencies away from the Eastern Seaboard, by the end of the '30s. Representative Martin Dies of Texas chaired the committee to investigate un-American activities, which began compiling its own list of "front organizations," charging that they were really instruments of the Communist Party, and listed a dozen CIO unions (though not the American Newspaper Guild) as having leadership "tinged with Communism." Any group sympathetic to the Loyalist side in the Spanish Civil War made the list, as well as the American Student Union, National Negro Congress and American Civil Liberties Union. The committee estimated that roughly a million Americans had been "taken in," and Chairman Dies declared the "Trojan Horse situation" in this country to be the most dangerous in the world.

When America entered the war, this first bloom of anxiety faded, if only because there were more immediate worries. But ideological debate resprouted vigorously as soon as the war was over. When my prewar anti-Communist colleagues were sought out in postwar New York and Washington by Special Agents Clare and Hipsley, popular panic was festering its way to the full boil of the '50s.

The investigation of me thus linked two separate eras of American history when it turned out to be personally dangerous not to conform to anti-Communist crusades. When Clare and Hipsley were turned loose in 1946 to find out what they could about a 30-year-old under consideration for the Foreign Service, they applied hindsight to me with double-powered lenses, each ground to the same paranoid prescription. They were not the only ones. The most durable bridge from the anxieties of the '30s to the panic of the '50s was the group of people agents sought out as confidential informants—the professional "anti-Communists" on the publications where I had worked.

In the modern era of developing sensitivity to the proper relationships between the press and law-enforcement authorities, my file makes clear that some forms of collaboration have been going on for years. American journalists who have trouble abroad because they are suspected of fronting for the CIA are carrying the baggage imposed by intelligence agencies in Washington that have long been in the habit of cultivating "anti-Communistic" sources among the working press.

Hipsley, obeying Counsel's instructions to make contact with a *Time* staffer determined in advance to be anti-Communistic, reported back:

> Discreet inquiry determined that the best source of information now available was [three lines blacked out].
>
> [Name blacked out] was contacted and asked the undersigned to give him some time to make discreet inquiries so that he might document his own beliefs concerning Kimball.

It's one thing for an investigator to make "discreet inquiries"; for a colleague to do so smacks of a little more than volunteerism. Nevertheless, even given the time to substantiate "his own beliefs concerning Kimball" this confidential informant/collaborator was something of a disappointment to Agent Hipsley.

> [Name blacked out] was subsequently interviewed and furnished the following information concerning Mr. Kimball:
>
> Mr Kimball was a young reporter on the *PM* paper in New York City and in his activities there he appeared to be on the Left Wing side. He was active in the *PM* Unit of the New York Newspaper Guild and his activities there were a little far to the Left. He is at present employed by *Time* Magazine and his activities with that paper [sic] have not in any way been out of bounds. [Name blacked out] further stated that the New York Office described Mr. Kimball as a person of liberal ideas, very definitely not dangerous and that he was entirely controllable. [Name blacked out] concluded by stat-

ing that he and his informed sources were of the opinion that
the subject of this report was liberal in his ideas but that he
was basically a patriotic American and a respectable citizen.

Patriotic, not dangerous, controllable by the editors of *Time*.
What more could anyone ask? Again, that interview was never mentioned in Bannerman's summary of the renewed investigation of my
character and background for ACOPS.

Hipsley had more luck following up a tip sent down from Special
Agent Clare in New York.

The following persons, now located in Washington, D.C.,
were contacted. [Names blacked out] furnished the following
information which, for the purposes of clarity will be reported
by the undersigned and the meat of the discussion is as
follows:

Mr. Kimball was described as an excellent reporter and
exceptionally good writer. He was further described as being
very definitely a Leftist to what appeared an extreme degree.
In the course of the discussion both gentlemen admitted that
it would be almost impossible to agree upon the pure 'color'
of the subject. The definite information covered was that the
subject was an active member of the PM Unit of the New
York Newspaper Guild and that, to the knowledge of the
two men interviewed, he always agreed with and voted for
what was considered to be a straight Communist Party ticket
in Guild activities. As previously described in this report,
these two gentlemen stated that the Guild as a whole was predominantly Communistic and that there was quite a fight
going on between the radical and conservative members.
Both men concurred that to their knowledge Kimball had
never voted with the anti-Communist or conservative group
and that to their knowledge he always lined up with what
they described as the "Party side . . ." Both gentlemen agreed
that they knew Kimball had signed and endorsed practically
all the Red petitions circulating in the Guild at that time and
to their knowledge he had never signed or assisted the conservative group in their efforts to control the radical element.

Both men continued by stating that Kimball had lived with a Communist and that he was always seen drinking beer in their company. Both men agreed that it would take a real expert to determine if it was the Communists' beer or the Communistic politics that interested him. Both gentlemen agreed that Mr. Kimball was not a Communist Party member and they both agreed that he seemed to be "a fellow traveler."

This might best be described as combining the doctrine of guilt by association with guilt by nonassociation. I know I should have spread my beer drinking around more democratically, but the truth of the matter is that all those conservative guys seemed to be nursing peptic ulcers. To understand why, you might try to follow this testimony, confidentially speaking, from another one of Special Agent Hipsley's [Name blacked out] sources:

I knew Pete Kimball in the early days of the paper *PM*, we were never close friends and my knowledge of him is entirely through association. Mr. Kimball was a fair employee and a nice young man who seemed to get along well with everybody at *PM* and I felt that, personally, he was a nice fellow. My knowledge of him is that he seems to have been one of the "saner" characters at *PM*. As you probably know, there was a distinct separation in the *PM* organization between the radicals and the conservatives. I was lined up on the conservative side in the Guild and can only state that I know Kimball was not on my side.

[Name blacked out] continued by stating he would clarify this with "by my last remark I do not mean that I know Kimball to be a Communist. I just know he was not an anti-Communist or conservative. During this time I do not think Kimball had an important active part in the political fight in the Guild on the side of the Communists for I feel sure that I would have remembered it as I was so bitterly opposed to them." Again, [Name blacked out] stated that he wished to clarify his last remark "in that I do not wish to state that Kimball was not sympathetic or not involved with the Communist Party, or at least the radical element. I am merely giving you a complete picture of my knowledge concerning his activities." [Name blacked out] stated definitely "I know Kimball to be friendly with [Name blacked out] and other known Communists. I have no knowledge as to whether he was interested in their politics, their company or as a young employee of the paper merely staying in their company so as to have someone to play around with. I do know that the Communists were so thick at PM that to shun them you had to stay home." [Name blacked out] continued by stating "I have had no real contact with Kimball since 1941 and the real Party Line actually formed in early 1942 after he had left the paper." In connection with this [Name blacked out] stated "that as Kimball had left before the real fight began, Kimball never showed which way he would jump or where he really stood. . . . I know he was not active in the anti-Communist or conservative ranks. What part Kimball played with the opposition is something I have no knowledge of. . . . and if someone could authoritatively clear up how far to the Left he went in his thinking, I would recommend him for a position of trust."

I discovered the identity of the *PM* informant so interested in my state of mind quite by accident. The government censor omitted to black out his name in another part of my file where the evidence against me was being summed up. The confidential informant turned out to be my fellow reporter covering the Ford strike for *PM*— former editor and then columnist for the New York *Post*, James A. Wechsler. Like many who were, by the late '30s, "so bitterly opposed" to the Left, Jimmy had been a Young Communist at Columbia earlier in that decade when he was editor of the *Spectator*. Ironically, Jimmy Wechsler himself later ran afoul of the McCarthy Committee, accused of dangerous proclivities toward the Left.

Discerning my "state of mind" without ever talking to me was beyond the capacities of these special agents—as indeed it should be. Since they never got around to reading anything I wrote, they learned nothing from that obvious source either. They did discover that whatever was going on in my head, it never led me to pal around with the anti-Communists or to line up on their side. If a degree of guilt could be gleaned from nonassociation, what might be uncovered from my associations? The technique of guilt by association led Special Agents Hipsley and Clare to focus on those with whom I had shared living space. Obviously, one lived under the same roof only with clones.

Shortly after I started to work for *PM* I moved from temporary digs at the Princeton Club to share a railroad flat on the top floor of a brownstone near the Chelsea waterfront in Manhattan.

My boss in the National News section, Kenneth Stewart, and his wife had a lease on the Chelsea apartment, but found it too confining for their two growing children. He offered it to me and another reporter on his staff who was newly arrived from California, Tom O'Connor. We didn't know each other, but were both single, strangers in New York City and looking for a place to live.

O'Connor, whose cherubic Irish countenance masked his Harvard education, had been an early Guild activist in Los Angeles. His father, he said, had been a Wobbly in the mines of Montana. O'Connor had a taste for Irish whiskey, and although our combined income was less than $100 per week we could afford in those days to buy whiskey by the case. The California style was a far cry from New Britain, and I remained pretty much on the fringe of O'Connor's entourage, although Tom and I became fast friends. He liked parties, and more than a few pub crawls in the Village ended up at our place.

Special Agent Edward Whalen of the FBI had already summed that all up when he reported from New Britain that Foreign Service "applicant is reported to have been the subject of much complaint for having wild parties in his apartment while an employee of *PM* in New York."

The Chelsea flat acquired another tenant when one weekend during *PM*'s first summer someone at the office asked O'Connor and me whether we would put up a homeless Spanish refugee for a night, seeing as we had a spare daybed in the living room. A fair-haired, blue-eyed Catalonian, about 20 years old and just off the docks, knocked at our door. The lad couldn't speak English, drank wine poured from a flagon held at arm's length above his head, sang

Spanish Republican ballads and could cook a wicked omelette. His name was Ricardo Sicre, and he stayed not for a night but for a year.

When O'Connor married and moved out, another *PM* staffer, Amos Landman, who had been living with his parents in Brooklyn, asked if he could take over O'Connor's share of the rent. Landman was a much more subdued type, with a habit of cocking his head quizzically after every sentence. His father was a well known rabbi, editor of the *Jewish Encyclopedia*, who would explain the Old Testament to me when Amos took me over for a home-cooked meal.

When State Department Special Agent Daniel H. Clare Jr. resumed the investigation three months after Whalen's FBI report from New Britain, he checked out the Chelsea address I had left four and one-half years before for the Marine boot camp at Parris Island, South Carolina. All three of my former roommates must have interested him very much.

Ricardo Sicre served in the Office of Strategic Services (predecessor to the CIA) during World War II. He was parachuted into Spain to cut off Franco communications with the German U-boat fleet, and became a United States citizen. He settled in Madrid after the war. He showed me a copy of his own CIA file not long ago which had him listed as (1) a Communist, (2) a British secret agent and (3) a postwar intimate of Francisco Franco.

The names of Landman and O'Connor were blacked out in the file first delivered to me. That apparently meant they were already in the government indices as suspicious characters, and therefore their privacy was protected. They, though not I, were called before Congressional investigating committees during the un-American probes in the '50s. They had been named by others as being present at Communist meetings in the '30s before they had gone to work on *PM*. They refused to testify about themselves or to name names of other alleged transgressors in return for their own clearance. Landman was fired by the National Municipal League in 1955 and O'Connor died of a heart attack two months after his appearance in 1952. Mine was a small price to pay in comparison for having shared the same roof.

Special Agent Clare's report on the association begins:

[Name blacked out's] contention that Mr. Kimball preferred the society of known Communists is given substance by investigation at 436 West 20th Street, where Mr. Kimball resided from 1940 until March, 1942.

Here 18 lines are blacked out, too horrendous for me to see. I can only suppose they involved accusations against my ex-roommates.

I could take an oath to this day that in all the time we were together—at work or at play, in public and private bull sessions, at Guild meetings and rides on the Hoboken ferry—O'Connor and Landman never said or did anything in my presence to indicate they accepted any outside discipline whatsoever to govern their free spirits. I knew them as talented, young colleagues, interesting to work with and fun to be with.

The possibility exists, I suppose, that I was considered too naive by the Comintern to bother to recruit. Membership in the Communist Party was supposed to be kept secret from nonmembers. But if the Cold Warriors were right, one might think that I rated from my housemates one teeny-weeny hint of invitation to join them inside the conspiracy. Or that an indiscretion would have been dropped during drinks and discussions lasting into the dawn. Never happened.

Both these former roommates were in New York City when the State Department ordered Clare to perform his special investigation. Landman had served with the U.S. Army in Europe and taken a postwar job as a publicist with the National Municipal League. O'Connor was 4-F because of a tubercular lung, and continued to work for *PM* and its successors when they bought out the paper after V-J Day. Both Landman and O'Connor were married and I was not, so our lives had drifted their separate ways. Special Agent Clare didn't try to talk to them anyway about the days when we belonged to the Guild together on *PM*, because they didn't fit Counsel for ACOPS' prescription as "anti-Communist former or present members of the *PM* staff closely acquainted with Kimball in New York." Clare's report continues with testimony from the best substitute he could come up with—the landlady at our Chelsea apartment—and concludes on an upbeat:

Mr. Kimball resided [18 spaces blacked out] until his induction into the Armed Services and, according to the landlady, he and his friends lived in a comparatively moderate manner, and of the three men Mr. Kimball appeared to be by far the most conservative and temperate.

Score one point for me on the wild-party charge. Score another for my Irish landlady's testimony about my relative conservatism. But I don't remember ever exchanging a word with my landlady except when paying the rent; the State Department's procedures for gathering intelligence were no more reassuring than the FBI's.

The ground rules of government investigations should terrify any American who has learned about our concept of justice as it is taught in our grade schools or in any institution of our democracy. No American ever learned that a body acting as judge and jury—as ACOPS surely was—would build its case exclusively on evidence from witnesses determined in advance to be prejudiced. Or to weigh such opinions more heavily than evidence. Or to ignore good reports, however pertinent and reliable, which, in my file at least, went uncensored—but unused. We do not learn, nor should we accept, that nameless moles can brand us disloyal for our lifetime. And beyond: apparently the government agencies conducting my investigation keep unsubstantiated allegations on file forever.

Since my file indicated that one source of information for the period I worked at *PM* had been the Office of Naval Intelligence, now known as the Naval Investigative Service, I wrote away for its full report. NIS wrote back that its policy was to purge its central files on a regular schedule—favorable material, after 15 years; unfavorable material, after 20. When NIS fed my name into its computer, the data bank was empty. There is something to be said for that policy, but it is not followed by the Washington headquarters of either the FBI or the State Department.

How am I to judge the confidential informants who sought to blacken my reputation? My conscience tells me that I should be more charitable toward them than they were toward me. My emotions cry for revenge. Beyond all that, however, is the principle which asserts that an accused should have the right to defend himself against his accusers. I have never had that opportunity.

I wrote to the State Department for the names and addresses of Special Agents Hipsley and Clare, if they were still alive. It might be fun, I thought, to compare notes, and let them meet in person the doddering college professor who evolved from the dangerous, young radical portrayed in their investigations.

The State Department said "no." It would be an unwarranted invasion, a department spokesman declared, of their privacy.

8

HOME FROM
THE WAR

THE "TIME SUPERVISOR" interviewed by the FBI in June had testified that I unwaveringly supported the cause of labor in any dispute and thus could not be trusted in any country where there was a possibility of Russian dominance. Counsel for ACOPS, the State Department's new vehicle for loyalty cases, had rejected that line of argument on the ground that "a continued support of the position of labor is not equivalent to disloyalty to the United States." In ordering another field investigation, he had stipulated that the State Department's special agents go back over the resolution on the North American strike and talk to anti-Communist members of the staff of *PM*. But that, after all, was ancient history. Even though the "superior investigators" had trouble locating anyone who had known me in the Marine Corps, the likelihood of turning up something juicy there was pretty remote. So, whatever Hipsley and Clare could find out from sources at *Time* was going to be crucial. Since Clare was covering New York City, where *Time* had its headquarters, he was chiefly responsible for checking out my current activities. And I was ignorant of the whole scenario, busy earning my living as a neophyte contributing editor in National Affairs, happily home from the war.

Whatever else those of us returning to civilian life after V-J Day had on our minds, subverting the nation was not it. It was just wonderful to be out of uniform and earning a living again in a place like New York City. Postwar housing was tight, and I was lucky to land a place in a room at the Princeton Club where transients occupied the other two beds. I was accustomed to barracks life, and it was mildly amusing to watch the old grads being tucked into bed after a few too many in the bar downstairs or to hear their troubles after they missed the last train to Darien. Once, a career Foreign Service officer was my roommate for a whole week. Stationed in Havana, he was back in the States supposedly for negotiations on sugar quotas. When I left for work in the morning, he was already drinking out of a large bottle of rum he kept alongside his bed. Some days he was still there when I came home at night. I don't know how the sugar quotas worked out, but I thought about that roommate when I learned that I had been judged unfit to be a fellow member of the Foreign Service.

I could take breakfast at the Princeton Club and walk to work— from 39th and Park to the Time–Life Building. There, on the 28th floor, a complete set of that day's newspapers—*Times, Herald-Tribune, News, Mirror, Wall Street Journal*—would be waiting for me on my desk. Even the Communist *Daily Worker*; *Time* believed its writers should be fully informed about everything going on. At noon, we would pop over to Toots Shor's for lunch, where, price controls still being in effect, chicken hash with asparagus followed by chocolate pie came to slightly more than a dollar. Working late, supper was oyster stew next door at Susan Palmer's or a quitsjmeitre and Heineken across the street at Holland House. From my window I could watch the skaters in the Rockefeller Center rink. My office mate, Ed Cerf, and I would sail paper airplanes when in the throes of writer's block to see which one of us could make a launch that would touch down all the way over on 50th Street. The ceiling of the office was covered with acoustical tile since it had once been the teletype room. We amused ourselves by shooting pencils into the ceiling with rubber bands until the place looked like a cave of stalactites. We were lighthearted lads trying to ease the pressure cooker that was *Time*.

Cerf had been a freshman trying out for the college paper at Princeton when I was the chairman and privileged to send the young candidate out on trivial errands. He had worked briefly for *Time* before being called up as a Marine reservist even before Pearl Harbor. His artillery unit had seen all the bad ones—Guadalcanal, Tarawa, Saipan, Okinawa. Because of his seniority, he rated the desk immediately adjacent to the window, or perhaps it was because he came back to work the week before I joined the National Affairs staff. We were the junior writers, the only ones sharing office space with another. Old Princetonians, ex-Marines, neophyte competitors in the big time, Cerf and I became fast friends. (Later on, he was best man at my wedding; I was godfather to his son.)

Cerf had been raised in Portland, Oregon, and had majored in classics in college. I used to kid him when he felt at sea on some story involving national politics, economics or Washington, D.C., familiar subjects to me. We played a game in which he pretended to be an ignorant provincial and I tried to explain as best I could the ABC's of what a *Time* writer on National Affairs should understand. He, on the other hand, claimed to know the name and position of every Big League ballplayer for the last 20 years and whether he batted and threw right-handed or left. We amused ourselves for hours quizzing each other on such matters.

But the FBI and State Department agents who came around to the magazine checking out my political views never quizzed Cerf; he knew me too well to be trusted by them. He died in 1954, so I was destined to see a great deal of his son and my godson, Barry, who grew up to take a PhD in anthropology at Columbia. He is not as smart as his father, however, about baseball players.

The work week at *Time* ended on Monday night when the edition went to bed that would reach subscribers in time to read the coming weekend. This meant that our days off were Tuesday and Wednesday, which had an incestuous effect on the social life of Time, Inc., employees. While the rest of the world played on Saturday and Sunday, we were hunched over our typewriters struggling to write about fast-moving stories in such a way that they would not be dated when they reached *Time* readers the following Friday.

Because of the out-of-phase *Time* workweek I saw few of my prewar friends still working for *PM*. I visited New Britain on my midweek "weekends" fairly frequently. My widowed mother had died in November, 1945, the month of my final discharge; my unmarried sister lived alone in the old family home. I was needed there to settle my mother's estate and similar family responsibilities, as I wrote the Board of Examiners of the Foreign Service in April, 1946. I would go down to the local Y and play volley ball with the young businessmen with whom I had grown up. One of these was the former FBI agent whom I identify as T-1, but he never mentioned to me that he had been interviewed about me by the bureau.

At *Time* there was a cadre of returning Marines besides Cerf and me. It was said that Roy Alexander, an assistant managing editor and gung-ho veteran of World War I, would hire any ex-Marine. Pat O'Sheel, the only Marine buddy those agents of "superior ability" ever managed to find, was working on *Life*. Herb Merrilat, another ex-Marine and former Rhodes Scholar, was a writer in Foreign Affairs. Warren Goodman, a former Marine pilot with whose torpedo-bomber squadron I had flown as a combat correspondent on a mission to Rabaul, was writing Business. The Semper Fi group would lunch together, trade anecdotes about our new jobs and congratulate ourselves for being civilians again. We had no trouble finding one another.

And because Old Tigers never die either, Cerf and I socialized a good deal with old friends from Princeton. John Brooks was around for a while, but fled to *The New Yorker*. Brooke Alexander was a writer for *Fortune*; he had been on the *Princetonian* staff when I was elected. Sam Welles was a writer in Religion. Wes Pullen, a fellow member of the football squad in my day and just back from the Navy, was working on the business side as a go-fer for Roy Larsen, one of the Henry Luce originals who had become president of Time, Inc. Cerf and I would condescendingly invite Pullen to lunch so he "could meet a couple of writers." (He ended up as a Time, Inc., vice president in charge of the whole broadcasting operation.) As a permanent resident of the Princeton Club, I would run into out-of-town alumni when they checked in. Young bachelors Kimball and Cerf would show them the sights. Not a controversial individual in the lot of those old acquaintances, nor anyone considered worth the time of a loyalty checker.

The pressures on a *Time* writer were such that during the working week there was little time for distraction beyond the churning of stories in the back, middle and front of the mind. A writer in National Affairs would be handling several stories at once, so the agony was multiple. Each story would then pass through several echelons of editors, each of whom would make corrections and notes in the margin. Corrected stories were all duly retyped on a set of carbon copies which were distributed around the office with one going back to the original writer. He would be expected to absorb the gist of the edits and crank out a new version. We described the process by comparing our copy to a piece of cheese being nibbled to death by an army of mice. Any writer who loaded his copy with left-of-center overtones would not long have survived such scrutiny by his superiors. *Time* was no place for an undercover Red propagandist to hide.

That did not mean that there was not ample room for editorial debate. The premise articulated by Henry Luce was that the truth was never a neutral statement of seemingly contradictory facts. It was the writer's job to search out the correct interpretation from the data. To that end the writer would be provided firsthand reporting from *Time*'s field correspondents in all corners of the earth, all the competing publications he was able to read, a library morgue stuffed with clippings on every known subject and person, and a researcher–checker to get answers to his queries and to put a dot over every word going into the magazine as verification of its accuracy. The writer worked from these raw materials and rewrote everything around a central theme. You were paid well at *Time*, given more time than daily reporters to think, backed by the logistics of an unequaled editorial support system and forced to hone carefully every word under the eagle eye of a talented editor. How could that result in anything short of the ultimate truth?

The overall method was described as group journalism. The National Affairs section, known internally as NA, would gather together in the office of our editor at about noon every Thursday, the first day of our working week. This was the story conference at which the contents of the next issue would be roughly blocked out, subject to revision as breaking news evolved, and each story set down on the working table of contents and assigned to one of the writers. Once assigned, a writer usually saw the story through to the final copy for teletyping to the printer in Chicago. Only on rare occasions—after three or four unsatisfactory rewrites—would a story be taken from one writer and given to another. More often, a story might be edited beyond recognition by one or several of the mice.

Story conferences were free-wheeling affairs, the place where everyone had a chance to present his ideas. The theory of group journalism was that a bunch of bright people kicking around ideas together might come up with something better than any single individual had brought into the room. The process was picked up eventually by the advertising business and called brainstorming, although imagination at *Time* was supposed to be disciplined by ties to the facts. Story suggestions each week were wired to New York by correspondents in the field; the Washington Bureau would file a long report backgrounding the news behind the news there. It became my job in the summer of '46 to digest all these story possibilities and to act as a summarizer at the weekly story conference when we gathered to hammer out a tentative schedule. My selection for that position of trust never made the investigatory reports either.

The year 1946 was a lively one for news—a nation reconverting from wartime to peacetime. Washington was debating how quickly to unwind economic controls; returning veterans were looking for jobs, housing and education; labor unions were seeking to catch up after four years of frozen wages and benefits and to consolidate the entry of blacks, women and the new generation into the labor force. Minorities returning home from military service were taking a second look at the customs of discrimination in their old hometowns; black markets and meat shortages persisted beyond the mobilization for war, and the first peacetime Congressional elections were in the offing.

The National Affairs editor decided at the weekly story conference who would initially take on such stories. As new possibilities arose in the news during the week, he parceled out the new assignments. We wrote nearly twice as many stories as could eventually be published, so there were a good many on the story list which we all knew were marginal. The new recruits were assigned more than their share of those. The cover stories went to the old hands. Otherwise, it was pretty much the luck of the draw. My luck was to draw not a few stories that should have interested the folks in the State Department.

One story assigned to me was a strike by the United Automobile Workers at the Allis-Chalmers farm machinery plant outside Milwaukee, a bitter, violent dispute which dragged on for weeks, then years. The situation was made more interesting to a young journalist who had once worked for a paper which refused to take advertising by the fact that Allis-Chalmers was a major *Time* advertiser. Its ads ran regularly as the double-truck spread in the magazine's centerfold, a premium spot.

I had cut my teeth reporting for *PM* on the 1940 strike at the Ford Motor Company, but I didn't know much about the Allis-Chalmers strike except what was filed by our Wisconsin stringers. These reports indicated quite clearly that the company was out to break the union and the union was equally determined to extend its organization throughout the farm machinery industry. There were the usual charges by management that the strike was Communist inspired.

My special awareness of labor's side in such controversies was formed even earlier than my reporting days at UAW headquarters in Detroit or my experience at *United States News* in becoming an early Newspaper Guild member. As an adolescent growing up in a New England manufacturing city where my father and uncle headed two of the largest factories, I had been brought up on the "union problem"; it had been openly discussed in front of the little pitcher with big ears. Having come of age during the New Deal, having lived abroad when Hitler and Mussolini dissolved labor unions in the totalitarian states, having covered as a reporter the first stirrings of unionism in United States production plants, I had assumed that the rights of working men and women were part of the agenda we had put on uniforms to protect. It was a conviction that I have continued to hold past the age of 65 though hard heads counsel me that I am long out of style. I still don't cross a picket line when the cafeteria workers go on strike at Columbia, though I now fudge the issue by holding my classes in my apartment.

I wrote the Allis-Chalmers story for *Time* pretty much as I saw it: an unyielding local management using every means at its disposal to avoid dealing with an "outside" union. I recognized the emotions on management's side from my New England youth; it was all spelled out again in the correspondents' file. The union goals? I knew from my contact with the Ford workers in Dearborn that they needed no shortwave message from Moscow to join the union. There is no such thing as "objective" journalism; it is the projection of a sense of fairness which gives credibility, fairness to both sides in that each can recognize its own perspective of events somewhere in the account. In the end, a *Time* writer was expected to point the reader toward the weight of the truth. That weight, I concluded, was not with the Wisconsin executives at Allis-Chalmers.

I don't remember any argument over my copy with either my immediate supervisor or the nibbling editors up the line. It ran pretty much as written, by *Time* standards of word changes and fixes.

The reaction from Allis-Chalmers, however, was something else. The company pulled its big advertising spreads out of the magazine beginning with the very next issue. I braced myself for a reaction from the editorial hierarchy. There was none. *Time* Letters ran a few comments, pro and con. Nobody said boo to me. A few months later Allis-Chalmers advertising resumed its former place in the centerfold.

The episode fulfilled none of the cliches enunciating advertisers' alleged control over the editorial product. I was pretty proud of *Time* and felt pretty good myself for receiving that sort of backing.

If a writer handled a story which reappeared in the news the next week, he usually wrote the encore. It was my bad luck to draw the congressional fight over whether wartime price controls should be repealed. The debate over that went on for weeks, too important to omit but about which there was precious little to add after the first week. Much has been written about how *Time* slants the news, as if the orders came down from on high to the obedient writer. My experience chronicling the fate of the Office of Price Administration in 1946 illustrates the process was a good deal more subtle than that and, on occasion, the touch too light to make any dent.

The head of OPA was Chester Bowles, who had been appointed to the job during the war by Franklin D. Roosevelt. Harry Truman had fired Harold Ickes and was generally getting rid of left-over New Dealers. There were signs on the hustings that the populace was weary of meat shortages and black markets in nylons and auto tires.

Suppliers blamed it on the continuation of wartime controls. Bowles, an original *PM* stockholder and one-time member of America First, was by 1946 fighting a valiant rear-guard action against the interest groups lobbying Congress to take the lid off prices, and Harry Truman seemed about to throw him to the wolves.

As the writer who had drawn the running story on price control, I earnestly tried to apply the master's degree in economics I had taken at Oxford. I was personally partial, I will admit, to the memory of F. D. R. as opposed to the crowd of Missouri cronies whom Truman had moved into the White House. Also, I enjoyed those cheap lunches at Toots Shor's made possible by price control. In covering the congressional fight over OPA for *Time*, I took pains to make clear that there were two sides to the argument. Documented, of course, by good quotes and lively anecdotes insofar as possible from the Washington file.

The proprietors of the magazine were well known for their preference for the Republican Party and the free enterprise system, so there was a bit of derring-do, I suppose, in my down-the-middle approach to the drive to repeal government controls. No one spoke to me on the subject, and the mice did not chew on my copy any more than usual. One Thursday morning, however, I received an invitation to lunch that day from no less a person than Manfred Gottfried.

Gottfried shared the title "Editor" on the *Time* masthead with Henry R. Luce. An original stockholder and staffer, the story about him around the shop was that he had written the world's most expensive book on economic affairs. He had sold off his *Time* stock early on and taken a year's sabbatical to turn out the work. The book sold only a few hundred copies, so the story went, but had he held onto his stock, it would now have been worth many millions. He returned to the magazine to hold down a wide variety of posts. His exact duties were vague, but he was known to have access to the ear of Henry Luce. So, a lunch with Manfred Gottfried was an unexpected opportunity for a beginner like me.

Gottfried took me across the street to Holland House, where we received an immediate table. Then, patiently, like an old professor, he spelled out his analysis of the economic forces being stifled by price controls. Once price controls were removed, Gottfried explained, prices would seek their natural—lower—levels. Consumers and producers alike would prosper. He didn't lean on me or talk about the installment of the story I was slated to write that week. It was a purely intellectual exercise. I paid no attention to Gottfried's advice when I returned to my office, and didn't even mention Adam Smith in my story that week. My attitude was partly puckish and partly conscience, but mostly Gottfried's analysis had struck me as absurd. Nothing more was ever said to me on the subject, and the week finally came anyway when I had to write: "OPA was dead, dead as a doornail, its blood spattered over the green baize carpet in the well of the House of Representatives." Or something like that.

It would not be accurate to suggest that group journalism as practiced at *Time* was entirely free of editorial direction applied from above. The methodology of rewriting and editing in the office everything sent in from the field made stories vulnerable to pundits who thought they knew better. I wrote a story one week about a racial incident in a place called Mink Slide, Tennessee, where a group of returning black veterans had been judged to be too uppity by the local patriots. The correspondent on the spot had filed a magnificent account, chock full of anecdotes, case histories and the ultimate details which are the grist of a news magazine story. All I had to do was to get out of the way, and let the facts roll.

I was proud of my story about Mink Slide, verisimilitude enhanced by my own recollections of Saturday nights in Southern towns adjacent to military camps. When Tom Matthews, the managing editor, sent word that he wanted to see me, I went prepared to receive a rare word of praise. Matthews had my copy on his desk. (One of the features of that desk was that there were sometimes several weeks of uncashed paychecks piled in a corner; Matthews, a member of the Procter family of Procter & Gamble, didn't need to bother.) He asked me where I had gotten the stuff for my piece. I described the great job I thought the stringer had done in rounding up the background and modestly admitted to my own sensitivities from personal experience. Matthews shook his head. "It won't do, Kimball," he said; "it couldn't have been like you have it here. Haven't you ever read Faulkner?" Matthews rewrote the story himself, straight out of fiction.

Matthews to his credit was chiefly responsible for introducing the idea into *Time* that readers wanted to stretch their vocabulary above the traditional journalistic stereotype of the 12-year-old mind. He would insert some marvelously appropriate but erudite word, then supply a footnote worthy of Partridge. The fabled Timestyle ("backward ran the sentences"; "as it must to all men, death came last week to. . .") was gradually undergoing change, but a writer out to have some fun could still get away with passages which approached a parody. Cerf and I conducted a monthly pool in which the winner won lunch for getting the best Timeism into the book. First sentences, picture captions and Timestyle adjectives were the principal categories. In the first-sentence category, in a story about the appointment of a new ambassador, I managed: "Precedent favors the deserving politician who sets his cap for diplomatic honors." For a caption under the picture of a jewel thief who got caught, "He bobbled the baubles." Writing about a bosomy young Hollywood starlet, I was allowed to make reference to her "cinemammary" charms. I can't remember Cerf's victories. *Time* stories etched themselves in acid into the memories of their authors. I could only write them line by line, rereading from the beginning every sentence I had managed to sweat out previously before adding the next—a distressing habit which ruined my writing facility forever.

If some of these efforts had crept into my file, I might have deserved a derogatory assessment. But although looking up published materials is simple enough, my file shows no evidence that either the investigator from the FBI or the two from the State Department sought to find an example of my writing from *Time* any more than they had from *PM*, *United States News* or even the *Daily Princetonian*.

A knot in the stomach, swelling in size as the weekend approached, was the occupational disease of *Time* writers. Since stories were originally assigned on Thursday, they had to be nursed through shifting events before being turned in on Saturday, revised on Sunday and finally locked into print on Monday night. And they had to be written with sufficient perspective to stand the test of time while the magazine was run off the presses, put through the mails and delivered days later to readers expected to be made to feel up-to-date and fully informed. All this while an army of highly skilled nitpickers looked over our shoulders.

The perfect *Time* story, in my experience, was a railroad wreck. There was no conflict of editorial interpretation. The writer would have at his disposal every last jot and tittle gathered from eyewitnesses at the event—who was sitting in the signal tower as the Limited with so many cars went clickety-clack over which numbered switch at exactly what time as how many passengers in the dining car slurped up which items on the menu. Query: How many foot-pounds of steam were released when which type of locomotive went off the rails at exactly when? Reliving the news!

Stories about politics, social issues or controversial public figures were more of a strain. The search for truth ran smack into value judgments at almost every turn. A shift in adjectives describing an individual could make him a saint or a sinner. The choice of a premise determined the editorial thrust of the whole piece. The process of making and defending such writing decisions could be exhausting—most especially when the writer cared deeply about being accurate and fair.

A state of tension was institutionalized by *Time*'s unique system for pairing research with writing. Research meant sending out queries to correspondents, finding the appropriate clippings in the morgue, digging out useful reference material from the library and, finally, checking the accuracy of each word just before it was sent to the printers. Researchers were all women; writers were all men. In the misogynist environs of Time, Inc., in the '40s, women enjoyed the same civil liberties as Pullman porters. If an error appeared in the magazine, the fault was judged to be that of the checker who had placed a dot of approval over each word of the offending passage, not the writer who had composed it. Writers were meant to be supplied with facts assembled by dutiful handmaidens, and if the editorial slant of an adjective or the accuracy of an anecdote appeared subject to question, the researcher was first to go to the writer and delicately suggest the need for change. Since such dialogues were bound to occur at the end of a grueling week, when the writer was already limp from several rewrites, the atmosphere for such parley was not beneficial to compromise. Like as not, a writer might take the position that some dumb broad from Kansas was out to mangle his poetry with her literal mind.

I like to think that I was more sensitive than most in these exchanges, thanks to the advice of Janet Fraser. In 1946, just a month before I took my Foreign Service oral examination, an attractive young woman from Syracuse, New York, joined the National Affairs staff as a researcher. Only 22, a tall, good-looking lady with straight black eyebrows over her big brown eyes and a smile that lighted up the room, she had been working as a reporter since she was 16, staying on full time with the Syracuse *Post Standard* during the war years while she studied history and journalism at Syracuse University. Her father, also a newspaperman, had died when she was only 12, and her mother had gone back to work as the secretary to successive Syracuse mayors, all Republicans. Since her mother had recently been remarried—to the Republican District Attorney of Onondaga County—Janet was now free to come to New York City on her own.

I took Janet home the first week she came to *Time*, after the office party for her predecessor who was going abroad. She shared a fourth-floor walkup apartment with two other working girls. So it was clear my intentions were honorable. It was supposed to be against office rules for writers to mingle with researchers, although it was not clear who had made the rule, honored in the breach on more than one occasion. Some thought it was the creation of the departmental head researcher, who used to boast to her underlings that she alone was privileged to lunch with the writers. (When Janet and I were married, I had left *Time*, but we still got a kick out of keeping it a secret and mailing the wedding announcement to her departmental researcher boss on the day of the ceremony, Janet's Tuesday off.)

Janet recalled that the first time she saw me I was lounging on top of a desk, explaining to the research staff in National Affairs why they should support a strike vote to strengthen the union's position during the contract negotiations between the Newspaper Guild and management. She had been a Guild member in Syracuse, where people got fired just for joining. One issue in the *Time* negotiations at that time was a proposal requiring all new employees to join and pay dues to the Guild, which, among other things, would have the practical effect that no one could be fired for union activity. In those days such provisions were rarer than now, and the contract benefits being sought—maternity leave, severance pay, equal protection for clerical as well as editorial staff, union coverage in outside bureaus—seem mundane today. The unit took a strike vote to strengthen the hand of its negotiators, a move that has become almost routine in present-day union practice.

When the contract negotiations were coming to a head, as one who had been through the mill before at *PM*, I lent a hand at writing the pamphlets explaining the union's bargaining proposals and went to the meetings where they were hashed over. I lobbied the members of the National Affairs department for their support (the role in which Janet first spied me), persuaded Cerf to join the Guild and approached Otto Fuerbringer, the editor in charge of National Affairs that week, to help explain the issues to the folks upstairs.

No one could deny the fact that pay and benefits for the editorial staff were first-rate, but the founders were still running the corporation with a highly paternalistic hand. And not a few of the Ivy Leaguers among the old hands regarded a CIO union inside the shop as something closely akin to revolution, not to mention rank ingratitude. Still, some of the very top talent and recognized names on the magazine were Guild officers. On the surface, at least, things were very civilized; the rank and file even lobbied their superiors in middle management to support the Guild contract demands among top management, and several went out on a limb to do so. When the contract was settled without any job actions, Managing Editor Matthews ordered a catered celebration on the editorial floors, with red-coated waiters passing out free champagne, compliments of Time, Inc. The class struggle was genteel in Rockefeller Center.

The head researcher kept a black notebook containing the names of every researcher on the staff and every time an error occurred in a story checked by a researcher a black mark was entered opposite her name in the book. Three black marks meant a pink slip for the careless offender. Janet was once the researcher on a story about a county seat in the South, and had dutifully supplied the writer with a favorite reference work, the WPA guidebook for the region, one of that remarkable set turned out by unemployed writers during the Depression. The story came through for checking with a mention of the statue to the memory of the Confederate dead in the courthouse square, the eyes of the sculptured soldier in gray looking ever toward the South. It made a nice turn of phrase, but before Janet could put her dots over the line, she had to be sure the writer was taking no liberties. In the guidebook she found a photograph, no less, of the Confederate memorial, including a crucial geographical coordinate. There could be no doubt that the statue existed, nor in which direction it pointed. She bestowed the authenticating dots and went about her other chores.

When the story appeared in print, letters poured in from the county seat. The statue still stood in the courthouse square all right— but the Confederate hero no longer fixed his eyes anywhere. A lightning bolt had hit the memorial a few years back and split the head of the statue into smithereens. One black mark for Janet.

Paragon that I was, researchers would leave even my office in tears. Janet explained that I failed to mask my cool contempt for the unlucky researcher who had omitted to supply material I had suddenly discovered to be indispensable to finish off a balky piece in the terminal stages of deadline fever. I was pretty good at avoiding the scenes I could overhear from the office next door, where the writer had the reputation among researchers for never letting the facts get in the way of his flights of phrase.

The one trait I couldn't abide in a researcher, however, was the attempt to coach a writer into a story line before he had a chance to think one out for himself. It was rare for a National Affairs researcher to take such liberties with a writer in the throes of composition. But there was one such, a longtime research veteran of uncertain age. Her specialty was labor; I had heard that she had partially lost her hearing in a picket-line fracas while working as a young woman in the garment trades. She had been taken on, I had also heard, to bring some real-world savvy to a staff largely recruited from the ivory towers of the Ivy League.

Miss Real World was one of that breed of ex-radicals I had first encountered on *PM*. She walked about with a furtive air, as if some conspirator were about to do her in. Her desk was loaded with tomes on ideological struggles throughout history, and she subscribed to all the journals of intellectual opinion from *New Masses* to *New Leader*, covering the range from self-professed Communists to old-line Marxists disaffected from Stalin and his Soviet regime. There seemed to be very little middle ground in the lives of ex-radicals; it was always them or us. Their hates were passionate; their self-righteousness was intense. I tended to get myself into trouble with such types, as with the diehard Republicans who frequented the Shuttle Meadow Country Club in my hometown, because I found baiting them irresistible. They were usually devoid of a sense of humor.

In the genteel atmosphere of *Time* the Guild unit was permitted to meet in one of the *Life* editorial conference rooms after hours; the unit chairman was a *Life* editor. The discussions tended to be lively, as befits the employees of publications supposed to be on top of the news.

Miss Real World belonged to the Guild, of course, but had decided that it, too, had fallen upon evil days since her pioneering in the Labor Movement, as she was wont to describe it. She had no use, she made clear, for the crowd in charge of the Time–Life unit and was not shy about describing the entire leadership of the New York local as an arm of Moscow. That, too, had a familiar ring. As a new boy on the block I was struck once again by a phenomenon I had noticed on *PM*. The active Guild members who seemed to care most about the economic protection of the brothers and sisters inside the shop were also those most concerned that the union should play a role in the political debate within the country at large. Bleeding hearts, some might describe them; anti-Communist opponents within the ranks declared that they must be Commies to carry on so. The bitter minority, here as at *PM*, huddled together at meetings, nodding their heads at one another to register their mutual agreement concerning the wicked plots being hatched by the majority.

Miss Real World's constant companion at Guild meetings was a National Affairs writer named Gilbert Cant. Much as they were opposed in principle to the likes of me, these fast friends, researcher and writer, both had reason to become miffed at me for other than purely ideological reasons.

During the war, Cant had been in charge of the section labeled Army & Navy. When we two Marine veterans joined the staff, the powers that be decided that those Army & Navy stories would now be assigned to Cerf and me. With peace, those stories didn't amount to much, so it was no big deal to us; we were not even aware that they had been someone else's regular beat. But when Special Agent Clare came looking for a potential confidential informant, this might have been one of several reasons Cant volunteered. I came to suspect that Clare chose Miss Real World as well, my own unsubstantiated suspicions having been triggered by an event of which I was aware and which I still remember well.

The first postwar year was a time of restlessness in the ranks of organized labor, whose wages had been frozen throughout the round-the-clock years of military production. Time, Inc., was not the only place where unions began playing catch-up. As an ex-labor reporter on *PM*, I drew my share of these almost weekly stories about collective bargaining disputes all over the country.

Often as not, I drew Miss Real World as my researcher on these assignments. She crowded me so closely with her own versions of events that taking an admittedly unfair advantage I complained to the acting editor of the department, Otto Fuerbringer, and asked him to get her off my back. In the balance of power at *Time*, a researcher hadn't a chance in such an exchange. Fuerbringer talked to her and the head researcher of the department from then on assigned her to the other writers for the most part.

There is no way a young man starting his career, falling in love, just feeling so good in those first fine days after the war could have known where impertinence and impatience might land him. I can forgive myself a lack of prescience; the story, as it unfolded in the portion of my file developed by anonymous informants at *Time*, is too absurd for anyone to have foreseen.

9

THE FINAL WEIGHTS
GO ON THE SCALE

THE LATEST EVIDENCE from *Time* was what everyone was waiting for. The final weights to be dropped on the scale. The first 30 years of my life had already been peeled away by the FBI and State Department security agents and their informants. Now the FBI agents sent out by Counsel for ACOPS for this third rerun of my investigation were down to the core—the place where I was currently earning my living.

Special Agent Daniel Clare Jr., looking for dependable anti-Communist sources at *Time*, bypassed Thomas Matthews, the managing editor who had hired me. Matthews was the son of an Episcopal bishop, as well as being an heir to the Procter fortune, amassed through the sales of Ivory soap ("99 and $^{44}/_{100}\%$ pure"). Not pure enough for an investigator. My office mate, Ed Cerf, was skipped too—too friendly to be reliable. No contact either with other Princeton, Oxford and Marine alumni around the office who knew me personally. My immediate boss, Otto Fuerbringer, editor of the National Affairs department, swore he was passed over too by Clare, who never showed any interest in what I actually wrote or did on the job.

Clare, instead, found two other sources more to his liking. Both conceded that they had not known me personally before January,

1946, when I came to work for *Time*. It was by then August—eight months working in the same office with me, not counting summer vacations.

The information picked up at *Time* is part of that contained in Document 56 in my file, the field report of Special Agent Daniel H. Clare Jr., written in New York City on August 28, 1946. Of all the 99 documents in my file it is the only one in which the government censors chose to mask the gender as well as the name of a confidential informant. A blank suddenly appears in Document 56 whenever the sentence being quoted contains a personal pronoun or personal adjective. Everywhere else in this and all other documents "he" and "his" appears unconcealed. An awkward bow to feminism? The security mind at work? Elementary, my dear Watson.

As it reached me, Clare's journey into *Time* magazine was reported thusly:

A confidential appointment was arranged with [Name blacked out]. [Blank] weighed [blank] remarks with great care and gave every appearance of being scrupulously fair in [blank] remarks. [Blank] asked that what [blank] had to say would be held in absolute confidence by the department.

The passage is worth scrutiny on several counts. Note how carefully Agent Clare builds up the credibility of his source. Sounds like the Boy/Girl Scout Oath. Note the informant's request for anonymity.

I suppose it is another dark side of my own character which made me suspect independently of [blank] personal pronouns that this anonymous source was probably a woman, and therefore almost certainly a researcher. Was it Miss Real World? (The government steadfastly refuses to disclose the identity of unfriendly sources.) I blush to document my suspicions of this informant's womanly touch:

[Name blacked out] stated that Mr. Kimball was a brilliant writer; that he had an exceptional technique; that he possessed a gift for words and genius for finding the right word for the right place. [Blank] acknowledged his extreme value as a writer and conceded that he was well informed in the labor field, and that it would be extremely difficult to find his equal. [Blank] said that he had a personal charm of great magnetism and that he was persuasive, convincing and presented his ideas with forceful lucidity.

Even my kindest friends—male or female—have never gone so far overboard. In informant circles the soft touch is often used to lull an unsuspecting pigeon for the coup de grace.

[Name blacked out] reluctantly admitted that [blank] distrusted Mr. Kimball's political viewpoint. Within a week after he joined the staff of Time, Inc., he had stamped himself in [blank's] opinion as someone to be carefully watched. He immediately became associated with the Communist element in Time, Inc. He participated in the agitation of that group.

She who "reluctantly admitted" my subversive tendencies was identified in my file as a "leading witness" by Counsel for ACOPS when he eventually reviewed my case. One of the things that happens to people who have been victims of circumstantial evidence is that they begin to use the same kind of thinking in their own defense. Miss Real World fit so well. I began to convince myself this informant must be her. The dossier continued:

[Blank] explained that, at that time, the Time Unit of the Newspaper Guild was considering a strike against Time, Inc., and that while more conservative members wished to bargain with the owners along recognized lines, the radical element insisted on a strike regardless of cost. Mr. Kimball joined the strike advocates and was active in attempting to gain the cooperation of other members to strike. He wrote pamphlets, spoke at meetings and definitely aligned himself with the Communist element. At the present time, the Time Unit of the Guild is in turmoil on the Communist question, and the more conservative members are attempting to throw out the

Communists and to institute an American regime. In that battle Mr. Kimball has consistently and without exception supported the Communist element, voted for every resolution they proposed, has solicited votes on their behalf, and has battled the conservatives on every issue. His interest in keeping the Time Unit aligned with the Communists has been manifest on numerous occasions but it is tempered by a subtlety and smoothness that has made it possible for him to avoid any outright commitment as to his Communist standing. [Name blacked out] contended that it was [blank] impression that Mr. Kimball was not a member of the Communist Party. [Blank] described him as a confused liberal. [Blank] asserted that he was much too smart to blunder in that way and that, if his sympathies were as strong as [blank] believed them to be, he would realize that his effectiveness was much greater as a non-member than as a member. [Blank] conceded that his activities in the Guild did not necessarily stamp him as a Communist, but when pressed for details [blank] stated that there were certain things that seemed to prove his disaffection to the American system.

On his quick trip into the misogynist world of Time, Inc., Special Agent Clare may not have been aware of the special relationship between a writer and a researcher. The context is crucial, especially in a shop where the war between the sexes had been refined to a fine art. Did Clare know that all writers were men, all researchers were women, and that there was no hope for their advancement? Did anyone tell him that if an error was printed in the magazine it was charged against the female researcher, never the male writer? Probably not. And certainly Miss Real World would not have volunteered my request to have her transferred.

The confidential informant from *Time* shifted the attack to broader terrain in the manner of the ideologues of that day:

Mr. Kimball is an apologist for Marshal Tito, for instance; and has consistently defended him and the Yugoslavian Government in connection with the current controversy with this country.

I was writing National Affairs from January to August, 1946, and had no professional occasion to get mixed up with the Balkans. The National Affairs section was allocated jurisdiction over State Department and congressional news under the subhead "Foreign Relations," but that was limited to stories involving ambassadors, treaties and such. *Time*'s Foreign section in those days, where Whittaker Chambers was a senior editor, preferred Mihailovitch, a Yugoslav leader whom Tito had put to death for collaborating with the Nazis during World War II. I would like to be able to claim vision omniscient beyond that of then Secretary of State Jimmy Byrnes, since Tito eventually was accepted by the State Department as an independent bulwark against Soviet Union influence in Europe. But I don't remember "consistently defending" any of the personages of postwar Europe while dallying in the corridors of the Time–Life Building.

Bearing in mind that I had worked there only a few months, the confidential informant's memory, pressed for more details, reached a crescendo worthy of a district attorney delivering his/her final summation to the jury:

> Mr. Kimball was a great admirer of Joseph Curran, the Maritime Union Leader, and in the past frequently extolled him as the type of labor leader needed to straighten out the situation in this country, but when Mr. Curran made his speech denouncing Communists and threatening to throw them out of the Union, Mr. Kimball turned on him and has consistently denounced him as a bad labor leader and one disloyal to labor. His reaction toward Mr. Bridges underwent a similar metamorphosis when Mr. Bridges seemed to be about to fall from Communist grace, and he has denounced Mr. Bridges for his lack of loyalty to "Labor." These are specific and well supported sentiments.

So much for the gifted young man "well informed in the labor field."

Joe Curran, president of the National Maritime Union, and Harry Bridges, the head of the International Longshoremen and Warehouseman's Union, were both members of a Committee for

Maritime Unity which was bargaining in the summer of 1946 with shipowners for new labor contracts and threatening to tie up all ports if their demands were not granted. *Time* ran a cover story on Joe Curran in its issue of June 17, 1946, for which Miss Real World was the researcher. "Around their boss, Joe Curran, sits the most effective group of Commie officers on the East Coast," the story said, which Miss Real World authenticated with little dots over each word. The next paragraph reported that the union's publicity director had been Leo Huberman, an old colleague of mine on *PM*.

I think it is entirely possible that I might have spoken sharply to Miss Real World concerning the story's implication that Huberman was a Communist, although the bit on turning against Curran after some speech denouncing Communists is still Greek to me. Harry Bridges was born in Australia and the United States for years tried to deport him back there on the ground that he had concealed his membership in the Communist Party. A militant leader of a tough union on the West Coast docks, he was constantly at odds with businessmen and politicians alike. The government never did succeed in deporting him—with or without my alleged metamorphosis, about which I can dredge absolutely nothing from memory. I dare say, though, I would not have been above saying most anything to Miss Real World which I thought might get a rise out of her. Expensive fun.

The informant pressed on and was quoted to charge that I was "a personal friend and admirer" of persons so reprehensible that six lines of their deeds were blacked out in the documents furnished to me. (Could one name have been Huberman's?) The task so exhausted the government censor that he/she goofed in editing the final section of Agent Clare's summary of his confidential conversation with this informant of unmentionable gender:

> [Name blacked out] contended that Mr. Kimball's actions and associations and spoken comments stamped him as one of divided loyalty. [Blank] expressed *herself* [italics mine] at a loss to understand his purpose in working for Time, Inc., for [blank] maintained that, as a writer for that Republican conservative publication, he had slight opportunity to color his stories. At the same time [blank] maintained that he was so

gifted that in spite of editorial vigilance he was able to inject his leftist viewpoint in his writings.

The cat, excuse the pun, was out of the bag. (Later on, in summing up the testimony, Bannerman's reference to "her opinion" was likewise missed by the censor.) The slight non sequitur regarding my opportunity or lack of opportunity to subvert the editorial process at *Time* seemed to have escaped Clare. It never occurred to him to stop by the generous *Time* morgue and take a peek at the clips of the stories I had written. Nor to talk to those whose "editorial vigilance" was referred to. To the extent that I was also applying my talents to Guild publications, there are no examples of those either. It is possible, of course, that government intelligence didn't believe what it read in the American press anyway, or didn't believe that what a journalist wrote bore any relationship to what he really believed. The theory of "objective" reporting was still in full sway.

But one might have expected that Clare would talk to at least one editor who handled my copy along its tortuous path to the linotype machines. The FBI, to be sure, had interviewed my "*Time* supervisor" two months previously, but a lot of copy had gone under the editorial pencil since then. After all, if the editors of *Time* had managed to protect the public from my subversive urges, they of all people would remember the unedited "leftist viewpoint in his writings."

With some sense of hierarchy, Clare did call on the publisher.

Mr. James Linen, Publisher of Time, Inc., was also interviewed. Mr. Linen was also associated with the Office of Strategic Services, and his forthright Americanism has never been questioned. However, he knew Mr. Kimball only as a highly competent member of his writing staff, a very desirable employee, and a valuable addition to Time, Inc. He was unfamiliar with his political beliefs and stated that he had every reason to believe that Mr. Kimball was loyal to this country.

Clare's disappointment in passing on these few kind words seems apparent to me.

For balance, he went on to seek out a male writer in the National

Affairs department and one of the anti-Communist caucus of the Time Guild unit, Gilbert Cant, who had lost his command of the Army & Navy section when Cerf and I had joined the magazine. Cant did not rush over to my office to let me know about his official visitor. I eventually found out his name, however, when the State Department calligraphers goofed again. His informant credentials were deemed to be in order.

> [Line blacked out] was subsequently interviewed. His anti-Communistic sentiments were ascertained through [Name blacked out] and others, as well as through an examination of papers relating to the struggle in the New York Newspaper Guild to overcome the dominance of the Communists. [Line blacked out] which repudiated the "North American Aviation telegram." There is no question as to his Americanism.

In my research of the minutes of the New York Newspaper Guild for 1946 I found the record of a second meeting held on June 18, 1941, to reconsider its vote of eight days earlier condemning President Roosevelt's use of troops. In another long session, this time at a place called the Fraternal Clubhouse, the debates and parliamentary maneuvering lasted once again into the wee hours of the morning. A substitute resolution—upholding the President and condemning the strikers for not waiting for mediation—was narrowly adopted 365 to 362. Cant, then a Guild member at the New York *Post*, was one of the speakers advocating reversal. (The minutes of this second meeting rang a bell, and I am sure I attended that one and, inconspicuously it would appear, voted with the losers.) The measure of our mutual involvement five years previously was that I had a dim recollection of his speaking at Guild meetings in behalf of the anti-Communist side, but not much more. Evidently, he had even less acquaintance with me except that I had not been one of the relatively small group on *PM* who had sided with his approach to Guild politics. My researches showed he had been among the losing slate of candidates in the two elections in which I won minor posts.

Special Agent Clare began his account of the interview on this upbeat note:

He . . . conceded that Mr. Kimball was an excellent crafts-
man, smart, brilliant and persuasive, and completely qualified
by reasons of his intellectual ability for a position with the
State Department.

Hark, the lullaby.

[Name blacked out] expressed grave doubts, however, as to
Mr. Kimball's political loyalty, but conceded that there was
probably, as he described it, no question of his basic loyalty.

Interesting sentence, that, for those weighing me in the scales of
national security. Doubtful political loyalty, but, as informant described it, no question of his basic loyalty. Not the sort of ambiguous
straddle one would ordinarily expect from a Timewriter.

He mentioned Mr. Kimball's participation with the leftist
movement of the Time element of the Newspaper Guild, his
sympathy with the Communist side of international questions,
and his familiarity with those acknowledged to be Communist
party members.

Three sweeping generalities. One can look in vain in my file for a
single detail of corroborating documentation. The witness continued:

[Name blacked out] said that he personally liked Mr. Kimball, and felt that he had great possibilities, but that he felt
that Mr. Kimball was confused; that he suffered from the
weight of maintaining himself as a "super-liberal"; that he
maintained that position in the face of all logic to the point
where his liberalism degenerated to a narrowness of viewpoint, which defeated its own ends. Mr. Kimball, according
to this source, is the type of liberal who rushes to the defense
of all labor movements and cries "persecution" at every opportunity.
At this point, [Name blacked out] feels that Mr. Kimball

is at the cross roads of his political development; that he is completely confused and that his viewpoint is still dominated by his immaturity and his desire to be known as an ultra-liberal. He can turn either way, [Name blacked out] believes, either to outright Communism or towards a more balanced liberal viewpoint.

Shades of Special Agent Hipsley's interview with Kenneth Craw-ford, when the agent sought to sum me up as one who in 1941 "teetered for a while as far as his political beliefs and loyalties were concerned." After five years and a world war, I was still being classi-fied as standing confused at the political crossroad, one foot on the path to "outright Communism." I wouldn't care to be hanging by my thumbs on the edge of a precipice for that many seconds. But my fate was by now in equally precarious balance.

[Name blacked out] feels that his employment by the United States Government as a Foreign Service Officer would be ill-advised; that the danger of Mr. Kimball's making a leap in the wrong direction is ever present, and that until he has straightened out his political philosophy he would be in danger of permitting his Communist sympathies to overpower his fundamental Americanism. [Name blacked out] stated that he could not recommend Mr. Kimball for the position involved, even though he recognized his suitability in every particular except that of political loyalty.

That about sealed it. Wrapping up his report to Chief Security Agent Fitch, Clare explained away the thin size of his sample:

In addition to the informants already mentioned, numerous other sources in the newspaper field were interviewed but their knowledge of Mr. Kimball was too vague to be of value in appraising his qualifications or political opinions.

How Gilbert Cant could have formed a less vague knowledge of me is beyond my comprehension. I barely knew him. Cant was older than Cerf and I. His office was in a different corridor from ours, so that we never had occasion to be wandering past his door. During my 11 months at *Time*, I cannot in truth remember sharing a meal, a drink or a prolonged conversation with Cant. But neither the thinness of Clare's sample nor the thinness of Cant's knowledge hindered Clare in reaching his own final appraisal:

> Investigation would appear to establish that, without reasonable doubt, Mr. Kimball's political loyalty is divided; the fact is conceded, and it is only the matter of degree which is disputed by various informants, and the preponderance of considered opinion appears to indicate that the degree is potentially dangerous.
>
> In accordance with instructions, Mr. Kimball was not interviewed.
>
> Daniel E. Clare, Jr., Special Agent.

Clare's report is dated August 28. *Time*'s National Affairs section that week contained a story on Joseph R. McCarthy Jr., upset winner in the primary contest for Senator from Wisconsin. I had written the wrap-up. Thus Clare and I were working on deadline together, but I was oblivious to the coincidence—or to the irony.

On its march through the bureaucracy Clare's report was logged in at Washington headquarters on August 30. Despite the fact that the request to "expedite" the new investigation had been marked "urgent," Hipsley's work at the department's doorstep in Washington was not received until September 20, three weeks later. Perhaps that was because Hipsley's interviews turned out to be rather more ambiguous than Clare's and contained a couple of strong plugs on my behalf. Hipsley avoided drawing any conclusions on his own, leaving that to Fitch, the next man up the ladder. For reasons unexplained in my file it took Fitch another two weeks, until October 4, 1946, to pass on his conclusions to the boss of his division, CON Director R. L. Bannerman, the last stop on the way to Counsel for ACOPS. The file includes Fitch's drafts painfully worked out in longhand in which he inserted the word "Communist" in a couple of places. Document 51, logged in at the Office of Controls, October 8, 1946:

DEPARTMENT OF STATE
CHIEF SPECIAL AGENT
OCTOBER 4, 1946

TO: CON—Mr. Bannerman
FROM: CSA—Mr. Fitch
SUBJECT: Penn Townsend KIMBALL
(Your request 14 August 1946)

Conclusion

Investigation discloses evidence of a material nature tending to affect adversely the applicant's loyalty to the Government of the United States and its institutions.

It reveals much information both pro and con in regard to the applicant's loyalty, and though no one placed him in the Party, it is noted that but few of the applicant's most enthusiastic supporters are able to recommend him without explanation and reservation in supporting his stand on past activities.

It reveals that the name Penn Kinball [sic] appears on a list of strike defenders in the case of the North American Aviation Company in California, which strike was said to have been Communist inspired, and for the purpose of hampering Roosevelt's preparedness program. It further reveals that the applicant has willingly and knowingly associated with and consistently supported radical and Communist groups and their programs. It also reveals that the applicant has not followed blindly, as he is too smart to blunder and that his effectiveness is much greater than a Communist Party member because of his winning personality and superior ability. It was pointed out that because of the applicant's political beliefs a divided loyalty is bound to exist and, therefore, he should be considered a dangerous individual.

The investigation seems to indicate, in view of the dangers inherent to this situation, that careful consideration should be given the determination as to whether the applicant should be employed in the Department of State.

Attachments

Report dated September 19, 1946 by Special Agent Hipsley covering investigation of the applicant at Washington, D.C.;

Report dated September 19, 1946 by Special Agent Hipsley covering investigation of the applicant at Washington, D.C.; [sic]

Report dated August 28, 1946 by Special Agent Clare covering investigation of the applicant at New York, New York.

This report supplements report sent your office March 6, 1946.

(Signed) T. F. Fitch

CSA:swa

At the next higher level in the bureaucracy it took another two weeks, from October 8 to October 24, to move along the "urgent" and third of my security clearance checks. Bannerman, the director of the Office of Controls (CON), was also head of the departmental Security Committee which had first cleared me, then uncleared me and then been subjected to review by the newly constituted Appeals Committee for Personnel Security (ACOPS). One might anticipate that he did not relish the prospect of being overruled in his first brush with the latest layer of bureaucracy between his department and the Assistant Secretary of State for Administration, Mr. Donald Russell (known by the code letters A-R on office documents addressed to him inside the department). Bannerman picked and chose carefully from the already screened sources as quoted and paraphrased by Clare and Hipsley in Documents 56 and 53 and evaluated by Fitch in Document 52, testing his ideas out in longhand, too.

The numbers on the documents returned to me jump around from the normal chronological sequence in this part of my file. Ordinarily the numbers become lower as they progress from the older to the newer documents, so that my application to take the Foreign Service exams in July, 1945, is Document 96 while an internal request for security information when I applied for a Fulbright grant to do research in the United Kingdom in January, 1974, is Document 7. Bannerman's longhand notes are numbered 60, although they were made subsequent to the report to him by Fitch, Document 52. The clue to that clerical mystery is that these later notes are mistakenly bunched with Bannerman's earlier memo (Document 59) ordering the third round of field investigations. The cause of the confusion might be that Bannerman's longhand notes are worded differently from the typed memorandum bearing his name and initials, properly numbered 51.

The longhand notes read as follows:

Kimball, Penn Townsend

This case was originally submitted as disapproved on 7-12-46. That action was based on preponderance of evidence which reflected doubt with regard to loyalty and left wing sympathies.

The case was returned 8-6-46 for further development. (See ACOPS memo).

Kimball was thoroughly investigated in D.C. & N.Y.C. He was formerly employed by PM and was a very active member of that unit of the A.N.G. He was Vice President of the PM unit and actively participated in the Right-Left wing battles. Those informants that are conversant with CP activity consistently describe K. as a left winger, liberal, C.P. sympathizer and two described him as a fellow traveler. Those informants that are not conversant in the C.P. field described K. as a brilliant, well educated liberal who was loyal and trustworthy, thereby recommending him.

The premise of discussion, loyalty, resolves itself to a preponderance of evidence and reasonable doubt. On this basis there is sufficient testimony to raise such a doubt and conclude in disapproval.

Witnesses such as: [Six lines blacked out] identified K. with C.P. element of Guild activities. K is not described as a C.P. member but is known to associate with known C.P.'s such as [line blacked out].

In summarization K. has a reputation in the Guild as being

actively engaged on behalf of C.P. element and has never faltered from that stand. In 1941 he is reputed to have been vigorously in favor of the Guild's protest to FDR's use of troops in the C.P. inspired North American Aviation strike. This was during the preparedness program, therefore such opposition reflected C.P. sympathies rather than American.

These longhand notes neatly separated the sources who had said favorable things about me from the negative informants by the simple device of categorizing all the positive witnesses as "not conversant in the C.P. field." That would include Kenneth Crawford of *Newsweek*, the publisher of *Time*, an Executive Assistant to the Secretary of Labor and a *Life* writer, among others, matched against the informants selected as "conversant with CP activity." When I later discovered the identity of three of the six [names blacked out] witnesses cited by Bannerman and matched their names against their testimony, Bannerman's statement that all had "identified K with C.P. element of Guild activities" proved to be a gross exaggeration. The final typed memorandum prepared from these notes was scarcely more circumspect.

The memorandum is notable for the brisk fashion in which it boils down 19 single-spaced pages of findings by two investigators into two and one-quarter pages. The summarization process eliminated completely any kind words without bothering to explain them away by declaring such sources to be ignorant of the Communist Party. Bannerman's specific description of me as "vigorously in favor" of the Guild's protest during the North American strike evaporated in the finished draft, which in its two paragraphs on that episode did not even try to link me personally with the Guild vote or "telegram" or circular (apparently there was nothing in Clare's investigation to support Bannerman's original description). By describing it as an "outlaw Communist inspired attempt to slow down American production," the report left the reader to infer that Bannerman wouldn't be talking about it if I had not been part of the conspiracy. Guilt by association was cited in two separate places, although I have no way of knowing who was named or how they merited Bannerman's description as "known communists." The tone of Document 51 is clear: it would take a brave and foolhardy government employee not to go along with the Security Committee's original contention that I was "a definite security risk"—now supposedly documented in detail.

SECRET

Office Memorandum   ·   UNITED STATES GOVERNMENT

TO: Counsel—ACOPS (for A-R) DATE: 24 October 1946
FROM: CON—Mr. R. L. Bannerman [initialed RLB]
SUBJECT: KIMBALL, Penn Townsend

Reference is made to the case of Penn Townsend Kimball, who was born at New Britain, Connecticut, on 12 October 1915 and who has passed written and oral examinations for the Career Foreign Service. Mr. Kimball is an applicant for the Foreign Service, and inasmuch as he has never been on the rolls of the Department, only the various reports of investigation are being submitted for consideration of this case.

The Security Committee originally disapproved the appointment of Mr. Kimball by its letter of 12 July 1946. At such time it was the contention of the Committee that Mr. Kimball was a definite security risk and that his loyalty to the United States was questioned.

In response to a memorandum from Counsel, ACOPS, under date of 6 August 1946, additional investigation has been conducted. As a result of the findings of this additional investigation, the Security Committee remains of the opinion that any consideration for the appointment of Mr. Kimball should be disapproved on the grounds that he is a definite security risk.

Informant [line backed out] was interrogated and stated the following with respect to the subject and his activities while employed by the newspaper PM: "In some instances his thinking and his liberal beliefs may have seemed to be entirely sympathetic with the Communist Party line. As I know Kimball to be an independent thinker and consider him to be completely patriotic, I do not think that he ever followed the 'proposed Communist Party line' in his thinking, as a person who stood for Communism. He may have followed the party line, and probably did in some instances." [Name blacked out] further stated that, "Kimball took an active interest in the New York Newspaper Guild. This Guild was predominantly radical, and the radical members spared little effort in their attempt to indoctrinate Kimball with their views and beliefs, so that they could bring into the fold a young man of his intelligence and background."

With respect to the Newspaper Guild, PM unit, statement regarding the North American Aviation Strike in 1940, the following information is submitted: In early June, 1940, there was a strike at the North American Aviation Plant, and the President used Army personnel to protect the workers who did not conform to the strike order. This strike has been described as an outlaw Communist inspired attempt to slow down American production. On June 10 a meeting was held by the New York Guild and a motion to send a telegram of protest to the President of the United States was carried by a large majority. This telegram as a whole stated that the Newspaper Guild objected to the use of troops in the strike, as the President by his action was disregarding a basic American principle.

The vote authorizing the sending of this telegram was 163 to 30, and at the same time the membership rejected a resolution expressing loyalty to President Roosevelt and voted to align the Guild with the Conference for Inalienable Rights, a known Communist front organization.

Other associates of Kimball while an employee of PM were contacted and their knowledge of the subject is reported as follows: [Line blacked out] stated that, "the subject was an active member of the PM unit of the Newspaper Guild and that he always agreed with and voted for what was considered to be a straight Communist Party ticket in Guild activities and he always lined up with what they described as the Party side." They both further agreed that he seemed to be a "fellow traveler." [Name blacked out], a former employee of PM, summarized his knowledge of Kimball as follows: "I was lined up on the conservative side in the Guild and can only state that I know Kimball was not on my side." This same informant further stated that he "knew Kimball to be friendly with [two and one-half lines blacked out]

[Line blacked out] stated the following: "Mr. Kimball did not carry a Communist Party membership card but was, without the possibility of reasonable doubt, sympathetic to the Communist regime, vocal in the defense of its principles, and an adherent of the 'Party line.' Mr. Kimball associated and indicated preference for the society of known Communists."

The Security Committee has taken note of the request to interrogate former associates of Kimball while serving on active duty in the Marine Corps. In view of the fact that all of his former associates during that period of time have now returned to civilian life and their whereabouts are unknown, it has been impossible to ascertain any factual information regarding his views and activities during that period of time.

Following Mr. Kimball's release from the Marine Corps and upon his return to civilian life, he associated himself with the staff of Time, Inc. Certain associates of his have been contacted with respect to his activities with this publication and their statements are reported as follows: [Line blacked out] that, "within a week after he joined the staff of Time, Inc., he had stamped himself in her opinion as someone to be carefully watched. He immediately became associated with the Communist element in Time, Inc. Mr. Kimball is apologetic for Marshal Tito, for instance; and has consistently defended him and the Yugoslavian Government in connection with the current controversy with that country. He is also a great admirer of Joseph Curran, the Maritime union leader, and in the past, frequently extolled him as the type of labor leader needed to straighten out the situation in this country, but when Mr. Curran made his speech denouncing Communists and threatening to throw them out of the union, Mr.

Kimball turned on him and has consistently denounced him as a bad labor leader and one disloyal to labor."

Kimball is reported to be a personal friend and admirer of [two lines blacked out]

In support of the contention by the Security Committee that the application of Mr. Kimball be disapproved, all reports of investigation are submitted herewith, along with his application for employment in the Career Foreign Service. Your attention is directed to the various statements of the informants reported which tend to bear out the contention that the subject is a definite security risk.

Attachments
CSA Reports of Investigation
Application for Designation
HET [initialed]
CON:EAEisenhart:rnc

SECRET

There are three mostly illegible scrawls across the last sheet of the memorandum. The handwriting is different from Bannerman's so one can surmise that they were written by someone on the receiving end. One looks a little like "But what of the definite loyalty?" A second reads like "Grant the PM story." Then, a three-word notation, "NO Mr. Kim." Rehearsing the final verdict?

The internal correspondence shows that Bannerman "omitted" to attach the supporting documents to his summary until jogged by telephone by Counsel, ACOPS, on October 28. The next day, October 29 (no mulling things over at this stage), Counsel turned in his TOP SECRET memorandum to the Appeals Committee on Personnel Security, his last word (Document 13) on the subject of Penn Townsend Kimball. (Do you suppose there is a black sense of humor among the members of the blackout squad at the Department of State? The number of Document 13 is inexplicably out of chronological sequence.) It ran three and one-half pages, single-spaced, and indeed read like a lawyer's brief. There was, however, no lawyer representing the defense.

TOP SECRET
Office Memorandum · UNITED STATES GOVERNMENT

TO: ACOPS DATE: 24 October 1946
FROM: Counsel, ACOPS
SUBJECT: Penn Townsend KIMBALL

The subject is an applicant for the career Foreign Service. It appears that on July 12, 1946, an adverse recommendation was made by the now superseded Security Committee on the basis of an FBI report. The case was referred back to ACOPS by Mr. Russell on July 30, 1946, with the statement that the record did not show Kimball to be a security risk and that additional investigation should be undertaken along three lines preliminary to a decision whether the case was adequate for consideration by ACOPS as involving security risk.

The investigation requested has, to some extent, been made and the Security Officer has reported by memorandum of October 24, 1946, that on the basis of the additional investigation "the Security Committee remains of the opinion that any consideration for the appointment of Mr. Kimball should be disapproved on the grounds that he is a definite security risk." Assuming, as I am orally assured, that this is the recommendation of the Security Officer, it is believed that the case is now properly before ACOPS for consideration.

The legal mind at work. After 84 days of investigation, telephone calls and exchanges of memoranda, the charge was now properly before the court. The little aside about being "orally assured" that Bannerman's memo represented the recommendation of the Security Officer rather than the "now superseded Security Committee" was to keep straight the new chain of command inside the Department of State. But there was never to be a hearing on my case before ACOPS, much less one in which I would have the opportunity to cross-examine witnesses or appear in my own defense. Counsel, ACOPS, played all the roles—prosecutor, defense, jury and judge—though not without some qualms.

It should be noted, however, that I believe the investigation to be adequate only in that it is sufficient to justify a decision by ACOPS; if the case were not one of an applicant for employment the facts would call for an interview with the subject, which has not taken place, and a more intensive exploration.

What might have happened if I had formally accepted the job offer tendered to me the previous spring? I had already been cleared as of that date, the very day that Bannerman first passed along the FBI intelligence that my name had appeared on a union circular. The record of the era that was launched by Senator Joseph R. McCarthy in Wheeling, West Virginia, nearly four years later, does not speak well for the protections afforded by being on the State Department rolls. It is an interesting theory, nevertheless, that applicants for government jobs have fewer civil liberties than other Americans. Swallowing his scruples over what he considered a less than intensive exploration of my background and the lack of a face-to-face interview with the subject of a major evaluation, Counsel moved quickly to the main point.

1. It is my conclusion that, although the record on the first submission showed no substantial security risk, the record at the present time indicates such a risk to be present and that the applicant should therefore be rejected on that ground.

What was there in the record amassed between August 6 and October 29 that Counsel found so convincing as to reverse his original opinion?

2. The file indicates that the applicant is a person of more than average talents. A Rhodes Scholar in mathematics [sic], the file shows that he is highly recommended for character and intellectual attainments by people who knew him as a student; these include Dean Gauss of Princeton, and one of his associates at Oxford, Mr. Philip Kaiser, Assistant to the Secretary of Labor. He took to a career in journalism while still a student at Oxford, writing for the *Washington Post*. From October 1939 to May 1940 he was in Washington,

working for the *United States News*. Mr. David Lawrence, the publisher of the *News*, has recommended Kimball highly on the basis of personal acquaintance and Kimball's father, a manufacturer in Connecticut; Lawrence has stated that he offered Kimball a job, apparently since Kimball's return from military service, but that Kimball declined the job. From May 1940 to March 1942 Kimball worked on the newspaper PM. From 1942 through 1945 he was in the Marine Corps, in which he rose from enlisted man to the rank of Captain, serving in the Pacific as a combat correspondent, in addition to other military activity. Upon his return from the Marine Corps he took a job with *Time* magazine where he is now employed.

I couldn't ask for a more favorable job resume from a government official, despite the fact that he had just declared me beyond the pale. The mistake in identifying me as a student of mathematics at Oxford, when I had actually taken a degree in politics, philosophy and economics, was picked up and repeated from an investigator who had checked me out originally. Once an error gets into a government file, it is immortal. Compared to Bannerman, Counsel had gone out of his way to set the record straight on David Lawrence's good opinion of me. Of course, Counsel had to justify overruling Bannerman in the first place and might simply have been playing the Washington game of protecting one's posterior. Yet the memo has the tone of a man searching his soul.

3. The original adverse report on Kimball was based primarily, it seems, on information regarding his activities on *PM* and on *Time*; it was buttressed by general statements from persons who knew him as a youth in Connecticut, that he was "liberal", "Socialistic" and the like. No one has alleged that he is a Communist or fellow traveler, or that he has adhered to Marxist doctrines.

These remarks were immediately followed by one inch of white space, marked "FBI," in the document turned over to me. Then Counsel resumes:

The only adverse information with regard to the *PM* period was that Kimball's name appeared as a member of the Grievance Committee of the New York Newspaper Guild, *PM* unit, which issued or signed a circular defending a strike of the North American Aviation Company in 1941.

Here followed in the released document another inch of white space marked "FBI."

It would seem likely that the first FBI interruption is either a digest of the bureau's trip to my old hometown or the statement of my "Time supervisor" and the second the "blind memorandum" connecting me with the protest on the North American strike. Not exactly powerful stuff, Counsel was prepared to concede in justifying his original skepticism over the whole affair.

On the ground that a continued support of the position of labor is not equivalent to disloyalty to the United States and on the ground that the personal opinion of David Lawrence should be deemed under the circumstances to outweigh the opinion of the *Time* supervisor, the conclusion was reached by Counsel, as has been noted, that on the record there was no security risk. It was obvious, however, that a much more thorough investigation would have to be made to determine just what the facts were with respect to Kimball's participation in Communist Party line activities. Accordingly, the additional investigation was requested.

4. The record shows fairly clearly that, while Kimball was on *PM*, he was definitely identified with the group that followed the Communist leadership. In his favor, it may be said, as pointed out by Mr. Kenneth Crawford and Mr. James Wechsler, leader of the anti-Communist group in *PM*, that the real break between Communists and anti-Communists on *PM* did not take place until some time after Kimball had left *PM*. These informants also point out that Kimball would have had to live as a hermit to avoid close association with Communists and fellow travelers on the *PM* staff. Crawford, who knew Kimball personally very well, and whose authority and responsibility in such matters are high, is definitely

favorable to Kimball and recommends his appointment as a Foreign Service Officer. [Four lines blacked out.]

The names of Crawford and Wechsler had been blacked out in all the other documents returned to me. The censor working on Top Secret Document 13, so oddly numbered out of sequence, may have been a different person from the one applying the brushstrokes elsewhere. Since paragraph 4 was generally favorable about my alleged associations with "Communists and fellow travelers on the *PM* staff," the censor working on that page may have decided they needed no cloak of anonymity. The four lines blacked out might well have been the unfavorable portions of Wechsler's testimony. In any event Counsel seemed to be making a telling point in my favor. But it was only a buildup to another idea.

5. The crucial question is thus whether in the four or five years since Kimball left *PM* his close association with Communists and Communist ideas continued to such an extent as to give rise to reasonable doubt as to his security; for it may be said that when he was on *PM* he was still young, eager, and while intellectually able was possibly emotionally impressionable. On this subject the latest evidence indicates that the Communist association of the *PM* type has continued.

No thorough investigation of the four years which Kimball spent in the Marine Corps has been made but one informant states that from his own knowledge Kimball did not adopt the Communist Party line while he was in the Marine Corps, although there was adequate opportunity to do so. He cites the fact that Kimball did not participate in any of the Communist-inspired movements to compel demobilization and that, as a combat correspondent, he did not engage in writing Communist line articles. This is, however, outweighed by the information which comes from Kimball's present associates on *Time*, other than his supervisor who was interviewed by the FBI. It now appears that there is a split in the *Time* staff between Communists and anti-Communists, along a line familiar to the New York Newspaper Guild; and that Kimball is still associated with the pro-Communist group. This association, while not particularized in great detail, includes his espousal of the Tito-Yugoslav position in the Yugoslav-United States controversy and his denunciation of Curran, the Maritime Union leader (whom he formerly admired) after Curran denounced the Communists. He appears to be still a close friend of [two lines blacked out]. There is no indication from the report with respect to any present association between Kimball and [name or names blacked out].

Counsel did not seem to me to be dispensing even-handed justice when he decided that everything good and decent I might have done over 30 years of life was "outweighed" by the "information" which came from one *Time* researcher and one *Time* writer who could not have known me longer than eight months. Yet it was their testimony which tipped the scales against me on the "crucial question" of my loyalty to the United States of America.

6. The conclusion of the two leading witnesses [Names blacked out] both of *Time* is the same: it is that while Kimball is not a Communist and while he is extremely able intellectually, he is essentially immature in his political opinions; and this immaturity, coupled with his intellectual skill and ability, push him in the direction which he thinks is "super-liberal", but which ends up with associating himself, and his views, with Communist-led groups.

On the surface the script comes straight out of the theater of the absurd. The sum and substance of the case against me was my activity in a white-collar union consisting of editorial professionals and commercial office employees on a national magazine of conservative leanings. No issue of specific content had been raised concerning the positions taken by the Newspaper Guild unit at *Time* or the New York local beyond the successful pursuit of bread-and-butter demands in a trade-union negotiation. The union had not gone on strike; it had signed a contract with *Time* management in an amicable settlement for collecting union dues and improving the wages and benefits enjoyed by its employees.

There was not a single "for instance" of what my "participation in Communist Party line activities" could have been, or of what party line I might have followed except the researcher's convoluted account of my convoluted attitudes toward a couple of waterfront labor leaders and the charge of my "espousal of the Tito-Yugoslav position."

Better than half of Counsel's memorandum was a dossier of favorable information from relatively prominent people who had known me for years previous to my brief months at *Time*. How could the hearsay from two obscure staff members there weigh so heavily on the scales?

The concern of that moment, only a few months after the surrender of Germany and Japan, was that our ally in that war, the Soviet Union, would turn on the Free World and put it under Communism. Its instrument in the United States, the Communist Party, would subvert first individual Americans, then the groups and institutions where they could establish positions of leadership and eventually the government itself. Along the way, the CP and its masters in Moscow would scheme to undermine the ability of America to resist. It was thought that many Americans were in danger of becoming dupes of the process, missing the main point of the ultimate threat in their dealings with subordinate issues. It was a patriotic duty to monitor the process, to sound the alarm, to blow the whistle on the dupes and to root out the enemy within.

That plausible premise is what gave the confidential government informants their clout. Counsel for ACOPS sounds like a decent fellow, trying hard to be fair. At the start he stood up for a "dupe" like me against Fitch and Bannerman. They had led the initial attack on the basis of a single scrap of information from the FBI. The additional investigation of me left something to be desired, and Bannerman's summary passed along to Counsel for ACOPS was stacked against me. The Chief Security Officer and the Chief Security Agent were not ones to overrule themselves. So, it was Counsel for ACOPS turn again to try to swim against the tide. It is asking a lot of an individual within such an official system to take that kind of chance.

7. On this record, and this being the state of Kimball's mind, I can not recommend that the Security Officer's adverse recommendation be overruled. I am of the opinion that the case falls within paragraph 4 (c) of the Security Criteria of ACOPS of August 12, 1946.

[I searched the archives in Washington for a copy of ACOPS Security Criteria as of August 12, 1946, but was unable to find them.]

A personal interview, it is true, might throw considerable light on Kimball's mind, but unless requested by A-R [Assistant Secretary Russell] as a matter of personnel policy (as, for example, desirable because of the unusual qualifications of Mr. Kimball), I do not recommend that such an interview be directed at this time.

TOP SECRET

At the end, Counsel, ACOPS, was still wrestling with his conscience. I have tried unsuccessfully to find out who he was (is). I wonder if in later life he ever came across my name again, triggering a flash of recollection. Sorry for me? Angry with himself? Only doing his job? The real victim perhaps of a security system that asks so much of a person in his position—and provides so little.

The system was moving swiftly now. On November 1, 1946, the chairman of ACOPS, Saxton E. Bradford (what a wonderful roll to those State Department names!) forwarded another TOP SECRET memorandum of his own to Assistant Secretary Russell:

1. The Committee has reviewed the record in this case, made available to it by its counsel.

2. The Committee accepts the recommendation of Counsel that this application be disapproved, and so recommends.

Saxton E. Bradford

That's all there was to it. Assistant Secretary Russell initialed Bradford's two-sentence memorandum and marked the TOP SECRET verdict "approved."

On November 12, 1946, R. L. Bannerman sent a memo to Selden Chapin, director of the Foreign Service. (By now the classification had sunk to CONFIDENTIAL): "A-R has advised the Security Office that the appointment of Penn Townsend Kimball to Foreign Service rolls has been disapproved on security grounds."

On December 4, 1946, the whole batch of materials on my case was turned over to CON for safekeeping in the State Department's permanent security files. *Time*'s December 2, 1946, cover was Ambassador to Argentina George E. Messersmith. The cover story in the Foreign Relations section of National Affairs detailed the Ambassador's watchdog role in monitoring the spread of totalitarianism of both the left and right throughout Latin America. The author was Penn Kimball. What a spot for a Soviet mole!

10

THE CASE IS
CLOSED

WHEN I WAS officially declared a national security risk in November, 1946, the paper work was routine. The routine, however, did not include notifying me. The "state of Kimball's mind," so crucial to the final decision, was—total ignorance. I had been condemned by my own government, without a hearing, without the opportunity to be informed of the charges against me or to cross-examine witnesses or comment on their credibility, or to make a statement in my own defense. Thus stood human rights in the United States of America in November, 1946, one year after the end of the world war to safe-guard our freedoms.

Life went on for me, none the wiser.

While the hassles over my political loyalty were going on within the State Department, I had already made up my mind to quit my job at *Time* after less than a year, and to cast my lot once again with an experiment in meaningful journalism.

The attraction of journalism as a profession is that it is one in which an individual feels that his contribution can make a difference in the state of the world. At *Time*, writers unhappy with their editors' revisions of their story would fight for a paragraph, then a sentence, then a word. In a medium with an influential readership, ran the rationalization, every blow for freedom is worth more than pages of truth in some unnoticed pamphlet. That theory kept many a good man chained to his typewriter at *Time* past the point of no return.

I felt no overpowering gripe with my career to date at *Time*, just the gnawing feeling that I wanted to be accomplishing something more. The generation that spent a large portion of its youth in a war in which it believed came home with big dreams for making a better future.

Drawn to the underdog by some curious chemistry, brought up to expect high standards of myself as well as others, blessed with a quick if not deep mind, combative in temperament (fat little boy with glasses from the posh side of the tracks?), resentful of authority (God knows why!) and idealistic to a fault (the line between hoping for the best and expecting the worst is sometimes mistaken for cynicism), I was perhaps destined for lost causes.

In November, 1946, I agreed to sign on come the New Year as a senior editor of *New Republic*, a distinguished though small-circulation journal of progressive opinion that was gearing itself to reach for larger audiences in the growing postwar market for news magazines. It was a repetition of my leaving *United States News* for *PM*, I suppose, a gravitational pull toward the left of center, wherever that was. As a matter of fact, I tell my students, I feel as though I have been doing the same thing all my life, only in different settings. I thought that at *Time* I would be for many years only a small cog in an established and successful enterprise. *New Republic* meant a piece of the action in an enterprise headed in the right direction for postwar America. (Or so I imagined. Ed Cerf, as small a cog as I was, became National Affairs editor of *Time*, then assistant managing editor, then managing editor of *Life*. I lasted five months at *New Republic*.)

I can't remember how the job offer materialized. The Straight family (married into the Whitney family), who had long made up the magazine's deficit, was now prepared to dip into capital to finance a new format, a new staff and a new target audience large enough to attract sufficient advertising to make the publication self-sustaining.

I was attracted by a $1,500 annual increase over my *Time* salary. Satisfying my conscience—and with a raise; that was a combination hard to resist. I accepted.

It was a psychological adjustment to move from my *Time* office, where handmaidens waited on me hand and foot, to a dusty cubicle overlooking an airshaft and with a pair of scissors for clipping my own paper. The price of liberalism. I had been so rash, or ignorant, as to quit *Time* just 10 days before Christmas, thus forfeiting my share of the year-end bonuses. I have spent many times out of work just before Christmas, and I think that has something to do with the severe depression that overtakes me at that season of the year.

I started with *New Republic* after New Year's, prepared to work as usual over the weekend. As I sat at my desk on my first Saturday the temperature dropped lower and lower. The office was in a building heated by Con Ed steam, which was turned off on weekends, and no one had budgeted for supplementary heat in the initial projections.

The idea for invigorating *New Republic* was to combine its noble tradition as a journal of liberal opinion with some of the more up-to-date forms of presenting a summary of the week's news which were proving to be so successful for the not-so-liberal news weeklies such as *Time* and *United States News*. Michael Straight was newly returned from wartime service with the Army Air Corps and ready to take a direct hand in managing his family's favorite philanthropy. Straight had recruited a promising staff: In addition to William Walton, my ex-colleague at *PM* and *Life*, who was placed in charge of the Washington Bureau, Theodore H. White and William Harlan Hale (later managing editor of *Horizon*) were hired as general editors and writers. The art director was Hank Brennan, lured away from *McCall*'s to redesign the new package (he later became Luce's art consultant for all of *Time–Life*). The man in charge of the publishing side was William D. Patterson, who went on to help make *Saturday Review* a success in new format.

Straight was a handsome, attractive, intelligent young man. He spoke and wrote well, and since he had spent most of his formative years in Britain, he sounded to me a lot like the mildly Fabian Socialists I had known at Oxford. (Straight confessed in a book published in 1983 that he had joined the Communist Party while an undergraduate at Cambridge University in the 1930s. No one was ever the wiser until he turned himself in to the FBI in 1963, having broken with the Communists before the war.)

It was an article of faith of the new enterprise, moreover, to eschew those ideological divisions so characteristic of the left-of-center press in America: most of them preach to the already convinced. *New Republic* and its rival *The Nation* had circulations of only 30,000 to 40,000 apiece. The hope underwritten by Straight was to broaden the base to attract a larger segment of the millions of liberal Americans who had supported the New Deal until its interruption by World War II. Interpretation of the news from a liberal perspective would be the rule rather than editorials telling people what they ought to think. It was a premise not unlike Ingersoll's for *PM*, which might have been a forewarning of the chaos that had marked *PM*'s beginning and the steady deterioration that had contributed to its end. But magazines were less hectic to put together than a big-city daily. Combining the best features of the news weeklies and the dissenting journals of opinion seemed a natural to one who had just been through the cheese-nibbling process at *Time*.

But Straight made a serious mistake right at the start. Without so much as a by-your-leave from the rest of the new staff, he hired as editor in chief Henry Wallace, recently tossed out of Harry Truman's Cabinet for questioning the Cold War. Although his father had founded *Wallace's Farmer*, there was not too much evidence on the record to authenticate Wallace's editorial ability. His presence made the magazine a lightning rod for all the factional quarrels between the members of the liberal coalition that had rallied behind Franklin D. Roosevelt.

Wallace's appointment had barely been announced when the New Deal coalition began to break up under the postwar pressures exacerbated by Stalin's regime in the Soviet Union. The old Committee for Political Action splintered into two rival groups. Americans for Democratic Action (ADA) declared themselves to be anti-Communists who understood the Stalinist threat and were ready to carry on the liberal heritage of F.D.R. minus any popular front that might include apologists for Communism at home or abroad. The Progressive Committee of Americans (PCA) accused ADA of wasting liberal energies on Red-baiting and playing into the hands of illiberal forces that were inducing the United States to back reactionary regimes around the world on the ground of containing the Communist threat.

The staff on *New Republic* voted to give both organizations a wide berth and to steer an editorial course that judged news on its merits, unencumbered by litmus tests for ideological purity. That was fine until some of Wallace's old pals came to New York for a PCA convention and invited him around for an unannounced social visit. Wallace with his usual innocence dropped over to the Commodore Hotel where the PCA convention was taking place. Next morning the New York press made the connection that Wallace had given the PCA his personal imprimatur. That was only the beginning of the troubles with Henry Wallace, which ended up with his running for President on the Progressive Party ticket while *New Republic* endorsed Truman.

Wallace was rebuilding an old farmhouse in South Salem, New York; his wife was remaining in their Washington apartment until the work on the house was finished. I was sick of living at the Princeton Club. Mike Straight's sister Beatrice was not occupying her part of a family-owned townhouse on East 92d Street, and he offered its empty bedrooms as a fringe benefit to Wallace and me. I was glad to take up his offer.

Wallace was painfully shy. He made his own bed, mixed six different kinds of dry cereal for his breakfast, washed his bowl, then walked every morning from 92d Street to the *New Republic* office on 49th. He arrived back late and rose up early, and commuted by train to his home in Washington every weekend. We would breakfast together on Monday morning, when he would tell me how perturbed he was by the talk of preventive war he heard that weekend at the dinner tables in the nation's capital. A devout Episcopalian, his feelings about peace were deep and religious. He seemed to be carrying on a huge correspondence with farmers all over the world asking questions about hybrid corn developed by Wallace and produced as seed at the family agro-business in Iowa. When he smoked, he would spill ashes over his vest as he became enraptured with his own thoughts. One day he left a letter from his own son open on the hall table. It began: "Dear Mr. Wallace."

The man was an enigma to everyone who ever knew him. While I was living with Wallace, I brought around Janet Fraser to meet him. When he asked where she was from, she told him that she was born and raised in Syracuse, New York. Wallace then reeled off the name of every manufacturing concern based there, facts he had filed in his head as Secretary of Commerce under Roosevelt and Truman.

Wallace had been forced to leave the Truman Administration in the fall of 1946, after making a September speech in Madison Square Garden critical of United States foreign policy and what Wallace perceived was a drift from cold war to hot. Secretary of State James Byrnes was in Paris negotiating the postwar peace treaties when he heard the news that Wallace had gone public with his view that American foreign policy was leading us into war with the Soviet Union in Western Europe. He cabled Truman that Wallace was pulling the rug out from under him in the negotiations. Truman repudiated the views expressed by Wallace and dismissed him from the Cabinet at just about the same time that the Byrnes State Department was deciding that I was a national security risk. Without knowing it, Wallace and I were fellow victims of the paranoia building up in Washington. Purest accident had thrown us together on the staff of *New Republic* and as roommates in the house on 92d Street. What a field day the special agents would have had with that one! But they were no longer tracing my footsteps, and the Wallace connection never did make it into my file. I left *New Republic* before Wallace decided to run for President.

The launching of new publications, or old publications in new directions, is a war of nerves at which I have won my share of purple hearts. Starting with the unheated offices, I had the feeling that *New Republic* might turn out to be *PM* revisited.

Paper on which to print the magazine was in short supply, and as we gradually pushed up circulation, our shortages became more acute. Getting display on the newsstands was very difficult, a modest seller like *New Republic* usually being consigned to an inside shelf for delivery only upon demand. Mail-order subscriptions were an alternative, but direct-mail promotion was expensive. Never mind the content, the sheer mechanics of trying to get a magazine moving were backbreaking.

Mike Straight had grafted his new staff onto the trunk of the old. The relations between the newcomers and old-timers were, to say the least, awkward. Bruce Bliven, who had been editor in the previous dynasty, kept his old office, was available for counsel, but really didn't have anything to do. Longtime *New Republic* contributors suddenly found their copy being edited for the first time by a bunch of strangers. Some readers were put off when the graphics improved; they felt more comfortable with the dull, gray *New Republic* of old. Assembling a new audience without driving away the old is one of the trickiest exercises in publishing.

We were in a real bind with editor Henry Wallace. He couldn't write. And he didn't seem to have anything to say, beyond a fixation about the danger of war arising out of our confrontations with the Soviet Union. There was some division of opinion on that issue among staff, new and old, so that it became difficult to hone a clear-cut editorial policy.

Wallace's troubles at *New Republic* were compounded when he took a trip to Europe and committed the breach of protocol of criticizing United States foreign policy from a platform in a foreign country. He left the country on April 7, 1947, and I mark the date by the fact that Janet and I were married on the next day, April 8.

Janet was still sharing an apartment on East 60th Street with a rotating series of women who inherited the lease of the original inhabitant. The fourth-floor walkup continued to be a good measure of the height of my devotion. Since my only long-term base had been the Princeton Club and Janet's name was not even on the lease on 60th Street, we literally had no place we could call home in New York City. The combination of rent control and the wartime building moratorium made for a shortage of space to absorb the new households being created by returning veterans. Wallace's trip meant that Janet and I could spend our honeymoon alone together in the 92d Street apartment while she continued to work at *Time* and I at *New Republic*. We were married on a bright sunny day in the chapel of the Presbyterian Church on lower Fifth Avenue. Ed Cerf was best man.

The furor raised by Wallace's speeches abroad caused a sudden cancellation of his itinerary and he returned to the United States ahead of schedule. And that is how Janet and I came to spend our honeymoon with Henry Wallace. He was an unobtrusive companion since he rose so early and was off for his morning constitutional usually before we were even awake. The apartment was not far from the Ruppert Brewery and the morning air was often fragrant with the scent of hops. Who would want to get up in Valhalla?

The only problem was that the phone was ringing constantly with inquiries from the press and friends about the whereabouts of our news-making roommate. Janet would take the calls, but nobody believed her at 7 in the morning when she said she had no idea where Wallace might be. The young female voice on Henry Wallace's telephone so early in the morning did wonders for his image, nevertheless.

We soon managed to find an apartment of our own and moved out. The last time we saw Wallace a few months later, Janet was demonstrably pregnant. Henry greeted us warmly, for Henry, and took one look at Janet. "You know," he immediately said to her, "the only animal for which you can predict the sex of its offspring is a chicken."

We never did know what to make of Mr. Wallace, and neither did *New Republic*. The whole enterprise didn't seem to know where it was going, or how to get there. Wallace, the editor, was really not the editor. Mike Straight, whose ideas and enthusiasm had attracted us to the new venture, was not strong-willed enough to move aside old retainers who still controlled some of the key spots, such as managing editor.

Teddy White and I would commiserate together, sometimes with Bill Walton when he came up from Washington, over the lack of direction. The care and feeding of a weekly magazine, all three of us had learned at Time, Inc., was a single-minded process even though many minds were at work. There had to be a sense of direction, a conception of the audience we were trying to reach, and that had to be translated via the copy at hand as it traveled through the editorial process.

The magazine innovations (such as the satirical drawings by Robert Osborn) would be faithfully and sharply reproduced. But the cuts were engraved in Stamford. The New York City printing business had priced itself out of the market for magazines of decent circulation and lacked the room to accommodate huge presses and binders. So all our copy was sent out of town to be set and run. This devious route raised no problems for a product being written and edited for the ages, but was a headache when we began trying to key *New Republic* more closely to the news.

More and more I had the feeling that I was reliving *PM*. My sense of *déja vu* reinforced the conviction acquired there that it is not enough to have your heart in the right place. It takes competence as well as sensitivity to put out a successful liberal publication. Like *PM*, *New Republic* was staffed with excellent, individual talent. It managed, with the help of expensive promotion, to push its circulation up close to 200,000 copies a week, a phenomenal number for a journal of left-of-center opinion. But the place was a madhouse inside. I implored Straight to put someone in charge, to no avail.

In June, Janet was rushed to Midtown Hospital for emergency surgery. We had been married two months and I had been working for *New Republic* for five. I was at her bedside when she came out of the anesthetic, and she used to say she still remembered the moment as if it were yesterday. "I hope you won't mind," I told her, "but I've just quit my job."

During the period when Janet and I were both holding down full-time, paying jobs, we never had it so good. New York City was the perfect honeymoon spot for a pair of gainfully employed journalists. Janet was 23, and I was born again. I would drop by *Time* to pick up Janet after work, and kid Matthews, Fuerbringer and Cerf about stories in that week's issue.

When I quit *New Republic*, I embarked on a career of free-lance magazine writing while Janet supplied the family's steady income, not for the last time in our 35 years of marriage. When she came home at night, I would try to ask her interested questions about her day at the office. I would complain about chores such as sending out and collecting the dry cleaning. Once she came home and caught me listening to the ball game on the radio. That was a scene.

My free-lance assignments didn't all pan out. One editor who had commissioned a story idea from me was fired in midpassage. Another loved a piece, but would I mind doing it over to accommodate more pictures—and, of course, less text? I managed a few published articles, but I lacked the temperament to merchandise several ideas at once and then grind them out on a steady production schedule. I could see that free-lancing was not fraught with security. And Janet was expecting a baby. The time had come to begin consolidating my assets and reviewing my options.

AND SO IT WAS that on December 9, 1947, I wrote to the Office of the Foreign Service to inquire how I might go about reactivating my postponed appointment. I reminded them that I had passed the written and oral examinations and had withdrawn my name because of personal obligations. "Am I still eligible?" I wrote innocently. "Are openings currently being filled in this branch of the Department?"

The silence was deafening. My file shows that my query began bouncing around the bureaucracy. Memorandum to File, from CSA (Chief Security Agent), a job still held by Thomas F. Fitch, December 22, 1947:

> Mr. Howe, BEX [Board of Examiners, Foreign Service], called today regarding the case of Penn Townsend Kimball and stated that the last indication of security action in the files of BEX was a security approval granted by CON on March 11, 1946. I advised Mr. Howe of the information contained in the memorandum of November 12, 1946, to OFS from CON and told him that the subject had been disapproved on security grounds. Mr. Howe indicated that his request was based on an inquiry from the subject with regard to the status of his case.

That very day Joseph C. Green, Executive Director, Board of Examiners for the Foreign Service, put this one-paragraph reply to my query into the mail:

> Dear Mr. Kimball:
> I acknowledge the receipt of your letter of December 9, 1947, in regard to your status as a candidate for appointment

to the Foreign Service. I have directed that the matter be investigated and I hope to be able in the near future to reply to your question.

Sincerely yours,
Joseph C. Green

The old stone wall.

When the government machinery is grinding you into mincemeat, there is a momentum to the process which moves the paperwork across desks with an irresistible force. The system creates the immovable objects only when the victim tries to find out the score. My attempt to find out from the State Department how it had manhandled my application seems to have created, if not consternation, then considerable confusion. It was not its style to level with outsiders.

The fine touch of the bureaucratic brushoff requires detailed attention from the eye of an appraiser. The in-boxes and out-boxes which channeled the flow of my tiresome inquiries must have contained more spectacular stuff. But the record in my file of the phone calls, exchanges of memoranda, drafted and redrafted letters is a tapestry of obscuring the issue. One must look closely to catch the finer distinctions.

Note in the files of the Chief Security Agent, dated December 22, 1947, the same day Mr. Green wrote the stalling note to me:

Mr. Green of BEX will call Mr. Fitch on either Monday or Tuesday on this case. Mr. Fitch promised to let him see the file.

Handwritten comment by Mr. Fitch, dated January 12, 1948:

Mr. Green has not called.

Memorandum for file, from T. F. Fitch, Chief Special Agent, January 14, 1948, Subject: Kimball, Penn Townsend.

Today Mr. Green personally called at this office to discuss the investigation made by CSA of this applicant. After reviewing the file Mr. Green stated that he was somewhat at a loss as to how to tell Mr. Kimball that our investigation proved unsatisfactory.

It was agreed that Mr. Green would write Mr. Kimball stating that the case was still under investigation by CSA. Mr. Green said he would furnish me a copy of such letter. I stated that if Mr. Kimball still indicated a desire to be considered for the position for which he has applied after receiving Mr. Green's letter, CSA would be willing to interview Kimball with a view to obtaining information which might assist in resolving the case, and at such time would give it such other attention as the circumstances warranted.

There is nothing to do on this until we hear further from Mr. Green or possibly from Kimball, himself.

Letter from Green to Kimball, dated January 14, 1948:

Dear Mr. Kimball:

I refer to my letter of December 22, 1947, and previous correspondence, in regard to your candidacy for appointment as a Foreign Service officer, and in reply to the questions contained in your letter of December 9, I have to inform you that your case is still under investigation by the investigative division of the Department.

Note on the file copy of letter:

This letter was drafted after consultation with Mr. Fitch of CSA and in accordance with his suggestion.

The shoe had dropped—and studded with nails it was. My case was under investigation! Just what the doctor ordered for a hungry free-lancer with a pregnant wife. There had been a considerable escalation in semantics from Mr. Green's assurance that he had "directed the matter be investigated" to the news that "your case is still under investigation by the investigative division of the department." The language was fuzzy, but the implication was ominous.

The letter had gone to my old address in New Britain where my sister was living, and seemed to have taken a while to catch up with me. The bureaucratic code referring to the "investigative division of the department" gave no clue that there was a live body there to whom I should write and demand to be interviewed, as per Chief Security Agent Fitch's internal memorandum expressing his willingness to talk with me if it came to that. I wrote again to Green on April 4, to ask what his letter meant.

> The exact implication of this is not altogether clear to me. I presume that it is another continuation of the process that has apparently been continuing since I was informed, nearly two years ago, that I had passed the oral and written examinations for the Foreign Service. . . . On December 9, 1947, I addressed a set of questions to the Department that I hoped would clear up the matter. Your letter of December 22, 1947, indicated that I might expect a reply "in the near future." Since your letter of January 14 I have received no further communication.

There was, of course, no investigation going on at all at this time. That had all been signed, sealed and undelivered more than a year before. And no one wanted to tell me what had really transpired. In retrospect, the gobbledygook, the stalling might have been part of the internal battle going on in the State Department between the Foreign Service and its security arm, a battle which was to surface with a vengeance in the McCarthy period. The file shows that a representative of the Foreign Service phoned the chief security agent on April 13 requesting that "the investigation on above subject be resolved," and Green himself dictated a memo for the file: "Over and over again I requested CON to pursue the investigation with a view to obtaining definite evidence against Mr. Kimball supporting the suspicions which led to the disapproval of his appointment, or exoneration and a reversal of Mr. Russell's decision."

Now my fate was delegated into the hands of subordinates. Cromwell A. Riches (another of those wonderful State Department names!) reviewed the bidding for Green on April 13:

Mr. Kimball was given security clearance by CSA [Chief Security Agent] March 11, 1946. After he passed his oral examination, the case was returned to CSA for further investigation. This investigation resulted in disapproval on security grounds. A memorandum to this effect was sent to Mr. Chapin November 12, 1946. There has been no work done on this case since and Mr. Fitch is opposed to reopening it.

I have gone through the Kimball file with Mr. Hoffman [in the Office of the Chief Special Agent] and believe that we should accept the CSA finding as final. While Kimball was employed by *Time* and *PM* he was active in the American Newspaper Guild. Many of his associates in the Guild state that he almost invariably voted with the Communist faction. A man as capable as Mr. Kimball obviously could not be unaware of the struggle within such organizations between Communists and anti-Communists and he apparently threw in his lot with the Communists.

CSA suggests that Mr. Kimball be disqualified on technical grounds. If this is not possible they are willing that a letter be sent notifying him that he has been disapproved by the Assistant Secretary. He was actually turned down by Assistant Secretary Russell rather than Mr. Peurifoy. [John E. Peurifoy succeeded Donald Russell in January, 1947.]

Now the long elaborate investigation could be boiled down into a couple of emphatic conclusions by Mr. Riches. The whole thing would have been a lot neater if it could have been disposed of on a technicality. Unfortunately for this scenario, my application was in order. Next day, April 14, Green thereupon dispatched a one-sentence letter to me:

My Dear Mr. Kimball:

I refer to your letter of April 4, 1948, and previous correspondence in regard to your candidacy for appointment as a Foreign Service officer, and now have to inform you that your appointment has been disapproved.

Thus the secret was finally out, though in somewhat truncated form, following two false letters telling me my case was still under investigation. Janet and I were in the midst of moving from New York to Connecticut pending the birth of our baby. My reply was delayed until May 7:

> I was both dismayed and bewildered by this decision. . . .
> This action came without discussion and without warning of
> any kind. I was never informed that a reversal by the Board
> was even under consideration. I was never told that the slight-
> est cause existed for such consideration. . . . I am naturally
> at a loss to comprehend this breach of the assurances I re-
> ceived from the Board when I permitted my name to be re-
> moved from the April, 1946, list of appointments. I am
> equally in the dark as to what possible reason could have
> prompted the reversal. Up to and including my oral inter-
> rogations by the Board no suggestion was ever made that my
> qualifications for the Service were not entirely in order. Since
> then, I have never seen or communicated in person with any
> member or representative of the Board.
>
> In light of these circumstances, I respectfully request a full
> and frank explanation of the following points of information:
> (1) What are the reasons for the disapproval? (2) By
> whom was the ruling made? (3) What privileges are avail-
> able to me for a review of this decision, and/or a personal
> hearing, and/or consideration of my case by the Civil Ser-
> vice Commission?
>
> You will understand, I am sure, my anxiety over a situa-
> tion that seems to me unreasonable and unjust.

The file indicates that my letter of protest created some but not a great deal of fallout. The bureaucratic tug-of-war continued.

Riches, whose memo had recommended that the case be kept closed, became the go-between for Green at Foreign Service and Fitch, at Office of Security. Green was now sick of the whole business and tried in vain to pass the buck. He drafted this reply, dated May 12 but marked "not sent" in the file:

I acknowledge the receipt of your letter of May 7, 1948 with further reference to your candidacy for appointment as Foreign Service Officer and have to inform you that your letter has been referred for reply to the Chief Special Agent of the Department.

Riches to Fitch:

In accordance with our telephone conversation I am enclosing the letter from Penn T. Kimball, together with a draft of a letter from Mr. Green to Mr. Kimball for your initials if you approve, and the Kimball file. We shall appreciate seeing a copy of the letter you send Mr. Kimball before it goes out.

Scrawled across the bottom of this memo is a handwritten note: "Reopen case to Personnel Security Branch with CSA file." It is initialed with letters impossible to decipher.

The upshot was that Fitch wanted no part of sending me a direct letter signed by the chief special agent and passed the buck right back to the Foreign Service by drafting a version for Green's signature. As he explained in a May 19 memo to Riches:

In accordance with our telephone conversation of today I am returning your file on Mr. Kimball together with the draft of a letter from Mr. Green to him for initialing by me if approved.

In discussing this matter with you over the 'phone several days ago I did not convey the idea that I would reply to Mr. Kimball's letter addressed to Mr. Green on May 6th but I thought it possible that I make some suggestion with reference to what you might desire to tell him.

As stated to you in 'phone conversation with you today I thought that possibly a letter from Mr. Green similar to the attached might serve the desired purpose. However, you were doubtful as to whether Mr. Green would sign such a letter. Nevertheless, responsive to your request I am transmitting it.

Fitch's draft for Green's signature, a masterpiece of "responsive" communication, was likewise marked "not sent"—and eventually deposited in the file:

My Dear Mr. Kimball:

Answering your letter of May 7, 1948, you are informed that my communication of April 14, 1948, regarding your candidacy for appointment as a Foreign Service Officer was based on concurrence with a decision made by the former Assistant Secretary of State.

Decisions with respect to candidates for employment in the Foreign Service are matters of administrative discretion and are therefore subject only to review by persons responsible for the conduct of that Service.

The trouble with that version was that it meant Green would be admitting that he had lied in telling me that my case was still under investigation. Caught in the blizzard of State Department paperwork, Riches sent out a cry for help. He wrote a memo to Fitch's boss:

Office Memorandum · UNITED STATES GOVERNMENT

TO: CON—Mr. Nicholson
FROM: BEX—C. A. Riches
SUBJECT: Penn T. KIMBALL

In accordance with our telephone conversation this morning I am sending you the Kimball file. You will note that it includes Mr. Kimball's unanswered letter of May 7th and the suggested replies drafted by Mr. Green and Mr. Fitch. Whenever you have had the opportunity to study the case I hope we can get together on the preparation of an appropriate reply to Mr. Kimball's letter.

[initialed]
Cromwell A. Riches

Three weeks had gone by and the government agency in charge of our international diplomatic communications had not figured out how to answer a request from one citizen for the truth. Never was a thought given to answering my questions asking the reasons for the disapproval and an explanation of my opportunities for a hearing and review. The paperwork had all been directed at obscuring the fact that the State Department in TOP SECRET had declared me to be a "definite security risk," of doubtful loyalty to my country and its institutions.

The file does not disclose how the text was arrived at, but Green "with some reluctance," according to the file, settled for this final word to me on May 25:

My Dear Mr. Kimball:

I refer to your letter of May 7, 1948, and previous correspondence, in regard to your candidacy for appointment as a Foreign Service Officer, and now have to inform you in reply to the questions contained in the penultimate paragraph of your letter under acknowledgment that your appointment was disapproved by the appropriate officer of the Department on the basis of facts ascertained in the course of the investigation subsequent to your examination referred to in previous letters and that this decision is final.

One sentence—84 words long—a masterpiece of obfuscation. Document 21 could have been written by a committee. D. Nicholson, director of the Office of Controls (CON), initialed it before it was signed by Joseph C. Green as executive director of the Board of Examiners (BEX) for the Foreign Service. Within the State Department, the world will end, no doubt, with a bang—as a committee struggles over a penultimate paragraph.

When I received Green's letter, I had no idea of the serious government action against me which lay behind it. It was early 1948, the year in which Truman would win re-election, however surprisingly, against Thomas E. Dewey. A Republican Congress, to be sure, was doing battle with the Democratic President, including charges that his administration was soft on Communism. A later director of CON resigned after a House committee charged he had a second cousin who was allegedly Communistic. But, in far-off Connecticut, I had no reason to suspect I was part of the dress rehearsal for the drama to come.

I received the letter 10 days before our daughter Lisa was born on June 5, 1948. While Janet had managed to keep working at *Time* almost to the last moment, our life was on the edge of the new adventure of parenthood. I was now the sole provider, age 32 and with no steady source of income. I went down to the bank and took out a mortgage on the family homestead. It was not the moment to pursue a low-paying career abroad with the Foreign Service.

I really couldn't afford any more time from scratching for freelance assignments. But, as my family never ceases to remind me, I am constitutionally unable just to let things pass. The idea that someone like me could be the object of a full-blown security investigation simply never crossed my mind. More likely, some government bureaucrat might have noted that I had worked for *PM* and been an editor of *New Republic* and automatically decided that I was beyond the pale. Or the State Department might be proscribing me on the grounds of my having shared an apartment with Henry Wallace. (I didn't know the decision had been made months before my move to *New Republic*.) It didn't strike me as right. I couldn't let it pass. I went up into my brother's old room at the back of the house and pounded out yet another letter to Joseph C. Green.

Pacing around my typewriter a day or so later, I came up with an inspiration. I would put those State Department dodos in their place by sweeping their end. I would write a second letter to Connecticut's Republican Senator, Raymond E. Baldwin. Baldwin, a popular former Governor, had a reputation as a liberal; he had almost made the GOP ticket as vice-presidential candidate running with Willkie in 1940. As a member of a family with Republican connections, I figured the Senator might react to a letter from a constituent. And a Democratic administration espousing a bipartisan foreign policy might react to a Republican from the Hill. I pulled out all the stops, including date-lining my letter to Baldwin "Memorial Day, 1948":

Dear Senator:
   I have no reason to hope that you will have time to hear my story through.

It is, I suppose, an inconsequential tale. But its importance to me is understandably out of all proportion to larger considerations of state.

You see, I have just been informed that I am unacceptable to be a member of the U.S. Foreign Service. The exact reason is obscure, because the State Department has refused every request for an explanation. The implication is clear, however, that I am in some way unworthy of my government. And that is a heavy charge for any citizen to bear, especially when no one will tell him why.

Here my letter sketched out for the Senator my family background and academic and military career. It continued:

On the basis of these qualifications I was accepted as a candidate to take the examinations for the U.S. Foreign Service. I was officially informed that I had successfully passed both the written and oral examinations for that service. But after "an investigation by the investigative agency of the State Department," I was informed that my candidacy had been disapproved. The results of this investigation, however, were never communicated to me. When I asked for a personal hearing or an explanation of the disapproval, my application was denied. I was also informed that the disapproval was final and not subject to review.

The only conclusion that I can draw, in the face of this secrecy, is that I have been disqualified on the basis of my personal or professional career subsequent to my successful oral examination at the State Department.

Here I filled the Senator in on my work history and membership in the Guild.

I do not imagine that all the officers of our State Department have always been in wholehearted agreement with the editorial views of those organizations. But I cannot believe that this is sufficient grounds to disqualify me as a candidate for the Foreign Service. If such is the case, however, it seems to me that the situation merits the closest scrutiny.

Inasmuch as I was never interrogated by the investigative personnel of the State Department, I can only guess at the conclusions accumulated on the basis of hearsay. I would be perfectly agreeable to discuss any matters in this record, but this privilege has been denied me. It is beyond me how one can defend himself against allegations never brought into the open. This procedure does not strike me as a sound means of determining the truth or falsity of irresponsible evidence.

I am profoundly disturbed that the official record of my case includes the note that casts a doubt, however slight, on my character, loyalty or integrity. In my own heart, the absurdity of such charges is apparent, but this does not protect me from the damage threatened by the State Department's official action. It strikes me as a dangerous precedent to stand unchallenged. The motive that prompts me to call it to your attention is not my feeling of deep disappointment, but of conviction that it is contrary to every American principle of democratic fair play.

Sincerely yours,
Penn Kimball

Baldwin sent my letter of protest to the State Department on June 15, where it initially produced the desired effect. The department has to deal with a Senator. The file reveals a hasty conference was called, including Green and the director of the Foreign Service, H. P. Martin. Another reply—"not sent"—was drafted to Senator Baldwin for Martin's signature.

My dear Senator Baldwin:

I acknowledge the receipt of your letter of June 9, 1948, in regard to the desire of Penn Kimball to obtain an appointment as Foreign Service Officer and requesting information as to why he was not appointed.

Mr. Kimball was, as he states in his letter of May 31 addressed to you, successful in the Written and Oral Examinations conducted under the supervision of the Board of Examiners for the Foreign Service. There followed the usual careful examination which the Department conducts in the case of all candidates for appointment as Foreign Service Officer. In the course of his investigation it was ascertained that Mr. Kimball while in the employ of *PM* was a member of the Newspaper Guild. The evidence indicates that he consistently sided with the Communist element in that organization. Furthermore, many of his closest associates have been either Communists or persons openly sympathetic with Communism. In view of these facts the Assistant Secretary at that time in charge of organization and administration decided that it would not be proper to appoint Mr. Kimball to the Foreign Service.

You will readily understand that the Department does not in cases of this kind find it advisable to inform candidates of the specific reasons for their failure to obtain an appointment. Mr. Kimball has not, therefore, been given and will not be given all the information contained in this letter.

After mulling it over, Martin made an appointment to call on the Senator personally instead of sending the letter, and took with him to the meeting the Senator's inquiry (which never made it to the file). Martin dictated this account to Green (which did make the file) of the State Department's final word on Subject: Penn Kimball.

I had a very satisfactory talk with Senator Baldwin last Thursday afternoon about the Kimball case. I explained to the Senator that I had come personally to see him rather than answer his letter of June 9. The Senator was fully appreciative of this and listened intently while I explained to him the questions raised by the investigation report.

I followed very much the line taken in the letter which you proposed to send to the Senator. I made it clear that if Mr. Kimball were an employee of the Department, we would make further efforts to either clear him of the charges or establish a case as the basis of getting rid of him, but since Mr. Kimball is an applicant, we have felt it unwise to make the appointment in the face of the questions that have been raised.

Senator Baldwin said that he did not think that Mr. Kimball is a Communist, but that he fully understands the decision we have reached. The Senator said he would be the last person in the world to ask the State Department to take any chances as regards security in the selection of its personnel. He pointed out further that even if we were satisfied that the man is not a Communist or has Communistic leanings, should we make the appointment, there would be a possibility of someone raising the question on the floor of the Senate or the House, holding up as an example the Kimball case in which the State Department made the appointment when it had been charged that he is a Communist or Communist sympathizer. The Senator's feeling in this regard was that such would create an injustice to the man, the State Department and the Foreign Service.

I handed the Senator the letter he had written to me. He said he would write to Mr. Kimball, simply telling him that he had talked to the State Department and is convinced that this Department will not change its position; also, he will suggest to Mr. Kimball that he simply forget the matter.

The Senator was as good as his word. His letter to me, dated June 20, 1948, bore the disclaimer "Dictated," and was merely initialed by a member of his staff.

Dear Mr. Kimball:

I have talked personally with a representative of the State Department concerning your application. They will not change their position. Since the matter is one that is completely discretionary with them, there is nothing further that we can do about it.

I regret this situation very much, but I am helpless in the matter.

Yours very sincerely,
Raymond E. Baldwin

Our new baby was two weeks old. Born to an unemployed national security risk.

The remarkable thing about Senator Baldwin's "understanding" of the State Department's decision was how clearly this Republican Senator with a liberal reputation anticipated and responded to the oncoming wave of McCarthyism. But the doctrine of guilt by accusation prompted Joseph C. Green to register in the file a daring dissent from the Senator's solution:

Office Memorandum · UNITED STATES GOVERNMENT

TO: File DATE: June 23, 1948
FROM: BEX—Joseph C. Green
SUBJECT: Mr. Penn KIMBALL, Class 6 Candidate

The proposed action of Senator Baldwin, as reported in Mr. Martin's memorandum of June 21, may put an end to this case. It should be noted, however, that the Senator's attitude, which seems to be that the Department should not take the risk of appointing any person who has ever been charged with being a Communist or a Communist sympathizer, is not in accord with the position which BEX has uniformly adopted in such cases. It has been our position that candidates otherwise qualified and eligible for appointment should be appointed unless, after exhaustive investigation, there could be adduced proof that the candidate was a Communist or had Communist sympathies or evidence of such a nature as to create in the mind of a fairminded and judicious person suspicion that the candidate might be a Communist or have Communist sympathies. We have never taken the position that a candidate against whom nothing derogatory could even be alleged with sufficient evidence to raise suspicion in the mind of a judicious person should be excluded from appointment on the ground that his appointment might cause embarrassment to the Department or any officer of the Department.

[initialed] J.C.G.
Joseph C. Green
BEX:JCG:HWD

[stamped:]
1 / 5173 / 171
DEPARTMENT OF STATE
APR 26 1955
OFFICE OF SECURITY

Green himself must have selected the portions of his memo he wished to emphasize for future readers of my case, for they are underlined in the original. And that memo, alone of the documents in that part of my file, is stamped as having been noted seven years later by the department's Office of Security. I wonder how many managed to hold on to such a view concerning the rights of the accused during the McCarthy experience. I wonder how many hold to that view in Foggy Bottom today.

PART TWO

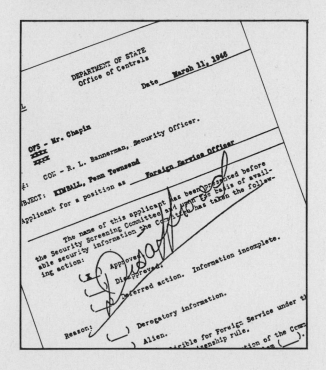

DEPARTMENT OF STATE
Office of Controls

Date _____ March 11, 1948

OFS - Mr. Chapin

COM - R. L. Bannerman, Security Officer.

SUBJECT: KIMBALL, Penn Townsend

Applicant for a position as _____ Foreign Service Officer

The name of this applicant has been presented before
the Security Screening Committee and upon the basis of available security information the Committee has taken the following action:

(X) Approved.
( ) Disapproved.
( ) Deferred action. Information incomplete.

Reason:
( ) Derogatory information.
( ) Alien.
( ) ...igible for Foreign Service under t...
...izenship rule.
...tion of the Comm...
...am ( ).

11

TRIAL BY POSTAL SERVICE

WHEN I CAME into possession of the documents in my file, it triggered within me a determination to do something about it, however long the odds. There was just something about the whole damn business that shouldn't be allowed to pass unchallenged. Something, if you will excuse the expression, un-American.

What to do was clear enough: track down all the missing links, including my accusers if I could. Try to persuade the government to reopen my case. Try to clear my name while I still had most of my marbles. I think anyone in my place would want to do the same. I didn't realize how hard that would turn out to be.

Access to government files is governed by the Freedom of Information Act of 1966, as amended in 1974, and by the Privacy Act of 1974. The Privacy Act gives you the right to retrieve your own records maintained by federal agencies, except for authorized deletions. Among the authorized deletions are the names of confidential informants, clues which might help you to guess who they are, and material which, if released, would be deemed harmful to national security.

Thus "freedom of information" is considerably circumscribed and susceptible to bureaucratic fiat. At that, bills were introduced into the 97th and the 98th Congress, with support of members of the

Reagan Administration, to restrict further the public's access to government files. And the White House in 1982 issued an Executive Order that placed new restrictions on what could be released.

Under these rules, you need staying power to exercise your rights. I have been in more or less continuous correspondence with various federal agencies regarding the files under my name since July, 1977. Each agency can release only those documents that it originated. Since my bulging State Department file contains copies of CIA, FBI and Naval Intelligence documents, I have had to pursue the chase in these agencies as well.

The process is not unlike a chain letter. One exchange leads to another someplace else. I learned of my FBI file from the documents sent to me by the State Department. When the FBI documents were released to me by the bureau, I first got wind of the existence of a CIA file under my name. In processing my request for this third set of documents from the CIA, that agency asked the State Department to clear material in its file on me from the Office of Passport Services. Those passport documents had not been included in the 99 documents originally sent to me by State. Indeed, even the crucial document in which Bannerman requested a special FBI inquiry of me and six other Foreign Service applicants never turned up in the State Department file. Leads one to suspect other holes in the net.

In addition to such clues that not everything is being efficiently retrieved, the chore of tracking down each new lead is laborious. Everything must be done by mail. The delays are exasperating. I was tempted to prod, also by letter. I was discouraged from seeking a personal meeting. As the citizen grapples with invisible bureaucrats, they confer with one another by interoffice mail. They keep the petitioner on hold via the United States Postal Service. Once documents are released, the Freedom of Information Act and the Privacy Act provide that the citizen can correct inaccuracies by asking that the record be amended. That procedure, too, can be conducted only by mail.

All this activity, every scrap of it, appears in my file. When a citizen writes to the government to inquire about what the files may contain under his name, that starts a file whether or not he had one before. In my case, of course, there proved to be files aplenty indexed under my name; in addition I amassed a hefty, second file-within-a-file in the process of trying to liberate my first one. The file-within-a-file reads like dull court procedure. Trial by Postal Service.

If you want to question an agency's judgment on what material is released or what facts are amended, you can appeal your case within the agency holding the file on you, but that administrative process is carried out privately with no opportunity for you or your legal representative to appear. Again you can make your arguments only by mail. If you don't like the outcome of that, there is nowhere to go except a federal court.

I have lost three appeals for the release of information expurgated from my file—one at the Department of State, one at the Department of Justice and the third at the Central Intelligence Agency. And I have come to learn that the gaps between a letter of request and a salient reply can stretch to months. Standard practice, it seems, is to route such correspondence through a bureaucratic maze until it expires. If the citizen expires before the government acts, so much the better. As my own days dwindle down—September, November—there's not much time for the waiting game.

WHEN I FIRST applied in July, 1977, to Secretary of State Cyrus Vance for copies of any documents kept in the State Department files under my name, I carefully followed the procedures recommended in a pamphlet on the Privacy Act circulated by the American Civil Liberties Union. I included my Social Security number, notarized signature and, as a clue leading directly to any dossier on me, a copy of the letter I had received so long ago from the Foreign Service in 1948 withdrawing my appointment.

Like that old exchange with Joseph C. Green, trying to discover the status of my appointment to the Foreign Service, my letter to Secretary Vance kicked around inside the bureaucracy long after the expiration of the supposed 30-day statutory deadline for action under the Freedom of Information Act. I wrote a note of complaint to Hodding Carter III, Assistant Secretary of State for Public Affairs, whom I knew casually. I received no reply from him either (do top officials in Washington ever get to read their own mail?).

I do know that my letter was logged in by his staff, then bucked on to the Freedom of Information staff, where Velma T. Smith and Barbara Cavanaugh punched my name into the computer for everything recorded from 1945, when I sat for the Foreign Service written exams, until 1977, when I asked to see my file. Ms. Smith, a GS-7 level employee according to the worksheet she had to fill out, spent 30 minutes at her part of the task, searching out the years after 1950 in the central files.

John S. Pruden, director of the Foreign Affairs Document and Reference Center, did not appear to be aware of this flurry of activity when he finally wrote me on September 12, 1977, in answer to my request to Secretary of State Vance in July. The "Privacy Staff," Mr. Pruden informed me, "has requested the appropriate offices in the Department to search their systems of record for any information they might have pertaining to you. I will notify you as soon as we have received responses from those offices."

Hearing no additional word from Pruden after another three months had passed, I wrote him on December 15, 1977—five months in all now having transpired since my original letter to Vance.

When that letter went unanswered for over a month and a half I wrote the Secretary for a second time on February 7, 1978, reviewing the record—my letter to him in July; my letter to Hodding Carter in August, not acknowledged from that office; my letter to Pruden in December, not acknowledged by anyone.

This time the director of the Foreign Affairs Document and Reference Center got back to me in the next mail—with the whole bundle wrapped in brown paper. John S. Pruden had now been replaced in that post by William H. Price. I would like to think that Pruden had been bounced for not answering my letters, but a more likely explanation was that my case had dropped between the cracks during the changing of the guard. "I apologize for the delay incurred in processing your request," Price wrote on February 9, enclosing a second letter dated nearly a month before, January 13, and signed by Deputy Assistant Secretary for Security Victor H. Diekos. It had been addressed to me at my home, but never mailed. From the file-within-the-file, I figured out later, a Mr. P. Sheils had drafted the apology for Price's signature. Peter Sheils turned out to be the case officer from the State Department Privacy staff assigned to my case, number 7708-019, in August 1977. Every time I wrote anybody in the department, the buck stopped there. Somebody, Price's ghost-writer went on to explain, had been holding up the unsent letter while queries were being sent out to other government agencies that had originated material contained in my State Department file. "I will forward those portions to you as soon as the reviews are completed," the letter of apology promised. There was no hint of the number of letters and the number of years, rather than months, involved in that disarming sentence.

Price's covering letter advised me that "There is no charge for search and review of documents requested under the Privacy Act. However, there is a nominal charge of 10 cents per page to cover the cost of reproduction. For those documents which you wish to keep, please send a check or bank draft drawn on a bank in the United States or postal money order in the amount of 10 cents for each page. . . . Enclosed is a franked enveloped addressed to the Privacy Staff so that you can return those documents which you do not want to keep." I have yet to pay a dime.

Secretary Diekos informed me that "a search of our files has located ninety-nine (99) documents, and they have been numbered 1–99 for ease of reference." His delayed letter went on to tell me that six of the numbered documents from my file had originated with the Federal Bureau of Investigation and could be released only by them. That, it turned out, took another nine months.

One of the FBI documents, moreover, was based on information from the CIA. That would continue to be classified until the CIA itself finally let me see some portions of its file documents nearly five years later, in August, 1982.

Still another document, according to Diekos, was being withheld because it had originated with the Naval Investigative Service, formerly the Office of Naval Intelligence. That, the Navy informed me, had been destroyed a decade before according to policy.

Because two different arms of the Federal Government were pursuing different policies as to preserving their files, this left the petitioning citizen in a no-win position. The State Department was maintaining information about me in its files that was derived from information which ONI had destroyed. But State wouldn't let me see it until released by the source. The source couldn't release it, because it could no longer find it. We are still going around on that one.

Along with the junk preserved for so long under my name in the State Department came a form setting forth the appeal procedure. A single paragraph explained that "A review of denials of access" might be appealed "within 60 days of the date in which the requester was informed of the Department's refusal to grant access to a record in whole or in part." I construed that to cover the instances where the names of confidential informants or whole lines of information had been blacked out by the censor. Requests for review had to be made in writing and sent to the Chairman, Privacy Policy Appeals Board (a name so clumsy it was seldom referred to correctly in the correspondence that followed), Department of State. "The final determination by the Privacy Policy and Appeals Board should be made within 30 working days." There was no information on who the chairman was or who would sit on the board making the determination.

A companion paragraph set out the procedure "to amend a record" by writing the Director, Foreign Affairs Document and Reference Center, Department of State. "The burden shall be upon the individual to support his request for amendment," the instructions declared. Guilty until proved innocent. "The requester should submit as much documentation, arguments or other data as seems warranted to support his request." Who would make the decision or how it would be carried out were not explained. No time limits were set forth for correcting the record.

Indignation prompted me to move immediately to set the record straight. I skipped the director of the Document Center, where my original queries had been stalled for months, and addressed my request to Diekos, the State Department official who had finally released the first heap of documents to me.

In a six-page letter to Diekos, the first of two such briefs in behalf of correcting the misinformation in my State Department file, I set these errors out specifically, and asked that my statement be incorporated in the records "in such a way that it will always be available to anyone in the Office of Security reviewing the files under my name" or sending them out for circulation. So much was guaranteed under the Freedom of Information Act. What else might be forthcoming from the Appeals Board was less easy to interpret. The law provided that I could address a request to the Appeals Board within the State Department for the information deleted from the copies of my file released to me. It was thus theoretically possible under this procedure, three decades after the action taken against me by the Office of Security, to learn the full content of the charges against me and the identity of my accusers.

The option of making an appeal to a State Department board further suggested to me that I might get the chance to appear personally and at last defend myself against those ancient charges. A board sitting in the 1970s, I speculated, might be sensitive to injustices done in the 40s, the incubation period before the advent of McCarthyism. No one would be personally motivated to protect department personnel and administrative divisions of a bygone age. And they could see and hear for themselves from this unthreatening old professor how wide of the mark was the material in my file.

In my formal petition to the Appeals Board, also contained in this missive to Diekos, I stated first what I wanted most: that the department rescind its 1946 action classifying me as a national security risk on the ground that the secret proceedings had violated my constitutional rights. If that action were not rescinded, I asked for the hearing now which had been denied me then so that I could reply directly to the hearsay upon which the department had taken action against me without my knowledge. To defend myself 32 years after the event, I said I would need full access to the record as well as to the identity of all those who had furnished the derogatory information used against me.

Meanwhile, I requested that my security file be embargoed so that it would not be circulated while the charges therein were undergoing review under some form of due process.

In that letter of protest to Diekos, lest there be any doubt in anyone's mind, I included the following paragraph:

Meanwhile, let the record show that I categorically deny the charges and inferences implied in the 1946 finding by the Department that I was in any way—then, before then, since then—disloyal to the Government of the United States and its institutions, a possible risk to national security in any position of public trust or private activity.

I indicated to Diekos that copies of the letter were being sent by me to Senators Edward M. Kennedy and Abraham A. Ribicoff as well as to a Washington law firm with close ties to the White House.

Lloyd Cutler, the political influential of the Washington firm of Wilmer, Cutler & Pickering, was a member of the board of directors of the Salzburg Seminar in American Studies, where I had taught, but didn't know me from Adam. The pamphlets from the American Civil Liberties Union had stressed the importance, however, of pushing one's legal rights at government officials hesitant to respond to requests under the Freedom of Information and Privacy acts. I had a friend working at the Cutler firm to whom I could legitimately send an information copy. Who knows? I speculated; somebody there might see in my case a worthy candidate for the *pro bono publico* work undertaken by all big Washington law firms from time to time. Worth a shot.

Kennedy was Senator from the state where Janet and I kept a summer home, but more than that he was an indisputably important figure on the Washington scene. When I had written a piece for *Life* magazine and then a book about Robert Kennedy, they had been moderately well received by the Kennedy staff and the Kennedy family. I had been invited to Bobby's funeral after his assassination and to ride the funeral train to Washington. A mutual friend said she would see that my letter got to the right hands on the Kennedy staff.

Ribicoff, Senator from my native state of Connecticut, was a member of the Senate Foreign Relations Committee and a key administration supporter for its ticklish policies in Israel and the Middle East. Both Senators would carry some clout with a Deputy Assistant Secretary.

I had known Abe Ribicoff for years (he, too, had been born and raised in New Britain), but our history had been less than chummy. In the brief letter I enclosed with a copy of my petition, I cited the fact that he probably had known me as long as anyone currently in public office. "Whatever my faults," I continued, "I am sure you will agree that one of them was never that of being subservient to outside influence—foreign or domestic." I dropped it in the mail, not overly optimistic about a response.

I overestimated my connections with the Senator from Massachusetts. My letter to him was shunted back to Boston with the rest of his local constituent mail, and I never did receive a reply. And I underestimated the senior Senator from Connecticut. His response dated March 10, 1978, was immediate and unequivocal.

Dear Penn:

I have your recent letter and enclosures concerning your request that the State Department amend certain records about you dated from 1946.

Unsubstantiated allegations which continue to cause damage should not remain part of permanent government files.

You have every right to pursue this matter to a conclusion. I have asked the State Department for its consideration of your request.

Best wishes,
Abe Ribicoff

The file-within-the-file shows that Senator Ribicoff at the same time he answered my plea with such a positive response whipped off a second letter, this one to Douglas J. Bennet Jr., Assistant Secretary for Congressional Relations, the State Department's troubleshooter on Capitol Hill. Bennet was the son of the man who had hired me on the staff of Chester Bowles three decades before. I had dandled him on my knee as a child, but there was no hint that he was personally aware of this initial correspondence being carried on in his name. A copy of Bennet's formal reply to Ribicoff—"Prof. Kimball requested amendment of his file and appealed the statutory deletions of information from those documents"—is part of the file-within-the-file, too. "I will let you know as soon as we have completed processing these requests."

Apparently the drumbeats were heard in the corridors of State that the Hill was asking about the Kimball case. Within five days of

Ribicoff's letters to Bennet and me, William H. Price was informing me on March 15, 1978, that "the Privacy Staff has forwarded your request [for amending my file] to the Office of Security for review. A decision regarding this matter is expected to be made within thirty days." As to my request for "full disclosure of documents about you contained in your security file," he continued, "the Privacy Policy and Appeals Board will now begin to act on your request. The Board will consider your concern in support of disclosure as well as the Office of Security's reasons for withholding this information. We shall provide you with an answer to your appeal within thirty days." Everything to be wrapped up by April 15. It seemed a promising development.

Price's letter from the State Department also released to me portions of the FBI and Naval Investigative Service documents about me which had not been included in the first shipment of my security file. The full documents were still undergoing review at the sources, I was informed.

Since I had been promised action within 30 days, I whipped off another letter answering the allegations in this most recent batch of material as best I could under the circumstances, so that these portions also would be subject to my request for immediate amendment of the security file now under review by the Appeals Board. I asked that "this letter be added to my letter of February 21 to Deputy Assistant Secretary of State for Security Victor Diekos in the Security Files of the Department and circulated any time that file is circulated until such file is purged, pending the action requested by me." My letter of February 21 to Diekos and this one of March 25 to Price turned out to be the only appearance on my behalf allowed by the board.

A few days earlier, the file-within-the-file disclosed, Price did indeed forward my February 21 letter of amendment to the Office of Security to "review Mr. Kimball's request for amendment and notify the Privacy Staff of your decision as soon as possible. As you know, OMB [Office of Management and Budget] Guidelines suggest that agencies complete their review within 10 days, and that only in extreme circumstances should the review exceed thirty days." My sending the first request for amendments direct to Diekos had only delayed things for a month while it steered a course through proper channels.

On April 5, a one-sentence memorandum declared: "A/SY/PSI/FIPS, at the request of Mr. Penn T. Kimball, has instructed A/SY/MGT/DIS that his correspondence dated February 21, 1978 be placed in his security file." On April 18, "A/SY/PSI/FIPS, at the request of Mr. Penn T. Kimball, has advised A/SY/MGT/DIS that his correspondence dated March 25, 1978 be placed in his security file." Meanwhile, I had heard nothing. Finally, two and a half months after my petition and in response to a letter from me complaining of the delay, I was informed by the Privacy Policy Appeals Board on May 8, 1978, that the "Office of Security has carefully considered your request and has agreed to include your letters as an integral part of your security file. The letters will be a permanent part of your file and any reviewer will have access to your comments."

So much the law grants—but not much more. The State Department's one-paragraph Amendment Procedures said nothing about how any "documentation, arguments or other data" I might provide could be used to correct misinformation in the file. A/SY/PSI/FIPS didn't tell A/SY/MGT/DIS what to make of any contradictions. The Appeals Board did not seem to share Senator Ribicoff's sentiment that "unsubstantiated allegations which continue to cause damage should not remain part of permanent government files." The word "amendment," as far as I could discern, means nothing more than sticking a few more pieces of paper into an already bulging file.

It was not even the board itself that made the decision to add those two letters to my file or to answer my other requests. Under State Department procedures, Price, the executive secretary of the Appeals Board as well as director of the Document Center, simply forwarded my petition to the same Office of Security that compiled the original dossier, asking it to judge the merit of my protests on its own, and then let the Privacy staff know the verdict. The Privacy Policy Appeals Board is no more than the messenger boy, tipping its cap for an answer.

When the Appeals Board relayed the news to me on May 8 that the Office of Security had "agreed to include your letters as an integral part of your security file," it also conveyed the news that it considered a personal appearance and hearing out of the question.

"Unfortunately, due to the time factor involved in this case, the Department has neither the capabilities nor the apparatus to convene a hearing of this nature and is unable to accede to your request to this regard." That decision was reaffirmed by the board chairman, John Thomas. With the marvelous logic by which bureaucracy justifies its own position, the board declared that my own written contradictions of statements being kept in my security file made it unnecessary for the State Department to reopen the question of its decision to classify me as a national security risk.

"Your letters chronicle your activities and the events of the 1946–1948 period and cogently present your concern about the Office of Security investigation and its ramifications. The inclusion of your letters in the security file will inform reviewers of your accomplishments and serve as a refutation of statements and conclusions made at the time."

To refute, in my dictionary, means to disprove and overthrow by argument, evidence or proof; prove to be false or erroneous. If the State Department had erroneously concluded me to be a national security risk in 1946, why wasn't it willing to own up and say so? Instead, government officials would be permitted to go on poking around in the security file maintained in my name. My word against the anonymous informants—forever.

So much for the amendment procedure.

There was no comment on my request to embargo the file, and no comment on my request that the 1946 action be rescinded.

On the issue of my rights of access to the names of informants as well as the other passages blacked out in the copies of my security file released to me, the Appeals Board informed me that this portion of my appeal was being treated as "a separate action."

If the members were deliberating at such length, searching their conscience about granting me the information I needed to challenge the credibility of my accusers from the past, surely they had not abandoned the possibility, I dared to think, of granting my request for belated vindication.

The delays continued through the summer.

On May 8, "the Board is presently consulting on a decision. A determination on your appeal is expected shortly." On May 10 Chairman Thomas wrote me that "I have extended the period for consideration of your appeal to the Department of State an additional twenty (20) working days . . . I will let you know the Board's decision by May 25, 1978." Hearing nothing for nearly a month after that deadline, I wrote another letter of complaint on June 20, this time directly to Secretary Cyrus Vance. On July 5, Thomas wrote again that "the Secretary has asked me to respond to your letter of June 20 . . . I sincerely regret the delay incurred in processing your Privacy Act appeal. Department guidelines establish a recommended time limit by which responses to appeals are to be completed. While every effort is made to comply with the suggested time limit, there are cases which require more time for deliberation, so that a proper and just decision will be reached. The Board's decision regarding your appeal will be forthcoming shortly and I will notify you accordingly."

I wrote back on July 10, enclosing a copy of a directive from Attorney General Bell urging all federal departments to avoid litigation on Freedom of Information matters "unless it is important to the public interest to do so, even if there is some arguable legal basis for withholding." The Attorney General warned that the Justice Department would defend such suits "only when disclosure is demonstrably harmful." The reluctance of the Carter Administration's chief law officer to become involved in defending excessive bureaucracy, I hoped, might nudge the Appeals Board to give my case the benefit of the doubt.

Chairman Thomas' July 5 apology indicating that the board was taking special pains with my case, plus the backing of the Attorney General's directive, triggered cautious optimisim on my part. After all, my case was now 32 years old. By no stretch of the imagination could the opening of my security file be classified as a threat to the national interest. But July lapsed into August and August into September while I awaited the decision which had been "expected shortly" as of May 8.

On September 8, the executive secretary of the Appeals Board, William H. Price, got around to "responding to your letter of July

10." Price conceded that the Department of State indeed considered the Attorney General's directive "germane" to my request. "Since the Privacy Act has been in effect, it has been the Department's policy to grant individuals access to as much information as possible. . . . The Privacy Policy Appeals Board is presently voting on your appeal and a decision will be reached soon." Cautious optimism escalated into temporary euphoria. By George, persistence might be paying off!

At long last, in late September, a full 6 months beyond the 30 days the appeals procedure is supposed to take, the Privacy Policy Appeals Board handed down its tardy verdict. It required two pages, single-spaced, for it to set forth an answer to what it chose to summarize as "your appeal to the Department of State for full release of information from seven documents previously denied to you by the Office of Security." There was no further comment on an opportunity to receive a personal hearing nor any reference to ordering my file removed from circulation, and, most certainly, no hint of vindication.

"The Privacy Policy and Appeals Board has completed its deliberation of your appeal," the decision began, "and previously denied information is now being released." Wow! Worth waiting for! I had to read on until page two to reach the anticlimax: "The Office of Security has re-evaluated its original decision to withhold the name and identity of"—a total of three people!

Name one was that of Kenneth Crawford, the one-time chief of *PM*'s Washington Bureau who had told Special Agent Hipsley that I was ". . . a completely loyal young man whose reputation and character were above reproach and who could be placed in a position of trust with complete confidence that he would serve his country honorably and well." I already knew Crawford's identity because he was the informant whose name had been blacked out as an anti-Communist witness by some State Department censors and left untouched as a friendly witness by other censors.

Name two was James A. Wechsler, whose identity was also known to me because a careless censor had failed to black it out in one line on the document containing Wechsler's concerns about the "state of my mind" in the 1930s and 1940s. So far, I had been kept in suspense for nothing.

Name three was a genuine surprise—"Mr. Eddie Lockett, as indicated in Document No. 53, Page 5." Document No. 53 was the one that recounted the journey of Agent Hipsley through Washington, D.C., in September, 1946, to interview persons known to the State Department to be demonstrably anti-Communist who also might have some knowledge of me. I had never even met Eddie Lockett, a member of *Time* magazine's Washington Bureau in 1946 when I was working in New York as a writer in National Affairs. I knew his name well in that relationship, however. Lockett covered the White House and specialized in the not-for-attribution sort of inside dope obtained from Washington bigwigs; I had written stories based on his behind-the-scenes revelations many times.

It was Lockett who had asked Hipsley "to give him some time to make discreet inquiries so that he might substantiate his own beliefs concerning Mr. Kimball." *Time*'s White House correspondent, the source of so many scoops, turned out to be a government informant and errand boy as well. In September, 1946, only a year after V-J Day, that was a less sensitive issue than it would be today. But it was a little frightening to reconstruct the situation in which I had been rewriting Eddie Lockett's copy for *Time* while he in turn was checking me out for the government. Congress in 1978 had become agitated by the revelation that American journalists had been used overseas to gather information for United States intelligence. Here was concrete evidence of the State Department working hand in glove with the White House correspondent of one of the most powerful publications in the country on a matter of *domestic* surveillance. No wonder that the Office of Security, even 30 years after the fact, had been a little squeamish about turning that loose.

I suspect that the possible repercussions of exposing such information may have occupied some of the seven months of dialogue over my file between the Privacy Policy Appeals Board and the Office of Security. At least that is a reasonable guess; nothing else in Lockett's contribution to my security file sounded onerous. "Very definitely not dangerous" and "entirely controllable," Lockett had concluded.

Three names, two of which I already knew, wasn't much to show after a good deal of trouble. I wonder, however, whether working alone I could have managed to obtain even that much. My file-within-

a-file includes a letter from Doug Bennet to Senator Ribicoff informing him, as promised, of the results of my appeal. "I am glad to
report that the Office of Security agreed to include Mr. Kimball's
correspondence to the Department as an integral part of his security
file. . . . Professor Kimball also appealed the statutory deletions of
information released to him from his security file. The Privacy and
Appeals Board reviewed this appeal and previously denied information was released to Professor Kimball."

The latter sentence was a somewhat sweeping description of the
release of the names of informants Crawford, Wechsler and Lockett.
If the letter from my old acquaintance in the State Department to
our mutual Connecticut neighbor in the Senate had a somewhat
familiar ring, the file-within-the-file offers a clue. It was drafted by
Case Officer P. Sheils. Thereafter, it was approved by F. M. Machak,
Foreign Affairs Document and Research Center, cleared by J. M.
Thomas and W. H. Price of the Privacy Policy Appeals Board, plus
L. J. Dupre and G. Winnett somewhere else along the long, gray line
of the State Department bureaucracy. The final draft thereupon was
lost, and according to the file-within-the-file, disappeared with "no
trace." When the loss was discovered, P. Sheils read the gist of his
draft over the phone to Ribicoff's administrative assistant. The next
week the letter itself turned up on the Senator's desk, dated October
31. Friends in the right place may help, but the play wasn't exactly
an end run around the permanent party in charge at State.

Eddie Lockett's name had been blacked out in the original file
releases to me with the notation "k-5." This refers to the paragraph
in the Privacy Act, 5 U.S. Code 552a, which states that "The head of
any agency may promulgate rules . . . to exempt any system of
records within the agency . . . if the system of records is . . . investigatory material compiled solely for the purpose of determining suitability, eligibility, or qualification for Federal civilian employment, . . .
but only to the extent that the disclosure of such material would
reveal the identity of a source who furnished information to the
Government under an express promise that the identity of the source
would be held in confidence, or prior to the effective date of this
section, under an implied promise that the identity of the source
would be held in confidence."

An "implied promise" not to reveal a person's identity is a loophole big enough for a steamroller. I am not sure what happened to the implied promise to Eddie Lockett between the time his name was blacked out and subsequently released. The same applies to Kenneth Crawford and James A. Wechsler. One day's promise repealed the next. But the final decision by the Privacy Policy Appeals Board flatly rejected my petition for access to the names of other informants against me and the full content of the documents used to rule me a security risk.

In regard to withholding the release of the names and identifying information of all other sources, there is strong reason to believe these sources would not have provided derogatory information to representatives of the Office of Security without expressed or implied assurance that their identities would be held in confidence. In addition, release of their names would also result in unwarranted invasion of their privacy and, therefore would violate the Privacy Act (5 USC 552a). In view of the above, A/SY reaffirms its original decision to withhold their identities.

It is further the determination of A/SY that the information deleted in Paragraph 2, Page 2, Document No 56 should continue to be withheld as it pertains to other persons whose personal privacy should be protected.

The Privacy Policy Appeals Board concurs in and upholds the Office of Security's decision to continue to withhold the above-mentioned materials.

The Department has now completed the administrative processing of your appeal. You may, of course, seek judicial review of this decision.

John M. Thomas
Chairman
Privacy Policy Appeals Board

I do not know who the members of the Appeals Board were beyond John M. Thomas, chairman, and William H. Price, executive secretary. It is not yet clear to me, either, what procedures were followed, except to forward my various requests to the Office of Security, which in the end agreed to nothing except the release of the names of Crawford, Wechsler and Lockett.

When I later made a trip to Washington to try to find out who sat on my Appeals Board and what they actually did, I discovered Thomas had left the department for a job in private industry. I finally tracked him down in New York City by telephone, but he didn't remember ever having heard my name, much less any details that would explain why my case took so long to produce so little. He said he suspected it was probably because of a backlog within the Office of Security. "Those chaps have been terribly overburdened," he said.

WHEN THE FIRST plain brown wrapper from the State Department arrived, and I discovered through the documents there that the FBI also held files under my name, I wrote to the director of the Federal Bureau of Investigation in February, 1978, requesting those documents too. Further following the drill I had learned from the American Civil Liberties Union, I indicated my Social Security number and date and place of birth below my notarized signature.

The FBI at first proved to be more efficient than the State Department, which might be expected of a well disciplined service. Fewer than three weeks had elapsed when I received a reply on March 8 from Allen H. McCreight, Chief, Freedom of Information–Privacy Acts Branch, Records Management Division, that number 60,608 had been assigned to my request. McCreight reported that the six documents still withheld from the first packet from State were already being processed and that other documents "have been located and assigned for processing and should be available for release within the next three months." The FBI, unlike State, owned up to that delay from the start. "Your continued patience and understanding are appreciated," wrote McCreight, who could teach a thing or two to the United States diplomatic service.

A week later, the State Department sent along those portions of my file based on information obtained from the FBI with a note that they had been reviewed and released—with certain exceptions. "The FBI deleted information from sections of the documents pursuant to 5 USC 552a (k) (5)—confidential sources of information." The same portion of the Privacy Act invoked at State. The note advised me that "if you wish to appeal these deletions, you may write to the Deputy Attorney General, U.S. Department of Justice, Washington, D.C. Your letter and envelope should be marked: 'Privacy Appeal, Denial of Access.' "

Since the State Department was taking the trouble to explain to me how to appeal to the Justice Department, and was also at that time considering a similar appeal from me regarding excisions from its documents, one could assume that the decision actually to withhold "exempt" portions of departmental records rested upon some official's discretion.

Though I realized I was becoming increasingly beset by paperwork in carrying out my crusade I forthwith pecked out on my typewriter a letter of formal appeal, per instructions, to the Deputy Attorney General, dated March 26. The letter requested release of information withheld from me, and also enclosed the "amendment" to the FBI portion of my file I had already submitted to Price at the State Department.

I was on a roll now. Eyeball to eyeball with the Department of State and the Department of Justice both at the same time.

It had taken me better than six months to pry the first installment of my file out of the State Department. The Justice Department and the FBI were in no hurry either. My March 26 appeal to the Deputy Attorney General was acknowledged April 24 by Quinlan J. Shea Jr., Director, Office of Privacy and Information Appeals. "This office has a substantial backlog of pending appeals received prior to yours and a shortage of attorneys. In an attempt to afford each appellant equal and impartial treatment, we have adopted a general practice of assigning appeals to Office attorneys in the approximate order of receipt. Your appeal has been assigned number 8-0574."

Now I had two numbers at the counters inside Justice—60,608 while I waited for my full FBI file to be processed, and 8-0574 on my appeal for access to information in that file which had already been deleted. On my request to amend the records according to my four-page response to FBI material used in the 1946 proceedings against me, Shea went on: "Since it appears you may be seeking correction and/or expungement of Department of Justice records, enclosed is a copy of 28 C.F.R. 16.48 and 16.49, which explains this procedure. Any request for correction of F.B.I. records should be addressed to Director Webster; it is not necessary to appear in person.

"We will notify you of the decision of the Deputy Attorney General on your appeal as soon as we can. The necessity of this delay is regretted and your continuing courtesy is appreciated."

It takes a little patience to stay the course on the Freedom of Information trail. On July 27, a little more than five months after my request to the FBI and just past the first anniversary of my first letter to the Secretary of State, Allen McCreight, chief of the FBI Freedom of Information–Privacy Branch, put a batch of documents into another plain brown wrapper and mailed them.

An FBI file, when it is released to a petitioner under the Freedom of Information and Privacy acts, is more difficult to follow than a State Department file. Although each document on file is organized on Form No. 1 supplied by the Government Printing Office, often more than one number is typed or written in longhand and it takes a while to figure out the system. Nothing as convenient or apparently all-inclusive as Documents 1 through 99. There is sometimes a file number in the FBI field office where the report originated, another number for the central files in bureau headquarters in Washington and a third number, in some but not all cases, assigned in the Records Management Division of the bureau's Freedom of Information–Privacy Acts Branch. The indices in the various FBI offices probably sort all this out, but the person who has been the subject of investigation has no way of telling of how much of his file is actually being released.

Most file documents contain a number of scrawls, dates and initials which are a meaningless jumble until one begins to sort out the mystery by cross-checking them with documents from other agencies which have been trading information with the bureau. That creates another parlor game as one flips back and forth among a pile of copies from various government files trying to trace out the web of cross-communication which went on in certain years of one's career. "This Is Your Life" as perceived by the security apparatus in Washington.

As I learned from McCreight's covering letter, the FBI's table of organization creates another obstacle for a citizen trying to find out what his FBI file contains about him. When you write to the FBI director in Washington, what you get back is what the bureau chooses to release from its files there. There are additional sets of files on you in every FBI field office throughout the country which ever kept tabs on you, such as Newark, New Jersey, which had jurisdiction while I was a student at Princeton, or the New Haven field office, which had jurisdiction when I lived in Connecticut. The petitioner under the Freedom of Information and Privacy acts has to write to each and every FBI field office in the country where he might suspect an agent had once filed a report on him. Trial by Postal Service is seemingly an endless process, like trying to capture fish with your bare hands.

Finally, it is FBI practice to black out the names of *all* its sources, favorable as well as unfavorable, making it that much more difficult to piece together the path of an investigation. The FBI, in addition, is wont to exclude whole pages from the files released to you on the grounds that the gaps concern delicate areas of national security, criminal investigations or the names of others under investigation at some time or other in the distant past as well as the present. Since my file went back a long way, my path probably crossed at one time or another with all kinds of people who rated a line in the myriad of FBI reports accumulated since then. Though preserved in my file, I have no way of knowing how much of this set of guilts by association was withheld from me.

McCreight's covering letter with my FBI packet conceded that not quite everything had been enclosed.

One document contained in our files was a copy of page L–17 of the New York Times for the Friday, June 14, 1940, issue. This entire page was an advertisement for the new newspaper, "P.M." Your name was listed under the editorial staff for National Affairs. This page is in very poor condition, being yellow and faded with age, and having been folded and taped so many times as to make it incapable of being mechanically reproduced.

The likelihood was that my FBI file had begun with the now "yellow and faded with age" clip from *The New York Times* of June 14, 1940, announcing the names of the original staff of *PM*. Probably not one for me alone. Special Agent [Name blacked out] compiled a report on the NEWSPAPER PM INCORPORATED, classified INTERNAL SECURITY-R, "setting out texts of memorandums originating with RALPH INGERSOLL publisher of PM showing his viewpoint on various issues, political and otherwise, and their application to the policy to be pursued by the newspaper PM, setting out personnel of PM as of June 14, 1940 according to a list prepared by PM and giving data on certain of these individuals."

The details came "from a confidential source designated as confidential informant #1 for the purpose of this report." These included "mimeographed memorandums and releases originating with RALPH INGERSOLL, publisher of PM. The first of these, which is headed 'Confidential Memorandum to the Stockholders from Ralph Ingersoll' . . . [bears] the title 'PM-THIS PAPER AS OF APRIL 1, 1940.' "

The copy released to me then skips to page 48, the top half of which is blacked out.

"The personnel of PM as of June 14, 1940, was set out in mimeograph form on a memorandum which was obtained together with the other documents referred to above. This personnel list is being set out below with names, addresses and titles as they appear on the original list. A summary of the information from the Bureau files is being set out where available." Then follows, at the bottom of page 48, two names beginning with "A" with their home addresses and phone numbers.

The next piece of the document released to me is page 77, where among the "K's" is "KIMBALL, PENN, National Affairs Writer, 39 E. 39th Street, CA 5-6200." The address and phone number is the Princeton Club where I lived the first weeks I was on the paper. There being no summary of information from the bureau files set out next to my name, and no more pages released to me, I presume that my notoriety at the FBI started with my going to work for a news-paper under surveillance.

These documents and others relating to my *PM* roommates and the North American Aviation strike circular in which my role was incidental until the State Department instituted its "special investigation" were referred to in McCreight's covering letter as

> four additional documents which, you will note, relate to our investigation of other events, organizations or individuals. Inasmuch as your name was mentioned in each of these documents, only those portions containing a reference to you have been processed along with additional material to indicate the context in which your name was recorded. Exemptions (b) (7) (C) and (b) (7) (D) were utilized in order to protect confidential sources and information concerning third parties.

The same exemption—5 U.S.C. 552a (k) (5)—for the names of confidential informants blacked out in the latest batch of documents was being claimed once more, with the addition of (b) (7) (C) and (b) (7) (D), which apply to "investigatory records compiled for law enforcement purposes, the disclosure of which would . . . (C) constitute an unwarranted invasion of the personal privacy of another person; (D) reveal the identity of an individual who has furnished information to the FBI under confidential circumstances or reveal information furnished only by such a person and not apparently known to the public or otherwise accessible to the FBI by overt means." The barrier between me and the confidential informants was thus raised another notch under the more sweeping discretion allowed when information was "compiled for law enforcement purposes." They were heading me off at every pass.

And there were still more documents to pry loose:

> Should you desire a check of our field office files, you are advised that a listing of them as separate indices has been published in the Federal Register, Volume 42, Number 190—Friday, September 30, 1977. It will be incumbent upon you to so designate your requests directly to them.

Still, the packet did contain some meaty materials.

By letter dated January 31, 1978, the State Department referred six FBI documents to us for a determination as to their
releasability. Five of these documents were contained in a file
concerning a Special Inquiry-State Department investigation
of you conducted in 1946. This file consists of ten documents, totalling 22 pages. All of the documents from this file
are being released to you in their entirety, with only minor
excisions for (k) (5) material.

At least I now had in my hands the full texts of those reports
from FBI special agents who went to New Britain, Princeton, New
York and Washington at Chief Security Officer Bannerman's special
request, plus the memoranda revealing that I was the point man in
1946 for an experiment utilizing the FBI to check out selected
candidates for the Foreign Service. Thus, I could document how
freely Bannerman had translated the FBI data in his summaries for
classifying me as a dangerously disloyal American. In this respect,
McCreight affirmed that the copy of my March 25 letter to Price at
the State Department challenging the substance of those data had, as
at State, been placed in my FBI file "so that it can be incorporated in
any future dissemination of information pertaining to you."
    The big news in his letter was that one of the documents I had not
yet seen from my State Department file contained information from
the CIA.

The sixth document which was referred to us by the State
Department contains classified information which was furnished by both the Central Intelligence Agency (CIA) and the
Office of Naval Investigations (ONI). This information must
be coordinated with these respective agencies before it can be
released. This process usually takes several months, and we
are, at this time, still waiting for their respective replies. As
soon as the CIA and ONI reply to our referrals, the sixth and
last document [also on file with the State Department] will be
released to you.

The verdict in my trial by Postal Service with the Justice Department was just about the same as the verdict from the Appeals Board in the State Department. In response to my appeal number 8-0574 regarding the first batch of FBI documents released to me, a letter from Benjamin Civiletti, Deputy Attorney General, informed me that my request for access to the names of confidential informants—which means to the bureau all informants—had been denied.

> After careful consideration of your appeal, I have decided to affirm the initial action in this case. . . . The only information requested to which access was denied is exempt from mandatory release under 5 U.S.C. 552a (k) (5) . . . Judical review of my action is available to you in the United States District Court in the district in which you reside or have your principal place of business, or in the District of Columbia, which is also where the records you seek are located.

In response to a second appeal sent November 1: "This office has a substantial backlog of pending appeals . . . and a shortage of attorneys. . . . Your appeal has been assigned number 8-2042." The exercise was still going on three years later, when I managed to extract another expurgated FBI document. By this time the Justice Department had relegated such requests to an Office of Legal Policy. Its reply, dated 12 October 1981: "The Office of Legal Policy . . . has a substantial backlog. . . . Your appeal has been assigned number 81-1533." With each form letter I was left standing in a new queue, each one longer than the preceding.

The form letters turning down my appeals found a different excuse each time. Civiletti remarked that "this material is not appropriate for discretionary release." Associate Attorney General Michael J. Egan claimed that "these pertain to investigatory records compiled for law enforcement purposes." Jonathan C. Rose, Assistant Attorney General, informed me that "certain information was withheld from you pursuant to purely internal agency practices."

THE REDUCTIONS IN RANK among the final arbiters—from Deputy Attorney General, to Associate Attorney General, to Assistant Attorney General—tells us something about the steady movement of Freedom of Information and Privacy concerns in Washington toward a place below the salt.

The formal "trials" were over as far as the Department of State and the Federal Bureau of Investigation were concerned. But I was to remain on trial. For more than half of my years the United States Government had been maintaining and circulating a file questioning my loyalty and warning any reader to think twice before placing me in a position of trust. My appeals verdicts changed nothing, nor have any of my efforts since. Today, I remain officially on record—into eternity, as far as I can discern—as a national security risk. Nothing I did, and nothing I said in my attempts to correct the record erased what unnamed informants and bureaucrats from ages ago did and said. Maybe that's what has bothered me the most.

The essence of the moral of my file is the contradiction between the Penn Kimball in the government documents and the Penn Kimball in real life. The flip side of the person my security file describes as a a person unfit to serve his country has, I think, served his country well as a journalist, a teacher and in government service. The 32 years between my secret classification as a national security risk and the partial release of my security file are a fair test, I would argue, of the quality of the predictions gathered by the government from its anonymous informants.

My own true life story, or some relevant chapters, I hoped might give a reader enough data to make up his own mind—the Penn Kimball of the official record versus the Penn Kimball perceived by a most interested party, myself. I thought I might claim the self-discipline to avoid making my version of the truth too self-serving. I cannot, of course, disclaim all the possibilities of bias. But matching my bias against the unstated and unanswered bias in the file makes the contest more fair.

Or perhaps there is no contest.

Confident in my own mind of the utter foolishness of the thought that a person like me should be regarded as a menace to national security, it occurred to me that my case was important for its sheer lack of credibility. If the whole engine of American surveillance—State Department, Federal Bureau of Investigation, Central Intelligence Agency—can waste so much energy to save the country against the likes of me, the safety of the Republic is indeed in jeopardy. If the quality of information gathered in my file is any indication, the enemy who might be coming is as good as here. Someone should sound the alarm about the real soft underbelly in the nation's defenses.

I want to tell my side of the story, and I am doing so, but I begin to think that it is not Penn Kimball who is on trial so much as the government whose avowed principles have always guided me.

12

INTERLUDE

BETWEEN THE DAY in 1948 when I received the final word on my application for the Foreign Service from my state Senator and the day in 1978 when the plain brown wrapper containing my file arrived on my doorstep, I lived a life filled, in retrospect, with irony.

Indeed, the irony began immediately. The word from Senator Baldwin to me, dictated but not signed, that there was no use arguing about my appointment coincided with the beginning of my lifelong involvement with politics. My political activities, within months, became involved with the appointment of Senator Baldwin to Justice of the Supreme Court in Connecticut. Thus the man who had warned the State Department that suspicion alone was sufficient reason to reject a young man from service to his country became an arbiter of justice in my home state.

My first job in politics, moreover, was as press aide to Chester Bowles, whose memo to America First had been the basis for the full page ad in *The New York Times* and for Lindbergh's advocacy of isolationism which I had broken in *PM* over the protests of stockholder Bowles. Bowles had come a long way in the intervening decade.

Bowles was 47, young by the standards of that era, when he announced that he planned to seek the Democratic nomination for Governor of Connecticut in the spring of 1948. He had been enormously successful in the advertising firm, Benton & Bowles, which he had started with fellow Yale graduate William Benton. As wartime head of price controls, he had held the line against the toughest of business lobbyists, earning the praise of F.D.R. Bowles was liberal, but understood a balance sheet; issue-oriented, but with practical experience in business. He had earned his spurs in government and was now talking about things that mattered: adequate housing for returned veterans, catch-up benefits for working men and women after the lean years of national mobilization, breaks for the consumer and, even more important, that the state and the nation could cope with and settle their problems under the right leadership.

The Bowles candidacy symbolized for me the right direction for American politics in the time of the postwar generation. I wrote Bowles a letter, asking if there was any way I could be of help. I received an immediate reply urging me to get in touch with his chief campaign aide, Douglas J. Bennet.

I did not know that the outlook was so gloomy for the Democrats in Connecticut that Bowles had been unable to persuade a single working newsman to quit a regular job to sign on as press aide. Nor was there much prospect of financial reward. I was immediately asked to take charge of the press side of the campaign. Any questions about money should be worked out with John Bailey, chairman of the Democratic State Committee.

I had been drawn toward politics as long as I could remember. Journalism, for all its satisfactions, is vicarious living. A political reporter is always just an observer on the scene, instead of being part of the action. The real fun, I considered, is in the thick of things, near the center of power. Not because power is heady (though indeed it turned out to be), but because power gets done things that need doing. Thus, after years of feeling sidelined in journalism the chance to be near the heart of even a long-shot political effort was exciting. Enough of lost causes, I thought to myself, it would be fun for a change to win. I accepted. Janet, taking care of our infant daughter, never arched her long, straight, beautiful eyebrows, though living on Party Chairman John Bailey's IOU's turned out to be pretty precarious.

Bowles himself was not overly optimistic: 1948 was the year of the expected Republican landslide for Dewey. Truman wasn't given a chance. In overwhelmingly Republican Connecticut, even Democratic Chairman Bailey was rumored to have supported Bowles only because, wealthy as he was, he would be able to pay his own way and not deplete the party's meager treasury. Chet Bowles in a way agreed. He saw the contest as a challenge to keep the liberal banner flying in the Democratic Party so that persons like himself would be in a position to help rebuild the party out of the ashes of the expected Truman defeat. When Elmo Roper, a weekend Connecticut resident, took a private poll of Bowles' chances a few weeks before Election Day, he predicted a Republican landslide. Bowles kept the Roper prediction a secret from his campaign staff.

When Bowles started his run for the governorship, Connecticut's solidly Republican press didn't give him a chance either. It was as if they had come to the conclusion in unison that 1948, since there was no real threat, was the year to prove wrong Democratic complaints that their candidates never received a fair shake on the news pages. I soon discovered that a press release written in a professional manner and delivered with an appropriate understanding of space and deadlines would be printed verbatim in the next edition.

Bowles, who had helped create the Maxwell House Showboat as a mass audience program on radio, knew how to use that medium well. Loose and relaxed, his short, informal chats on the issues were a new idea to Connecticut campaigning and we couldn't afford longer air time anyway. By preparing press releases built on a few key quotes in advance, we made these radio talks do double duty— standard operating procedure now, but a novelty in 1948 when politicians still cranked themselves up to deliver set speeches which drove away the audience.

When the Republicans awoke to the fact that they had a fight on their hands, James Shannon, the incumbent Governor, took to the air waves himself in the old-fashioned way. Full texts would be distributed on the day of the broadcast to the press corps assembled at the permanent Republican headquarters, across the street from the fleabag where we Democrats were behind in our rent. An old friend from New York newspaper days now working for a wire service in Hartford would slip me the text he had picked up at the morning briefing. I would write a reply for Bowles to broadcast somewhere in his campaign travels that day and for publication the next day in the column alongside the Republican handout. These instant rebuttals drove the Republicans up the wall, and they redoubled the security to make sure the texts went only to bona fide regulars from the supposedly friendly press. But they never did manage to plug the leak. We took a photo of Bailey looking out the window through a telescope, ridicule being the sharpest of political instruments. Bailey and I became close during this long-shot venture, although he was never very encouraging about my own ambitions to one day run for public office myself. "Kimball," he used to say, "you're the appointive type."

The Bowles-for-Governor staff all but ignored Truman in our own free-wheeling campaign; stacks of Truman campaign literature remained unopened in state headquarters. One enthusiastic group of supporters, without Bowles' knowledge, took out full-page ads in the paper showing Connecticut's large numbers of unaffiliated voters how they could split a ticket on the voting machines and cast their vote for Dewey and Bowles. This was a practical move in a state where the voting machines were set so that a voter was required first to pull the party lever, then move the individual buttons by hand in order to stray from a straight ticket.

In the event, Dewey carried Connecticut and Bowles upset the incumbent to win the governorship by 1,700 votes. Awaiting the returns at Bowles' house in Essex on election night we were full of ourselves for pulling off this local miracle. A volunteer worker from Yale carried the drinks, and reported that he had heard on the radio that Truman was leading in early returns from Illinois. We patiently explained how the heavily Republican downstate vote in Illinois would be along later. We were confident that Bowles in Connecticut was single-handedly swimming against the tide. With one small town out of 169 to go—Plainfield in the far eastern end of the state— Bowles enjoyed a slight lead. Bailey called up the state police to escort the returns from Plainfield by motorcycle. They put Bowles over the top for good. I was ecstatic, celebrating there among the underdogs, on the winning side at last.

Once elected, Bowles was confronted with the immediate problem of preparing a state budget for presentation to the legislature in February, only a month after his inauguration. Since I could claim a degree in economics, Bowles picked me as his liaison man for the new budget.

Between Election Day and Inauguration Day, I was performing my budget service for free since Democrats were not yet eligible for the payroll. Bowles, like many born to wealth, seemed to have no conception of the practicalities of life for less fortunate humans. He never mentioned money, and I was too proud to dun him, although Janet and Lisa were at home under the leaky roof of the old family homestead in New Britain. Still another unsalaried Christmas went by.

I was finally put on the payroll, with Bailey's help, as clerk of the Appropriations Committee. My job was to steer the Executive Budget through the legislature and keep any sticky Democratic or Republican fingers out of the till. I lived at close quarters that year with small-bore politicians as we rode around the state together "inspecting" the various facilities for which budget requests were under consideration. The camaraderie of these State Representatives and State Senators crossed party lines. They drank together, played cards together, traded stories and holiday cards. Then they voted the way they were instructed by the state chairmen who roamed the corridors. Most of them didn't give a hoot for the ideological divisions publicized at party headquarters. Many were marking time until it was their turn to be rewarded for faithful service.

One method for rewarding the faithful was the system whereby the state bought all its insurance from the big companies located in Hartford and then distributed the commissions through the Comptroller's office to any agents doing business in the state. When the Democrats were in, one list of insurance agents reaped the reward for being on the approved list; when the Republicans were in, the list changed. In neither case had any services been provided to either the state or the insurance companies. The latter could have cut their rates, perhaps, if they had not had to allow for the commissions. But none of these prominent businessmen seemed interested in the cost to the taxpayer of the insurance patronage system. When the question of raising taxes paid to the state by the insurance industry came before the General Assembly, it always could count on goodwill on both sides of the aisle.

This petty "honest graft" was the poison that made reform so difficult. It was the source of control Bailey used to maintain discipline in the ranks. The political press rarely laid a glove on the story of what really went on. One reason was that "honest graft" or political arm-twisting isn't that easy to document when the people involved have every incentive to keep their mouths shut. A powerful factor, however, was the convenience of a system in which the party chairmen were in control. When they said something was going to happen, it usually did. To stay on their good side meant that a reporter could receive his leak just before deadline as to who was slated to be nominated or which bills were going to get out of committee. In return, if the chairman had a little trial balloon he wanted to launch, he could usually find a cooperative writer. The net result was pretty much coverage by handout. It was a rarity for an independent legislator to be able to get his name in the papers after Bailey had passed the word that the fellow was making a nuisance of himself.

The suspicion among Bowles' staff was that he had pretty much delegated to Bailey the privilege and the worry of recommending the persons who should fill those jobs at the Governor's disposal— agency heads, regulatory commissioners, judges, middle-echelon posts in the state bureaucracy. The bickering over these favors pained and bored Bowles. Their distribution was, of course, crucial to Bailey's hold over the party. His assignment was to keep the peace and to minimize the complaints from the job seekers who were always trying to bend the Governor's ear.

The result was that Bowles, who had ridden into office as a knight on a white charger, made some perfectly dreadful appointments. He permitted an ex-convict who was important to Bailey's coalition in the city of Hartford to become a high official in the Motor Vehicles Department; he filled the local courts with hack politicians, and he let Bailey put his own law partner on the ticket as the candidate in 1950 for attorney general.

Word reached the staff of Governor Bowles early in 1949 that Senator Raymond Baldwin was interested in leaving elected office under the right conditions—thus removing himself as a potential candidate for Governor in 1950 and leaving his seat in the United States Senate open for Bowles to fill by appointment. The "right conditions," it was hinted, was appointment to Chief Justice of the Connecticut Supreme Court.

At the council of state in the Governor's office to which I was invited to consider this political gift from heaven, John Bailey chewed on his cigar, pushed his glasses up on his forehead and composed the reply. "Tell him that he can have a seat on the court, but Chief Justice is out. Tell him that when his turn comes for the top spot and if there is a Democratic Governor in office, it won't be held against him that he is a Republican." Baldwin took the offer on Bailey's terms. He rose to Chief Justice 10 years later, appointed by Democratic Governor Abe Ribicoff.

All of a sudden every important Democrat in the state laid claim to the vacant seat in Washington—Abe Ribicoff, then a first-term Congressman; Thomas Dodd; Congresswoman Chase Going Woodhouse. Bowles brainstormed doing something spectacular with the appointment, such as naming Eleanor Roosevelt or Walter Reuther. Every politician had his own idea to offer.

The most awkward approach came from John Bailey himself. He said he didn't want to contest an election, only warm the seat for a candidate who could be recruited when the time pressure was less severe and be groomed to fit in with Bowles' ideas of a strong ticket. He only wanted the post long enough, Bailey said, so that his children could gain admission to the Hartford Country Club where the swamp Yankees might make an exception for a Catholic who had attained high office. It was a touching plea from the man who had lined up the delegates for Bowles' nomination and held the party together long enough for his surprise election.

It was an impossible situation. To appoint Bailey to the Senate would have been perceived by the outside world to be a symbol of using the nation's most prestigious legislative body to take care of a local politician. Not to appoint him was perceived by the inside world of practicing politicians as a snub of rank ingratitude. Bowles never recovered from the rancor engendered by passing over Bailey. He appointed to the vacant Senate seat William Benton, his former partner in Benton & Bowles and one-time Assistant Secretary of State when I was under investigation.

SENATOR BENTON PROMPTLY invited me to join his staff. And just as promptly—only a year had passed since Senator Baldwin's letter

telling me to forget the matter of my Foreign Service appointment—
the question of my file surfaced. When Benton asked me whether
there was anything about me which could possibly be an embarrassment to him in the jungles of Washington, I told him the story of
taking the examination for the Foreign Service and writing in vain
two years later to try to discover what had happened to the appointment. As a former Assistant Secretary of State, Benton knew just
whom to call for a peek at my file. He reported back to me that there
was some stuff in there about my having worked for *PM*, but as a
onetime stockholder in the paper himself, he attached no importance
to such drivel. He appointed me his executive secretary.

It was well that I had told Benton all I knew before the announcement. Benton told me that Arthur Schlesinger Jr. called him
from Washington warning him that I was either a Communist or a
fellow traveler. I had met Schlesinger only once, when he was a guest
at a 1947 staff luncheon on *New Republic* while I was working
there. Schlesinger was at that time a leader of Americans for Democratic Action. According to a memo he prepared for the ADA and
circulated among friendly and influential journalists—syndicated
columnist Joseph Alsop was among the recipients—one editor, Penn
Kimball, struck him "as a smart and cool party liner, at least."
(James R. Boylan, editor of the Columbia *Journalism Review*,
found Schlesinger's bulletin among Alsop's collected papers in 1977
while doing research at the Library of Congress. His sharing of that
intelligence with me was one spur that decided me to write away
for my files.) Although the Schlesinger lunch occurred after I had
flunked my security check, presumably he had no more access to my
government security file than I did. More likely, it was a personal
response. I had been so bold, as I recall, as to contradict something
he had said at that supposedly private lunch. But irony, at least, is
even-handed. Schlesinger became the victim himself to similar black-
listing during the McCarthy era a few years later.

Looking through my file-within-the-file three decades after the
Benton appointment, there emerged an unsettling intelligence: Senator Benton's review of the material was nowhere recorded. Thus I
discovered that not everything about the circulation of a security file
necessarily shows on the record. In those days, the key findings were

still classified top secret. The fact that Benton got a rundown on my file without a note on a log to show it bothers me. How many others? Perhaps some less understanding.

The paranoia about national security rose to fever pitch during Benton's term in office.

I was in the Senate chamber that day in February, 1950, when Joe McCarthy made his floor speech ticking off his allegations on the number of Communists on the State Department rolls. ("I have here in my hand a list of 205 that were known to the Secretary of State as being members of the Communist Party and who nevertheless are still working and shaping the policy of the State Department.") Benton was the first and for a long time the only member of the Senate to come to the defense of the State Department against McCarthy's wild accusations. I drafted the speeches.

Joe McCarthy was no stranger to me. I had known him when he and I had both been attached to the same Marine command on the island of New Georgia in the Solomons. On Munda Airstrip in December, 1943, we shared a Christmas dinner of canned turkey washed down with medicinal brandy which he had scrounged from the rear area. McCarthy was the ground intelligence officer with a dive bomber squadron and the pilots would ferry him back down the line looking for supplies to barter with the Seabees, who made beautiful jewelry out of beachstones and metal salvaged from damaged aircraft.

The McCarthy I knew in the South Pacific was a genial, outgoing guy, popular with the enlisted men as well as the pilots in his squadron. During a lull in Japanese air activity, McCarthy would ride the back seat of a Douglas Dauntless dive bomber making milk runs to keep the enemy air strips on Bougainville full of holes. McCarthy would get the adrenalin out of his system by shooting the tail gun at the anti-aircraft emplacements as the pilot pulled out of a dive after releasing his bomb.

At McCarthy's behest and as press officer I wrote a story about his extracurricular rides which he said he wanted to send home to his friends in Wisconsin. He had a sign over his bunk "McCarthy for Senator," but no one took such things seriously at that early stage of the Pacific war.

When his squadron returned for its next tour of front-line duty, McCarthy waved at me with a fistful of clippings from Wisconsin papers. (Years later, McCarthy parlayed the incident into a political poster portraying Tail Gunner Joe superimposed on a sky full of spinning, flaming Zeroes.) My stories had fed into a tide that was eventually to carry McCarthy through the Wisconsin primaries and into the Senate in an upset victory in 1946. I was at *Time* then. I wrote the background story that explained McCarthy's surprising popularity back home. That article didn't hurt him either. It is more than possible that I helped launch McCarthy's postwar political career and even helped him to create the myth, and myth it was, of "Tail Gunner Joe."

That much of the irony was apparent to me as I helped Senator Benton in his single-handed defense of the State Department. The full savor of irony was still 30 years in the future, when I at last discovered that persons whose loyalty was in question, often on the basis of hearsay alone, were colleagues of those who had convicted me on no more just a basis than Joe McCarthy convicted them.

After working for Governor Bowles and Senator Benton, I was thoroughly hooked on politics. My major in politics at Princeton no longer struck me as very germane to my experience in the grassroots of state politics or the intrigues on the Hill. I longed for a chance to study the subject again from my new perspective. Yale Graduate School, not far from where Janet and I were living in New Britain, had a rule in 1950 (can you believe it?) that barred the admittance of married students. And the Yale Government Department informed me it wasn't very interested anyway in graduate students with practical experience in politics. The Sociology Department was more receptive to me, and I to it. Sociology was not even taught at Princeton in my day. I enrolled for a PhD in political sociology in the fall of 1950, while Janet supported me with a job at the New Britain YWCA. But that renewed entry into the Ivy League was short-lived. Unlucky Janet had developed a back problem which at last required surgery. I left Yale at the end of the second term to take my turn supporting the family.

I GOT MY JOB on *The New York Times* in the hit-or-miss fashion with which newspapers handled their personnel needs in those days. I went around to see Lester Markel, Sunday editor of *The Times*, during the spring of 1951 on the off chance that there might be something there. Markel had a legendary reputation as a hard task-master, with a vinegar personality and a perfectionist attitude toward backgrounding news properly. He had practically invented the Sunday paper in the form that set a standard for the country—a weekly Review of the News, book review, drama section, travel section, real estate section plus a Sunday magazine. His operation reported directly to the publisher. Although he used *Times* staffers to write for the Sunday sections, he was independent of their superiors on the daily. When you wrote—or more precisely, rewrote—for Markel, his verdict was the law. His own deskmen hammered copy into the shape he desired. Markel had need of persons who possessed a broad familiarity with national and international news and who could write, rewrite, edit and think of story ideas. I laid claim to all these qualities in my interview with Markel, but he informed me that there were no jobs to be filled.

A week later I received a telephone call in New Britain. There might be a job opening after all if I were immediately available; a member of the staff was unexpectedly leaving. My resume, happily, had been on top of the file, and the first call had gone to the last person through the office. Such was the hiring system in the pre-testing, pre-layers-of-personnel management, pre-computer, prehistoric days of the newspaper business. I rushed down to the city to close the deal. Markel offered me $200 a week, a fortune to an unemployed refugee from politics. I rushed over to the Astor Hotel and sent Janet a telegram at the hospital where she had been lying flat on her back for six weeks. I thought it would cheer her up, in contrast to the day I had informed her as she was coming out of the ether that I had quit my job on *New Republic*.

The Sunday paper went to the printers one section at a time, beginning with the magazine on the previous Monday, travel on Tuesday, and so on down the line until Saturday night for Section 4 containing the News in Review, which Markel insisted be right on top of the latest developments. When something big happened, such as General MacArthur's challenge to President Truman, Markel would order everything previously prepared thrown out so that the Sunday *Times* could give its readers every last tittle and jot of background and analysis. He could be a great editor. He could be a pain in the neck. But there was no doubt that Markel was driven by a fierce inner pride in the newspaper breakthrough which had been his personal creation.

I spent most of my time working as a deskman on the magazine section, although Markel would let the staff out on the street once in a while if they insisted. He liked "All About" stories that could tell the reader everything he could possibly want to know about some feature in the news. When the Russians threatened to cut off the supply of caviar to the West as part of the cold war, he let me go out and write a one-pager "All About Caviar." I came up with the genius idea of calling up Henri Soule, chef and proprietor of one of the most expensive and most fashionable restaurants in town, Le Pavillon. He trotted out samples of every variety of caviar he served, meticulously explaining the proper ways to eat it with chopped onion or lemon, on toast or black bread or, caviar Heaven, in great dollops on a spoon. All washed down, of course, with the finest examples of Le Pavillon's cellars. Such was the clout of a prospective mention in the Sunday *Times*. The fact that all this feasting took place at 10 a.m. cut down some of the delight, but Markel insisted that one day's reporting was plenty for an "All About" takeout. I had to check out as well the Iranian consulate—Iran could still gather caviar from the Black Sea—and an expert on fish eggs at the Museum of Natural History. Markel believed that there wasn't anything an intelligent generalist couldn't master if he found the right experts and asked the right questions.

The medium which a journalist happens to be working for at the time makes an enormous difference in his ability to carry out his professional duties. As one who switched from David Lawrence and *United States News* to Ralph Ingersoll and *PM*, from *Time* to *New Republic*, to free-lancing, to the *Times*, I experienced all the shadings as to who will take your phone calls or agree to an appointment. Trying to get past a corporate secretary in the name of *PM* or *New Republic* was almost as bad as the confession that I was doing a piece on spec. By the same token, working for *PM* helped a lot when I wanted access to the Auto Workers in Detroit. The guy covering the story for the Chicago *Tribune* did better at corporate head-quarters. Dropping the name of *The Times* would open most any door, although *Time* magazine when I worked for it had more magic in Middle America.

Markel avoided Harry Luce's trap of pretending to find the one and only absolute truth. He insisted that good interpretation meant mustering the arguments on each side of the issue, getting inside the skin as it were of the contending sides so that each would concede that at least *The Times* had its side of the case straight. Like the paper itself, truth was usually gray, somewhere in the middle between the zealots who saw everything in clear black or white.

On such stories as the cold war Markel would send for the photographs each time the members of the Politburo stood in Red Square to review the May Day parade. He would send for Harry Schwartz, the Russian expert on the editorial board, to study the pecking order on the reviewing stand for some clue to a change in the power structure inside the Kremlin. (Schwartz is famous on *The Times* for sleeping through the phone calls the night he had been preparing for all his career—the night Stalin died.) Give the readers as many facts as possible to understand the meaning of the news.

I covered the 1952 presidential primary in New Hampshire for both the *Sunday Magazine* and the Review of the Week. That was the year which really put New Hampshire in the political spotlight. Eisenhower and Taft were competing for the Republican nomination for President and a young upstart from Tennessee, Senator Estes Kefauver, was taking on President Harry S. Truman, who had not made it clear what his own intentions were.

New Hampshire, then as now, was among the least representative states in the union. The southern half of the state lived in the shadow of Boston; the northern half of the state might as well have been in Canada. There was no city of any consequence except Manchester, a faded textile center. The most substantial minority population was French-Canadian, and only a small percentage voted. A small railroad hamlet up in one of the passes, Hart's Location, roused its dozen or so voters at a minute past midnight every four years to vote for President and send the results to the wire services. The trend was almost invariably wrong.

With Yankee economy, New Hampshire had scheduled its presidential primary to coincide with the town meeting day in March when citizens voted on local warrants appropriating the tax money for the next fiscal year. That made it "first in the nation," but until 1952 nobody had ever paid it much attention. The Governor of New Hampshire that year was Sherman Adams, in charge of the State political machinery, who favored Eisenhower. So New Hampshire was built up for the benefit of the media as the first political test for the hero of World War II. The Eisenhower camp pushed out the word that the state was made for Bob Taft—conservative, nationalistic, homespun. Thus began the legendary game of managed expectations: defining for the visiting newsmen what kind of a showing could be interpreted as victory for your side and defeat for the other. If you were privately sure you would win, you publicly said that a close race would be a moral victory.

The scene was further enlivened by Kefauver, who donned a coonskin cap and began walking New Hampshire main streets, sticking out his hand at surprised townspeople and telling them, "I need yoah help." Nothing quite like that had ever happened in New Hampshire before. Harry Truman stayed in the White House and fumed. But another New Hampshire tradition was born: namely, that the voters in the Granite State liked to see their candidates close up.

Eisenhower beat Taft; Kefauver bested the President. But the more significant thing was that the press poured into the state as never before. And the politicians kept spending more money to give the press a better show. Television had not reached its element for covering political news, so viewers that year were not treated to the quadrennial glimpse of Walter Cronkite warming his hands on a potbellied stove. The most important thing about what happened in New Hampshire is what the media said had happened there.

Late that summer in 1952 I received a call from my old boss, Senator William Benton of Connecticut. Benton was up for re-election to a full six-year term and his longtime personal aide, John Howe, had suddenly been sidelined by a heart attack. I left *The Times* temporarily to help out.

Although the Benton candidacy was doomed from the start, one consequence was that Janet, Lisa and I moved from the apartment we had rented in New York into a house in Westport, Connecticut, and the family residence remained in that town for the next 22 years. After the election in which Benton was buried in the Eisenhower landslide along with Adlai Stevenson, I went back to *The Times* as a commuter from the suburbs. I became active in local affairs, becoming a fiscally conservative member of the local Board of Finance and also a member of a committee to rewrite the Town Charter to make local government more effective. At work, I was once more a dues-paying member of the American Newspaper Guild.

I had been inactive in the Newspaper Guild for three years when I joined *The Times* and reactivated my membership. *The Times* had a Guild contract, and the issues were the usual ones when a paternalistic, family ownership must deal with a union. One of the attributes of the Guild, which bargained for all the clerical and maintenance employees as well as the editorial staff, was the leverage the reporting staff members gave to the lowest paid part of a newspaper organization. *The Times*, for example, had taken the initiative to give jobs to blacks, a fact of some pride to the owners. The only problem was that the only jobs held by blacks were as elevator operators.

I was not directly involved in Guild contract negotiations, but I paid my dues and attended meetings. The collective bargaining crisis which occurred while I was with the paper came, not with the Guild, but with the Photo-Engravers Union. They made the metal cuts of photographs used in the paper. Among the aristocracy of the printing trades, the photoengravers collected among the highest wages. Some earned more than the reporters, a condition dating from the era when the printers were unionized and the editorial staff was not. In 1953, just before Christmas, the photoengravers' negotiations for a new contract with still higher wages broke down and they voted to strike.

Based on grim experience, the New York Newspaper Guild had adopted the policy to honor strikes called by printing unions by refusing to cross their picket lines. This was not the product of brotherly love so much as a question of practical necessity. If the reporters and editors had a quarrel with management and went out on strike, the executives could probably get out the paper on their own. They possessed the same skills and had access to wire-service and broadcast news. When the printing trades went on strike in those days, the paper had to close down. Even if the reporters went to work, there was no way in the technology of that era that management could operate the hot-lead linotypes, make the cuts, cast the plates and roll the presses in a highly unionized town like New York City. Thus, the printers, by honoring a Guild picket line, could make all the difference when it came to the crunch.

The *Times* unit of the Guild, with some dissenting, voted to back the photoengravers in the long-term interests of our union, not only at *The Times* but at any other paper in town where the editorial staff might one day seek the support of the printing trades. We and the Guild members on five other dailies hit the bricks—four weeks before Christmas—and took our turn on the picket line outside the *Times* entrance on 43rd Street. Nobody except the executives went to work in the Sunday Department, although as a group we were among the best paid on the paper. All the top reporters and sub-editors from the daily paper stayed out, too. The strike was settled within 10 days and everybody was back at work by Christmas.

One consequence was that *The Times* in negotiating its next contract insisted upon and won new categories which it claimed were part of management and should be outside Guild jurisdiction. The traditional union position was that you were management if you possessed the power to hire and fire. Now the paper was suddenly crawling with assistants who, the paper claimed, were in key policy-making positions. I was suddenly promoted to "Assistant to the Sunday Editor," not, I suspect, because of my performance on the job, but to be part of the cadre who could get out the paper in the future if the Guild ever again went on strike. The game was to create a slew of editorial professionals who, if they didn't volunteer for duty during a strike, could be fired without union protection. When the contract was signed, I was mailed an honorary withdrawal card from the Guild, dated December 31, 1953. I wrote the president of the New York Guild, Thomas Murphy, that I didn't want to withdraw from a union to which I had belonged from its earliest days and believed in as a matter of principle and in the best interests of my profession. Sorry, said Murphy, and good-bye from the Guild, the source of so many of my troubles with the United States Government.

Well, not quite good-bye forever. During all these years, from 1948, when I received the only hint the State Department would give me of my status there, to 1954, when I was "promoted" from labor to management on *The Times*, there were no additions to my file. It might have been a mere skeleton in a closet that was never opened, but for the fact that Senator Benton had obtained a peek at it. Like a ghoul that will not die, however, the file rose to life again in 1955, after an interlude of nearly a decade.

THERE CAME A DAY when I received the last of the documents in my FBI file. One was an FBI report from the New York office—File No. 100-113352, to Director J. Edgar Hoover on "COMINFIL INTO THE 'NEW YORK TIMES.' " I was named at the bottom of a list of 14 employees alleged to be part of a Communist infiltration of "All The News That's Fit to Print." The 13 names above mine were blacked out. I was identified as assistant to Lester Markel, who was identified as the "Number one pro-Communist on the New York Times with the ability to pick reporters, foreign and Washington correspondents, News Department executives and people in all key positions on the newspaper." The absurdity of that charge was exceeded only by the sweeping description of his power at a newspaper where every executive jealously guarded his own empire. For good measure, I once again earned the label "as one of the leaders of the pro-Communist faction in the Newspaper Guild."

The report was dated January, 1955—one whole year after my withdrawal from the Guild, and six months after I had left the paper. The source of the FBI intelligence was a member of the staff, "who has furnished reliable information in the past," but "has never had any connection with the CP." To protect its source inside *The Times*, the New York office warned Mr. Hoover:

> In the event any of the following information is disseminated, [Name blacked out's] identity should be concealed, by his own request. [Name blacked out] has advised that should it be-

come known to his employer that he is furnishing information
to the Bureau, his position would be in jeopardy.

It was a far cry from *PM* to the good, gray *Times*—apart from
my presence on the staff of both papers—and the FBI had definitely
broadened its reach in the 15 years since it had begun by following
the ads. No wonder it had taken extra months for Washington to
turn that piece of my file loose.

In contrast to their earlier investigaton, the FBI this time around
had consulted their files of newspaper clips more thoroughly. At last
they came upon my role in the VFW episode. "On March 16, 1936,"
the investigator reported, "as a student at Princeton University, he
was one of the organizers of 'Veterans of Future Wars,' formed to
'combat with laughter the failures of national democracy' . . . and
was Commander of the 'Veterans of Future Wars' for the northeast
district of the US." Suggestions of candlelit cellars.

It was also the first time that anyone paid attention to anything I
had ever written in my long career as a journalist. An FBI agent
reported that he had come across a dispatch I had written from the
South Pacific about the participants in the first air raid to reach the
Japanese naval bastion at Truk. "This article contained no political
expression of opinion," the agent declared. Another article proved
more gripping but—I should not have been surprised—the investigators failed to get it right.

After I left *New Republic* to embark on a career of free-lancing,
my old roommate Henry Wallace had announced in the spring of
1948 as a third-party candidate for President. I went back to interview him, in question-and-answer form, and sold a three-part series
to North American Newspaper Alliance. The series received big play
around the country and NANA paid me a bonus when I needed one
badly to buy groceries.

In the course of my interview with Wallace, I tried to get at the
reasons that had prompted him to undertake the historically forlorn
task of running for President as a third-party candidate. He said
(shades of Barry Goldwater) that he thought there was a huge silent
vote not reflected in the polls. The interview as printed in the papers
went on from there:

Your supporters contend that the third-party ticket will help elect more progressive candidates for Congress. Will you explain how this works?"

WALLACE: The third party is going to bring out several additional millions of votes, and statistics show that the bigger the vote, the bigger the progressive vote.

Won't the third party cut into liberal rather than conservative candidates?

WALLACE: Ordinarily there won't be any third-party congressional candidates. If there's a good man running on one of the two major parties, we'll endorse him.

How do you decide who is a good man?

WALLACE: He doesn't have to be 100 per cent liberal; he has to be 66⅔ right on the three crucial tests. One, the Taft-Hartley Act; two, the Truman Doctrine; three, universal military training.

In a memorandum sent to J. Edgar Hoover and subsequently forwarded to the director of security for the CIA the following summary of that interview with Wallace was put into my file:

On April 24, 1948, in an exclusive interview for the North American Newspaper Alliance, a newspaper syndicate, KIMBALL spoke to HENRY A. WALLACE and reported that the WALLACE candidacy for President "will help elect the more progressive members of Congress."

Thus Wallace's answers to my questions became words put by the FBI into my own mouth, with the ominous suggestion that I had been a Wallace partisan in 1948 when actually I was engaged in trying to elect Chester Bowles Governor on the Democratic ticket headed by Harry S. Truman. The FBI sleuths never did uncover the damning evidence that I had once again shared an apartment with a suspicious character, and I suppose I should settle for that.

The FBI, on the evidence, had left me alone for nearly 10 years —years in which I had been a free-lance writer or employed by politicians. Only when I returned to newspaper journalism and re-activated my membership in the Newspaper Guild was I under scrutiny once more.

For the next 20 years, my file shows, the FBI's interest was revived from time to time—and so was the attention of the State Department and the CIA—sometimes for reasons that I could discern and sometimes for reasons that I can still only guess. My document collection eventually grew to 269 pages for me to pore over, wonder about, carry around on my mind and rehash during those moments when I wasn't absolutely required to devote my attention to something else. Over the years after the first installment arrived in February, 1978, more pages arrived in dribs and drabs—from the FBI in Washington, from their field office in New York, from the Passport Division of the State Department and, five years later, from the CIA. It is surprising how much is still missed after leafing through such documents a hundred times. Connections between my FBI and State Department files would suddenly dawn on me when I spotted a tiny initial and date in the corner of a page. Some contained scrawls that took on meaning only later when another piece of the puzzle became available. Janet would chide me gently about my preoccupation when it became clear that I hadn't heard a word of her conversation at dinner. "Where are you, Penn?" she would ask, as if she didn't know.

During the years represented by my file, I thought I knew where I was, as well as what I was doing, and why, and the sort of person I had become. All that was nothing like the Penn Kimball in my file. Perhaps others, too, were misrepresented there, or had been victims of that time and now had cause to regret it. Baldwin's statement in Document 15 particularly stuck in my mind—

> Even if we were satisfied that the man is not a Communist or has Communist leanings, should we make the appointment, there would be the possibility of someone raising the question on the floor of the Senate or House, holding up as an example the Kimball case in which the State Department had made the appointment when it had been charged that he is a Communist or Communist sympathizer.

Baldwin was a kind man of unquestioned integrity. Acting on impulse, he might not have thought through the policy implications which presaged the McCarthy era. I still knew him. We had worked together after we both were elected in 1965 as members of the bipartisan convention to forge a new Constitution for our home state of Connecticut. There had been reunions of that group from time to time. Baldwin, about whose strange opinion in my case I then, of course, knew nothing, always greeted me warmly, by my first name. I wondered how his perspective might have changed—now well past 80—with the wisdom of time. I wrote to Judge Baldwin early in 1979 that I was engaged in some historical research during the period of the Truman Loyalty Program and the tenure of Senator Joseph R. McCarthy. I told him that I had recently obtained some documents about myself under the Freedom of Information Act. I enclosed copies of the documents in my file recapitulating his own exchange with the State Department over my case.

"If you have the time," I wrote, "I would appreciate whatever comments you might make in the perspective of hindsight regarding the comments by you quoted in these documents." I added that I hoped that my letter would find him in good health and wondered when we might be due for another reunion of the members of the 1965 Constitutional Convention.

"Many thanks for your thoughts in the matter," I concluded, then awaited with anticipation his reply.

It did not come quickly. After several weeks, I received his acknowledgment on his letterhead—Raymond E. Baldwin, State Referee, Court House, Middletown, Connecticut.

Dear Mr. Kimball:

I have your letter and have examined the enclosures which you sent.

It is a long time since I was in the Senate, 30 years in fact. I have only the vaguest recollection of the matter which you discussed and I am sorry that I can't help you further.

Yours very sincerely,
Raymond E. Baldwin

13

THE LIBERAL
COLUMNIST

AT THIS WRITING, I have been a teacher at the Columbia Graduate School of Journalism for 25 years. That life had seemed to me relatively benign and undisturbed—until I received my file in 1978. Although the episode itself had come to an end with Baldwin's letter to me more than three decades before, it was hardly buried in the past.

Leafing through the pages again and again, I found evidence that this Top Secret part of my life had been more public than I could have imagined. The official record documented the fact that as recently as 1974 a State Department bureaucrat looking over my application for a Fulbright research grant to study the British general election had pulled the file. The date coincided with that time of the year when the final nominations for Fulbrights are sent abroad to the receiving country. I figured at the time that I stood a pretty good chance. No Fulbright. Had the file anything to do with it? (I applied for a Fulbright again in 1978. A professional colleague who sat on the original screening committee said my application had been given a 1/1 rating, the highest possible for both the substance of the proposal and the qualifications of the applicant. Fulbrights are no longer administered directly by the State Department, although government officials participate in the final selection process with institutions abroad. In any event, I was turned down once more.)

Going back in time, the record also contained a routine note from the State Department to the Federal Bureau of Investigation in 1971. I was on leave from Columbia that year, serving as director of public affairs for the New York State Urban Development Corporation. The agency booked me to go on an inspection tour of new town developments in Britain and Finland and prefabricated housing systems in Russia along with a group of planners, architects and housing administrators. When I renewed my passport for the trip, the State Department flagged my name in its security file and forwarded the information along with my itinerary to the FBI. Was I being watched every time I went abroad?

In the fall of 1969 during the Nixon Administration I received a phone call at home in Westport from a State Department official inviting me to lecture in Southeast Asia for six weeks on American communications. I never heard another word about it. Sure enough, in my FBI file was a "request for biographic data" on Professor Penn T. Kimball from one MGGeesa, program officer in CU/STAL, the code name for I know not what, as a "Proposed U.S. Specialist-87 256," dated 10/23/69.

A reply from the FBI dated Nov. 25, 1969 directed MGGeesa to "data re Penn Townsend Kimball which was sent to your agency on 6-11-46"— the ancient field check ordered by the State Department concerning my appointment to the Foreign Service.

A reply from the Central Intelligence Agency, apparently to the same routine query, was one the FBI could not release to me. It was covered over with the notation "Confidential—Group 1—Excluded from automatic downgrading and declassification." I can only presume that the lectureship in Southeast Asia involved the approval of the CIA. The document is confusing, because the name at the bottom is G. Marvin Gentile, Deputy Assistant Secretary for Security, presumably in the State Department. Between the classified portion and his signature was an uncovered paragraph carrying the date 12/18/69:

A partial national agency check has been made in the name of Penn T. KIMBALL. Subject applied to Department as candidate for the Foreign Service while still in military service with the Marine Corps in late 1945. SY political investigation developed derogatory security information as to his "leftist" political views and associates. As a result of a dispute between Board of Foreign Service and Security Officials, a special investigation was concluded by FBI in June, 1946, and based upon the results and adverse recommendations for a clearance, subject was denied a security clearance by the Appeals Committee of Personnel in final decision on Nov. 1, 1946. There is attached the 1946 FBI reports, plus a summary report dated May 20, 1959, which brought his case up to that date. Please return the attachments to Mr. Flow, SY/E, R–2422, within 30 days with your decision.

One can imagine the reaction to that by a functionary in the Nixon Administration on the verge of dispatching me to a sensitive territory in Southeast Asia.

My government's interest in my travel plans had quite a long history, as my file revealed.

There was to be, in 1963, a celebration at Oxford of Balliol's 700th year. I had never been back to Europe since sailing from Le Havre in August, 1939. We were still living in Westport, and I was teaching at Columbia. Janet and our daughter Lisa submitted their passport applications to the office in nearby Bridgeport and I took mine to the New York City office in Rockefeller Center. They received their documents in the mail within a week or so. When mine didn't arrive, I attributed the delay to the higher volume of traffic from New York and thought no more about it until about a week before our departure. Still no passport. I called an ex-Bowles staffer then serving in the Kennedy State Department. He promised he would get right on it. My passport arrived in the mail a couple of days later, just in time for us to make our flight.

When I leafed through my file, there was a form from the Office of Security to the Director, Passport Office, with a check mark in the box "Attached is the SY FILE which appears to be identical to the above subject." Classification: SECRET. No information, however, in the file explained what the Passport Office intended to do beyond delaying their approval, nor was there any record of any exchange with my State Department friend.

When the Democrats came into power with the election of John

F. Kennedy, the thought crossed my mind that I might take up once more my favorite avocation, making the move this time from the sanctuary of Columbia University. Early in 1962, about a year after Kennedy's inauguration, I received a call from J. Leonard Reinsch, an Atlanta TV executive who had managed the Los Angeles convention which had nominated Kennedy. At a pleasant lunch at the St. Regis Hotel, he asked me if I would be interested in taking a post on the United States Information Agency Advisory Commission, a civilian body charged with monitoring the performance of the Voice of America and similar government activities in the international communications field. It was only a part-time activity, but I expressed interest and received a letter from Reinsch a few days later saying he had recommended me to the White House.

Almost simultaneously, the wheels began to turn regarding an even more attractive appointment to federal service.

The post in question was commissioner on the Federal Communications Commission. Newton Minow, who had already achieved notice for his speech describing the state of commercial television as a "vast wasteland," was the FCC chairman. Commissioners are appointed for seven-year terms with staggered expiration dates; no more than a bare majority can be members of the same political party. By coincidence, three vacancies for Democrats were scheduled to become available within a year and a half. With the right package of new appointments, Minow would be in charge of a working majority. He nourished the idea that a congenial team which caucused together on the big issues and then voted together might make regulatory history in improving the quality of TV programming.

My name had been suggested to him through a headhunter on the White House staff on the basis of what was by then my broad range of experience—in politics, journalism, teaching and, as newsman for the TV show "Omnibus," in broadcasting as well.

As a would-be commissioner I thought of myself as a maverick spokesman for the public interest in a field where I had special knowledge. My stint on "Omnibus" had been an expression of belief that commercial broadcasting need not be focused on the least common denominator of popular taste. Both networks and local stations seemed to me to be falling far short of their obligations in news and public affairs. It was an arena where I could bring to bear the political skills I had learned in the service of others exercising the powers of public office. The appointment offered the chance to be out there on my own this time, in charge of my own fate while satisfying those ideals which had drawn me into politics. I wanted the job.

Minow came up to New York City a few weeks later. We had lunch together, and he set out the script. The first vacancy became available July 1. The White House staffer was ready to put my name on the President's desk. Pierre Salinger, an old colleague and now the President's press secretary, was enthusiastic. Since I was a Connecticut voter and had been in politics there, Minow suggested that a letter from John Bailey to Bobby Kennedy might help seal the deal. Bailey in turn suggested that I come down to Washington and call on Senator Thomas Dodd, who as senior Senator from my home state would have the right to veto my confirmation under the rules of senatorial courtesy. That meeting went well; everything was going smoothly.

Bailey sent me a copy of a letter to Bobby Kennedy reporting that if I were appointed to the agency the appointment had the support of the Connecticut delegation and Senator Dodd. The Bridgeport paper carried a story the next day that I was being considered for the post, presumably leaked to the Washington stringer who covered Dodd's office.

I began checking real estate in Washington and secured a place for Lisa in a private school there. I waited in Westport for the phone to ring. Minow called to say I should be hearing any day now, and then called again to say that he would be on vacation in Chicago in August and I should be sure to let him know if there were any developments. No word. I went to a journalism convention at the University of North Carolina in Chapel Hill at the end of the month. I was on the way home via Williamsburg when the news came over the car radio. "The President today announced the appointment of a new member to the Federal Communications Commission." My heart leaped, until I heard the name. It was E. William Henry of Memphis, Tennessee. Minow had never even met him. He was as furious as I was baffled.

Could my unsuspected status as a national security risk have surfaced somewhere along the line? With the hindsight provided by my file discovered 15 years later, I remembered the long-forgotten invitation from Reinsch to join the USIA Advisory Commission. I assumed at the time that his recommendation of me to the White House had simply been overtaken by Minow's recommendation for me to be a member of the FCC. But the suggestion of my name for government service in the world of international diplomacy could logically have triggered all sorts of inquiries at State, the FBI, even the CIA. Nothing shows in the records.

Still, I lost something I valued and thought was mine. Never again was I offered a similar opportunity at the federal level to put my convictions into practical operation.

I KNOW I will never find out exactly how the course of my life might have differed if I had never been declared a national security risk. And the government has refused me the information so that I could try to get in touch with the full cast of characters who decided my fate so many years ago. I would like to understand their train of thought fully in order that the implications of my file to the public interest could be set forth clearly. What was it about those government informants and government employees of yesteryear that could lead them to so readily condemn a young man like me?

Reading what the informants had told the investigators about my life was a curious sensation. Here they were, reading my mind, probing my motivations, interpreting my behavior, explaining things about myself which only I could possibly know. Assessing my character, I suppose, was fair game. We make judgments all the time about other people in order to function in this world—when we choose friends, hire an employee or ask a person to marry. To express the opinion that somebody is disloyal to his country and a danger to its security, however, is more than an idle opinion. It cuts to the bone of a man's reputation.

The fact that so many had been willing to do this to me came as something of a shock. I had always thought of myself as a fairly decent fellow. Not without faults, to be sure. But I like to think I never walked over another human being for my private advantage. Reading the testimony against me by those who had worked alongside me in the pursuit of truth, as we like to say, gave me pause about the state of the art.

A newsperson would think twice, I had assumed, before bandying about slander at that level. A professional colleague would be guided by a sense of fair play when a government investigator came around asking questions about a fellow member of the staff. A sense of decency in such circumstances might operate to give another human being the benefit of doubt. In my case that is not what had happened.

As a teacher of future journalists, my need to understand why my detractors had behaved that way has been all the more acute. I have had something to do with the formative years of nearly 2,500 students who have passed through Columbia's Graduate School of Journalism, and intimate contact with nearly one-third that number. My students have found me an exacting, even stern mentor. That is because I see them as surrogates to infuse into society the ideals I have tried so many times to project on my own. Most of all, I have sought to help these young men and women to find within themselves the independence of judgment and the skill which might propel them to the achievement of excellence in a profession vital to the public interest.

They are presently in every sort of media post, all over the world. When they excel, it gives me vicarious pleasure. I hear from many of them from time to time. It is like having an extended family, constantly renewing itself. I like to think that, if asked, they might judge my own character and reputation with more charity than those in my file.

What was so powerful as to make the informants cast fact and fairness aside? What kind of individuals were they? If given a second opportunity in the hindsight of history, might they be willing—three decades later—to make amends?

I had this burning notion in my head that if I could round up once more all the informants against me, I could show the State Department how wrong it had been. That would be satisfying personally. But I persuaded myself, too, that there was something worth proving more important than my individual vindication. There is a message in my file that is important to every American.

Of course, I knew the names of only a handful of my detractors. At the top of my list was James A. Wechsler.

Wechsler, a senior informant in the chronology of my security file and a colleague of mine on *PM* in 1940–42, had been by 1978 editor and columnist for the New York *Post* for decades. He had been a longtime spokesman for the reform Democrats in New York City, a personal friend of Eleanor Roosevelt, Adlai Stevenson and Hubert Humphrey, and a frequent essayist on the topics of human rights and civil liberties. A Communist Party member during his college youth in the 1930s, Wechsler in the '40s, according to the investigator who interviewed him about me, was a self-styled "conservative" in the politics of the New York local of the American Newspaper Guild—which was a euphemism for defender of the faith against Communists.

It was Wechsler's advice to X-ray the state of my mind that was ultimately accepted as the acid test of my political loyalty: "if someone could authoritatively clear up how far to the Left he went in his thinking, I would recommend him for a position of trust." In the final decision against me Counsel for ACOPS had declared: "This being the state of Kimball's mind, I cannot recommend that the Security Officer's adverse recommendation be overruled."

The State Department's decision to give me Wechsler's name was an empty gesture; it had already surfaced as the result of human fatigue within the confines of the State Department Privacy Office. Stuck with the boring task of blacking out the name of every unfriendly informant in 99 documents, the censor slipped up in midpassage and failed to eliminate a revealing phrase, ". . . Mr. Wechsler went on. . . ." Thus the cover had already been blown as far as Jimmy Wechsler's involvement with State Department Security was concerned.

I can't say that I was totally surprised to learn from my security file that Jimmy Wechsler had done a number on me in 1946. An episode at *PM* had stuck in my mind. In 1940, management had sought to dismiss the paper's labor editor, Leo Huberman, as "incompetent." The Guild Grievance Committee, of which I was then chairman, had defended him. Wechsler, I recall learning at the time, had personally gone to Ralph Ingersoll to seek the removal of Huberman, his department head. Huberman was a self-avowed Marxist who had been chairman of the Social Studies Department at New College, Columbia, and had been a pioneer in adult education for trade union members. A pipe-smoking intellectual, his quiet manner concealed a tough streak of old-fashioned radicalism. The rap against him by the anti-Communist wing was that he was "soft on Stalinists." The Guild won the case in arbitration; then Huberman quit. Wechsler was thereupon appointed by Ingersoll to succeed Leo.

Jimmy Wechsler had his own troubles during the McCarthy era when, as an admitted ex-Communist, he attracted the attention of the witch-hunters in Congress. Wechsler was called to Washington to defend himself against the charge of being subversive. The rule adopted by the congressional committees investigating un-American influences in the land was that witnesses could be forgiven their past indiscretions if in return they would turn in the names in executive session of anybody else they could identify as loyal to the Communist Party. It has been written that Wechsler traded the names he gave then for his own skin, but I leave such harsh judgment to others with direct experience of that traumatic episode in our nation's history.

As the McCarthy era receded into history, Wechsler's role as editor of the editorial page of the New York *Post*, the only liberal daily in New York City, gave him a reputation as a champion of progressive causes. An impetuous liberal, of course, might have handed in his resignation on principle when *Post* publisher Dolly Schiff switched her paper's endorsement from Liberal Democrat Governor Averell Harriman to Republican challenger Nelson Rockefeller on election eve 1958 without even telling Wechsler about it. Wechsler swallowed his chagrin and carried on. When Mrs. Schiff sold the paper to Australian Rupert Murdoch, whom no one ever accused of being progressive, Wechsler carried on once more.

I had read his column through the years, and generally shared a sympathy for the causes he championed and thought about him as one of those, all too rare in the mass media, who were stout defenders of the underdog.

When the State Department special agent went to interview

Wechsler about me in Washington in 1946, his testimony as recorded in my file waffled a bit, like a suitor who was thinking he might hate himself in the morning. "As you probably know, there was a distinctive separation in the *PM* organization between the radicals and conservatives. I was lined up on the conservative side in the Guild," Wechsler was quoted, "and can only state that I know Kimball was not on my side." He thought about that for a moment apparently, and hastened to clarify it.

"By my last remark," Wechsler continued, "I do not mean that I know Kimball to be a Communist. I just know he was not anti-Communist or conservative." And then again: "I do not think Kimball had an important active part in the political fight in the Guild on the side of the Communists . . . [but] I do not wish to state that Kimball was not sympathetic or not involved with the Communist Party, or at least the radical element."

In a preview of the name game later so popular among the congressional investigators, Wechsler recalled in his conversation with Hipsley that, half-a-dozen years previously,

"I knew Kimball to be friendly with [Name blacked out] and other known Communists. I have no knowledge as to whether he was interested in their politics, their company or as a young employee of the paper merely staying in their company so as to have someone to play around with. I do know that the Communists were so thick at *PM* that to shun them you had to stay at home."

That sounded, I suppose, like a safe position to Wechsler.

When my security file arrived in the mail and I came upon Wechsler's equivocal comments about me in the long, long ago, the reminder that newspaper colleagues of mine like Wechsler had behaved so badly during the very earliest hours of national hysteria was both worrisome and annoying.

Weakness is in us all, and deserves forgiveness. Hypocrisy is a more serious matter. And the idea that this ex-Communist should be taken so seriously by the United States Government as a character witness concerning an innocent like me seemed unfair. Wechsler's quotes about me were summarized over and over again in my file—doubly damaging because of his political credentials as a card-carrying liberal.

I made up my mind that I would go and see Wechsler, confront him with the record and see what happened. In the same way that I had hoped that Justice Baldwin might in his old age produce an eloquent footnote to a piece of unfortunate history he could now view in the perspective of wisdom, I hoped Jimmy Wechsler might in his maturity repent in a somewhat different fashion. Both Baldwin and Wechsler—I indulged myself—in the full passage of time could not fail to realize how wide of the mark they had been in their dealings about me with the security establishment. Senator Baldwin, liberal Republican, had espoused Senator McCarthy's doctrine of guilt by accusation before McCarthy had even been elected. Columnist Wechsler, a reform Democrat, had anticipated the peculiar litmus test of that era of blacklists by musing on my possible guilt by non-association with avowed anti-Communists. What a wonderful piece, I thought, Jimmy Wechsler might write—turning a story of misguided patriotic zeal upon himself. Dreams of glory and retribution.

In recent years I have had a nodding acquaintance with Wechsler, an enthusiastic supporter of Columbia football and basketball teams. That is to say, I have nodded to him, and once found him in my seat by mistake at a Columbia–Princeton game. He moved, rather gruffily, with no hint of recognition. He used to spend weekends in Westport, where I lived for 22 years, and I interviewed him there once when I was doing my book on Bobby Kennedy, whom he greatly admired.

Was Jimmy's eyesight deteriorating as badly as mine in my old age, or was something else shielding him from vision of me? I very much wanted to see Wechsler and talk to him about my file. Beyond what he had to say for himself, perhaps he could lead me to the other informants from the staff of *PM* whose identities were concealed beneath the censor's black strokes.

The anonymous informants from *PM*—aside from Wechsler—threw off few clues. They had been interviewed by the security agents in New York and Washington years after I had left the paper to join the Marines. I had spent most of my professional life in those two cities before the government investigated me, but nothing said by the *PM* informants rang a bell. In those carefree days of my youth I was aware of no personal enemies. *PM*, unlike *Time*, was enormously outgoing in both its editorial policy and internal atmosphere.

The probability was that my detractors on *PM*, like Wechsler, were persons I never had very much to do with. Once I ran into an old staff member whom I knew was a good friend of Jimmy's, and tried, just for size, to find out whether he had ever been interrogated about me. He didn't blink. I called up on the phone long-distance one whom I knew had been brought onto the staff by Wechsler. Foiled again.

Without something concrete to go on, it was a tough task for an amateur sleuth, and I had never cultivated a taste for mystery stories. Those identified in my file as having put in a good word for me at *PM* were John P. Lewis, the managing editor, and Ken Crawford, the head of the paper's Washington Bureau. So, if the informants were not among management nor any recognizable friends, that left those who, like Wechsler, perceived themselves as the guardians of "the conservative side" in the Newspaper Guild. When I saw him, he might drop a name.

An excuse to make a probe seemed to present itself in April, 1979, when the Supreme Court handed down a landmark decision, ruling that public figures suing for libel were entitled to inquire into the "state of mind" of the journalists who write and edit controversial articles. Many editorialists took a dim view of the ruling as the latest in a series infringing upon journalistic freedoms supposedly protected by the First Amendment. "The mind is a private domain," said *The New York Times*, "beyond the reach of the courts." Others cited the potentially chilling effect on editorial freedom if one were forced to take the stand to explain one's innermost thoughts.

However, James A. Wechsler, rather surprisingly, joined the company of William F. Buckley to argue that "no chill is discernible in the air around here." He dismissed the "state of mind" protesters as hysterical. Wechsler's position at both ends of this span of time was at least consistent.

I wrote Wechsler the following letter just after I read his editorial:

Dear Jimmy,

I was reminded by your comments on the Supreme Court "state of mind" decision that I have been meaning to get together with you regarding a document released to me under the Freedom of Information Act. I am doing a book on my security file as amassed by the State Department 33 years ago when I took and passed the examinations for the Foreign Service. That unleashed a security check as a result of which, unknown to me, I was ruled unfit for the Foreign Service and a file established under my name which is circulated every time I apply for a passport, or a Fulbright or mentioned for government employment.

You were one of those interviewed in September, 1946— interestingly enough two months before my old Marine buddy Joe McCarthy was elected to the Senate. Perhaps you can remember the occasion.

In any event, I am endeavoring to reconstruct the spirit of those times by checking back with all the sources involved. Do you suppose you could find time to give me an interview at a place and time of your convenience?

Not a bad letter, I thought. Straightforward. A couple of lines to prick the conscience. The McCarthy dig, perhaps, was a little mean, but I couldn't resist. It put Wechsler on notice, however. He didn't answer the letter.

When I phoned Jimmy's office to try for an appointment, I never got through, and he never returned my calls. I persisted. One day, I finally caught up with him. He had been terribly busy, Wechsler explained. It was possible, he said, someone might have interviewed him about me years ago. There had been numerous such interviews. He couldn't remember them all. More specifically, since he hadn't the faintest recollection of anything involving me, it would be a waste of time to bother with an interview. He was awfully busy, he said.

Document 53 quoting Wechsler's testimony had by now been cleared of censorship and referred to him by name in every instance. I told Jimmy I would send him a copy of the document in the mail, and perhaps we could get together after that.

No reply.

Another round of unanswered phone calls.

When I finally reached him again, he said he was awfully busy. He said he'd like to talk to me when we had a chance to sit down somewhere, not in the midst of all this frenzy in the office. Perhaps things would be less hectic in the summer. Why didn't I call him back in a few weeks?

I asked him whether he had had time to look over the document I had sent him.

"The whole thing is comic opera," he replied. "Full of words I would never use. I would never refer to myself as a 'conservative' in a million years. This sounds as if it had been written by a bunch of semi-skilled intellectuals." Maybe we could get together about it when summer came.

The interview which Wechsler now disclaimed was one of those conducted by Special Agent Elmer Hipsley, whom the State Department had refused to help me locate on the ground that it would be "an invasion of privacy." I thought the contradiction might appeal to Wechsler's sense of humor. By deriding the interviewer, while absolving himself, he had given me an in to pump him concerning the other sources he might know.

On May 29, I wrote him:

I expect to be back in New York the week of June 11, and would still like the opportunity to chat with you about Special Agent Hipsley.

For reasons which I am sure you can appreciate, I am interested in establishing what other PMnicks besides you, Crawford and Cole were kicking around Washington in September, 1946. [Cole, who had spoken favorably of me, had been interviewed as a onetime colleague of mine on *United States News*. He worked for *PM* after I left, then joined the U.S. Department of Labor. Two other *PM* informants contributed derogatory comments, and their names were withheld.] You will note in the document I sent you that the "meat of the discussion" between Mr. Hipsley and these two gentlemen was summarized by him for "purposes of clarity." The State Department refuses to release their identity, so I have no direct way of checking what liberties Hipsley took with the truth. I gather from your own comments attributed to you that his reporting was not totally reliable. The Government thus seeks to protect itself in the name of protecting others. An interesting situation, don't you agree?

I thought that the mention of Elmer Hipsley might tickle Jimmy Wechsler's reportorial curiosity, but the ploy didn't work. No reply to my letter. In June I phoned Wechsler's office once again. The call was never returned. And that was that.

14

THE *TIME*
SUPERVISOR

SPECIAL AGENT Joseph F. McCorry had hit paydirt when he interviewed [Name blacked out] my "supervisor" at Time, Inc., who described me as "very definitely a left winger" whom he "would not trust in other countries, particularly countries such as France or any other country where there is a growing possibility of Russian dominance."

This juicy bit was seized upon by Chief Security Officer Bannerman, chairman of the State Department's Security Committee. "The Security Committee believes that particular emphasis should be given to the remarks and recommendations of the subject's most recent supervisor." That emphasis took the form of repetition. The few words from my "supervisor" at *Time* are quoted over and over in my file.

On *Time*'s pyramid masthead of editors my name was listed as "contributing editor," well toward the bottom, beneath those of a host of senior editors, a pair of assistant managing editors, the managing editor and editor Henry Luce. Any of the above could have been described as a "supervisor" in a general description of *Time*'s hierarchy.

A State Department agent ultimately did talk to James Linen, the publisher, who gave me a clean bill of health as a "valued employee," although, in truth, we were many floors apart and he couldn't have known very much about me. Tom Matthews, the managing editor who hired me in the first place, stood next highest on the masthead, but low on my list of possible candidates. He once worked for *New Republic*, a tendency that would not have appealed to a prowling agent from the FBI, and he was too friendly toward me to serve the FBI's purposes.

Working down the masthead from Matthews was his assistant managing editor, Roy Alexander, a bluff ex-reporter for the St. Louis *Post-Dispatch*. Alex, who had been a flier in World War I, had been in charge of the magazine's war coverage during World War II. The office joke was that anyone who came to him asking for a job in a Marine uniform had been automatically hired. There was an unusually large bunch of Marine veterans among the postwar hirelings at *Time*. Being one of that bunch, and sharing an office with another, Alex would drop by from time to time to shoot the breeze. One of his principal duties was to oversee the production process by which the magazine was put to bed late Monday evening via telex to the printing plant in Chicago. Although he later acquired a reputation as a conservative influence on the magazine's editorial policies, mostly we refought the war. Alex died in 1978 after his retirement from *Time*, one possibility for the role of "supervisor"/informant who would no longer be available to my search for the truth.

The National Affairs editor at the time of my investigation and the person who most closely fit the description "supervisor" was Otto Fuerbringer, a tall, handsome graduate of Harvard and the St. Louis *Post-Dispatch*. When I went to work in January, 1946, *Time*'s management was conducting an elimination contest among its wartime staff to pick senior editors to edit the key departments through the next phase of postwar development. Otto Fuerbringer and Ernest Havemann would rotate between the National Affairs section and the back-of-the-book, one week in one place, the next week in the other. It was a nerve-wracking experience for the writers as well as the contestants, as the revolving occupant of the corner office in National Affairs attempted to prove his mettle. Fuerbringer won out and Havemann became a *Life* special correspondent as a consolation prize.

When Henry Luce's wife, Clare, announced her retirement as Congresswoman (as one wrote in that prefeminist age) from Connecticut, the founder, editor in chief and principal stockholder let it be known that he would like to write that story himself. The National Affairs section used to lean over backward to keep Clare Booth Luce's often newsworthy activities out of the book lest we be charged with nepotism. Now that she was leaving the public scene, her husband, the boss, thought it might be time to give Clare her due.

Barely installed in his newly won position of responsibility, Fuerbringer was the one to whom Luce sent down from the 33rd floor his eulogy to Clare. Otto sent the first version back upstairs with suggestions to tone it down a bit. Some might say that took guts; others might say that Otto correctly judged his man. Henry Luce, though a man of strong opinions, was not the type to seek out sycophants. There were several more versions before the final one entitled "Fighting Lady" was permitted to be published in Henry Luce's own creation. Fuerbringer's career at *Time* continued to go forward steadily until he was named managing editor, the top operating post on the editorial staff.

Fuerbringer was an individual of conservative bent and a tough editorial pencil. He reputedly became known as the "Iron Chancellor" when he took over the reins at *Time*, a man feared by the younger writers under his aegis. I never had any trouble with him; when he wanted a piece rewritten, I always found him civil and a person who mustered his reasons logically. But if the FBI conceived of a supervisor as someone breathing down my neck, he could be said to have done that.

Years later I reviewed for the Washington *Post* a book about *Time* which had some cruel things to say about Fuerbringer. Drawing upon my own experience in the review I put in a word in defense of Otto, although I hadn't seen him in years. He wrote me a pleasant note of appreciation. I was on the admissions committee which admitted his son Jonathan to the Columbia Graduate School of Journalism and had the pleasure of instructing the child of a former boss (which is almost but not quite as satisfying as being asked for a job by your former commanding officer).

I doubted from the first that Otto could have been the confidential informant identified as my *"Time* supervisor." It wasn't his style. Even allowing for the fact that FBI reports were a mixture of direct quotes and a summary of the interviews as written up by the special agent who had made the investigation, it was hard to conceive of an experienced writer like Otto reducing his observations to thoughts so crudely expressed as "Kimball is always vitally interested in some sort of social reform and unwaveringly espouses the cause of labor in any dispute regardless of the merits involved in a particular case." And Fuerbringer would have known better in May, 1946, than to describe me as "a capable writer on foreign affairs." As of that date I had not written a line to be edited by Fuerbringer or anyone else on any topic except domestic affairs.

Still, I wanted to see him. As a top management person for so many years he must have been exposed to many such investigations of present and former Time, Inc., employees in connection with government jobs. Perhaps he would recall the scheme of things at that time, and suggest others whom the FBI could have considered my supervisor.

When Fuerbringer retired, after a stint helping to plan new publications such as *Money* magazine, he had been named managing editor of *Horizon*. He had recently left that job when the ownership of the publication changed hands. So, I resorted to my trusty Time–Life Alumni Directory, found his Greenwich, Connecticut, address and dropped him a line. I took a direct approach. I wrote him that I had come into possession of an FBI document which might have been based on an interview with him about me back in 1946. I wanted to talk to him about it.

Otto phoned me back promptly. He said that he didn't think he could help me much, but that he would be glad to meet with me when he came to the city.

It turned out that he was using an office on the sixth floor of a building on Fifth Avenue near 52d Street. Fuerbringer's office—No. 12—was next to last at the end of a corridor lined with offices. I knocked, and he opened. He looked about the same to me—tall, handsome in a square-jawed way, hair now graying, dressed in an expensive-looking, pin-striped suit and wearing a striped regimental tie. He sat behind a desk covered with newspapers and next to a file cabinet. I could see another empty desk in the smallish room and a few chairs lining the walls.

Otto explained that he had rented the place from an ad in *The Times*. The answering voice from the advertised phone number told him nothing was available except a "three-room" office. When he arrived, he found out that meant one room big enough to hold three desks. On my journey down the corridor I had noticed a couple of closetlike rooms with no windows; Otto's place had large windows overlooking Fifth Avenue.

When I asked him what he was up to, he told me he was a magazine consultant and he gave off vibes that he didn't have too much time to waste on nonproductive small talk.

I told Otto I had reached the age when we all begin to think about writing our autobiographies and that was one of the reasons I was bothering him. I asked him if he intended to write his own. He replied that he had lots of notes, but hadn't gotten around to doing anything about them. I gave him a rundown on how I had taken the Foreign Service exams and had even been offered a post.

I related I had recently learned that the FBI had made a security check in connection with my dormant Foreign Service application. An agent had come to talk to my "supervisor" at *Time*. Otto gave no hint of recognition to that. I asked him if he could help me reconstruct who was doing what on the magazine in early 1946.

He recalled at once the free-for-all competition for postwar promotion. He acknowledged my recollection that Ernie Havemann and he had alternated regularly in the slot editing National Affairs. But he said that Tom Griffith had sat in, too, and perhaps Whittaker Chambers and Duncan Norton-Taylor. I couldn't remember all those other guys handling my copy during that time. Finally, in June (the FBI agent, I had already told him, had been around during the last week of May)—he had been promoted to senior editor and put solely in charge of National Affairs.

Otto continued to speak in the most impersonal terms about the unknown informant. He did not seem captivated by the idea of solving the mystery. He threw out suggestions matter-of-factly. He agreed that Chambers was a possibility, but so was Roy Alexander, he suggested. Or Duncan Norton-Taylor, since he had been one of my rotating editors.

I took out the page from my FBI file which covered my life living at the Princeton Club and working for *Time*. Otto noted immediately that the FBI report said I wrote foreign affairs. Then, he concluded that in National Affairs we did write stories involving the State Department, and perhaps that was what the source meant. But he went on to say he found it amusing that someone in 1946 would single out France as a country where there was a growing possibility of Russian dominance; he pooh-poohed the idea in that tone I remembered from the days when, as a senior editor, he and some of his compatriots would tell me why they knew better than the dispatches from the field.

I found myself contradicting him—ridiculous position in the present circumstances—pointing out that this had been during the era when Europe was talking once more about Popular Fronts. He dismissed the person who could propound such an idea the way I remembered he used to dismiss me when I would argue that the Republican Party was not so good for the country as Henry Luce and Otto himself maintained. He made it very believable that he had not been the source of the quotation in my file.

In the first place, he became more specific, he would have remembered. And Otto said he had always made it a practice to tell the fellow involved when the FBI came around inquiring. He remembered that the FBI men he had talked to were never very impressive reporters. He couldn't believe their questions, he said, when the FBI came to him in their security investigation of Jim Keogh, an editor who went to work in the White House for Richard Nixon.

When he read the part that somebody at the Princeton Club had heard me express "leftist" views during the Roosevelt–Willkie presidential campaign in 1940, Otto attributed it as probably coming from a club employee. I thought it strange that he was not familiar with the political jibes of Old Grads toward "traitors to their class" such as F. D. R.

Otto said he was "astounded" over what I had showed him in my file. He said it was hard to believe that the State Department would pay any attention to such stuff—especially since there were so many around in those days who knew better about me. I took that as a compliment, as well as a denial of any complicity.

Otto had warned me that he didn't think he could help me much.

I couldn't blame him, really. The matter was certainly of more crucial interest to me than to someone with problems of his own.

Otto and I shook hands in his austere office and bid good-bye.

It was fascinating to me that Otto would mention Whittaker Chambers. I hadn't remembered having anything to do directly with Chambers, but his place on the masthead above mine might lead an FBI agent to rank him as my "supervisor." Of course, the FBI agent might have written his own version of the conversation. On the other hand, he might have been talking to someone at *Time* who was perhaps a good source, but not necessarily too familiar with me.

I wondered if the informant really was Whittaker Chambers. That ex-Communist turned FBI informer was on the masthead at the time as a senior editor in Foreign News. Summing up an interview with Chambers in his office in the Foreign News section might lead to the natural mistake of referring to me in the FBI report as a "writer on foreign affairs."

Moreover, the "supervisor's" premonition of the gathering cold war in Europe followed by only a couple of months Winston Churchill's famous "Iron Curtain" speech, and it was not unlike that being echoed in the Foreign News section in the summer of 1946. That section was a very early sentinel in the cold war; 1946 was the year Harry Truman fired Henry Wallace out of his Cabinet for making a speech critical of Secretary Byrnes' anti-Soviet policies. History shows that when I was being investigated in the summer of 1946, the first threads of the case against Alger Hiss were starting to unravel within the higher echelons inside the State Department. Chambers, of course, became a key witness in the Hiss case, and before that had been a source tapped frequently by the FBI.

But Foreign News was the preserve of the 29th floor and my office was on the 28th. Chambers and I never traded a word, to my recollection. He was considered something of an oddball around the office. When he went out to lunch with one of his colleagues, he would always take a seat with his back to the wall. He told them he feared the Soviets were going to try to assassinate him. Janet crossed his path when she was working in the Education section and Chambers was editing the back of the book. She complained that he would come to work after a weekend spent on his Maryland farm, where the crucial evidence against Hiss was eventually discovered secreted in a pumpkin, reeking of the manure still caked on his boots.

One insidious aspect of the system by which the government refuses to reveal the identity of the informants in your file is the maddening process of trying to figure out who they might be. It leads you to suspect everyone lest you overlook a clue. There was no way to track down the tantalizing suspicion Fuerbringer had raised. Whittaker Chambers was long since dead.

In the long series of communications to the State Department asking for the release of all the expurgated information in my file, I repeatedly asked the question whether their interpretation of protecting the privacy of informants included the privacy of the dead and gone. No one would ever answer that question. The names of all informants against me as quoted in my security file—whether dead or alive—continued to be withheld. The young man holding all the secrets of my file on his lap—my caseworker Peter Sheils—didn't bat an eyelid when I mentioned the name of Whittaker Chambers. Of course, he hadn't been born when Hiss and Chambers had their famous courtroom confrontation. My burning curiosity was nothing to him, except a possible threat to State Department security 33 years after my original sin.

The meeting with Otto, bland as it had been, drove me to more meticulous measures for trying to figure out the hidden identity of this crucial informant. Though one normally too impatient for puzzles, I began for the first time to count the spaces where the "*Time* supervisor's" name had been blacked out on all the documents and compare them with the number of letters on the names above mine in a 1946 issue of the magazine. Security Scrabble. But I was thwarted by right-hand margins and by my inability to be sure when and if the whole name was used or Mr. Surname. The longest surname on the masthead, Norton-Taylor (13 characters) had been mentioned as a possible suspect by Fuerbringer (11 characters) along with Roy Alexander (13 characters) and Mr. Chambers (12 characters). Most of the spaces seemed to me to be 12—but perhaps they were 13. Maddening for an amateur sleuth, with no gift for this test of skills.

Duncan Norton-Taylor—I had completely forgotten about him

until Otto mentioned his name. A National Affairs writer in 1946, with an office next to Cant's, he was the one whom we all envied because he could bang out cover stories with no more visible effort than as if he were writing letters home. His political views, I recalled, were somewhere to the right of Robert Taft's.

Norton-Taylor went on to become managing editor of *Fortune*, a natural for him. He was retired now, too, living somewhere in Maryland. Perhaps if the riddle were to be solved by laying a ruler along the blacked-out names in my file I had better check out that possibility as well. Yet there had been so little personal contact between us in 1946 or since that no such suspicion would have crossed my mind spontaneously. That was a terrible side effect of this business of confidential informants. It set you wondering about people, the innocent along with the guilty.

I wrote Duncan Norton-Taylor:

Dear Dunc:

Do you remember being interviewed about me by an FBI agent by the name of McCorry in May, 1946? The occasion was when we were working together on *Time* National Affairs, and I had taken the exams for the Foreign Service.

I am in the process of writing a book about those years, and am trying to reconstruct the mood of the era. My chief recollection was the ease with which you knocked off those cover stories and perhaps a few arguments in NA story conferences about the virtues of the CIO.

Saw Otto Fuerbringer the other day in the City and he reminded me of the round-robin arrangement for editing NA until he won the brass ring. They probably hit the 28th on one of your weeks.

I would appreciate it if you can remember anything about the man.

My letter to Norton-Taylor left him ample opportunity to confess. Down there in Oxford, Maryland, wherever that was, Dunc was not, I was sure, any more shy than he ever had been over calling a spade a spade. Within a week, he wrote me his answer:

Dear Penn,

If you say somebody named McCorry interviewed me in May, 1946, then I guess maybe he did. But I haven't any recollection of it, much less anything about such a man.

I wasn't in that round-robin arrangement. I had taken myself out of the contest, choosing to be something called a Senior Writer instead of an editor; I never did edit NA. I edited a short-lived section I think was called Armed Forces during the war (Ed Cerf was one of my writers)—but never NA.

It was all some thirty or more years ago. I'm afraid I can't be of any help.

So Otto Fuerbringer's recollection of the round-robin at *Time* did not square with Dunc Norton-Taylor's. And Dunc's memory that Ed Cerf, off fighting in the Pacific, was one of his writers in a section (not called Armed Forces but Army & Navy) during the war was also incorrect. That was the duty Cerf and I were assigned to take over from Gilbert Cant after V-J Day. Journalists pride themselves on their memories for facts, and over the short term a disciplined mind is remarkable.

But my file included recollections from my hometown neighbors going back to my boyhood and testimony gathered about *PM* before World War II. Now all that testimony had achieved immortality in the documents. Trying to set the record straight three decades after the event ran into the frustrating reality that people's memories fade or become reconstructed over time. In this sense the "history" written in my file is not correctable—ever.

Norton-Taylor's disavowal of a "supervisor's" role in *Time*'s National Affairs department drained me of the energy to search out and contact Ernest G. Havemann. I couldn't picture Havemann, whose hobby was race horses, having an assignation with the FBI. That left no place to go—except for Whittaker Chambers. And I hoped I never ended up where he must be now.

15

THE *TIME* RESEARCHER

IF I COULD BE CORRECT about anything, I felt it could be about the identity of the *Time* researcher who had been the confidential informant quoted for nearly three pages in my file. It was the only portion of all 99 State Department documents where the censor had blotted out the sex of the source. [Pronoun blacked out] must be a woman. Miss Real World's brusque manner, I admitted to myself, did not seem to go with the purr of her flattery as recorded by Special Agent Clare, yet the womanly tone of some of the remarks was, to me, unmistakable. "[Name blacked out] stated that Mr. Kimball was a brilliant writer; that he had an exceptional technique; that he possessed a gift of words and genius for finding the right word at the right place. . . . He was well informed in the labor field, and that it would be extremely difficult to find his equal. [Blank] said that he had a personal charm of great magnetism and that he was persuasive, convincing and presented his ideas with forceful lucidity. [Name blacked out] reluctantly admitted that [blank] distrusted Mr. Kimball's political viewpoint. Within a week after he joined the staff of Time, Inc., he had stamped himself in [blank's] opinion as someone to be carefully watched." That last sentence was another clue. Miss Real World had been tapped by *Time* editors as the resident authority on who could safely be called "pinko" or "red-eyed" in a story.

There were few labor specialists on the research staff of National Affairs, and nearly half of the anonymous deposition dealt with my alleged attitudes toward Joseph Curran and Harry Bridges, heads of the Maritime and Longshoremen unions, respectively; Leo Huberman, the labor editor when I worked on *PM*; and other matters so terrible to mention that five lines had been expurgated from the file document released to me. She was also a stalwart in the anti-Communist caucus of the Guild unit which had viewed the majority of members as agents of Moscow.

> [Name blacked out] explained that at that time the *Time* unit of the New York Newspaper guild was considering a strike against Time, Inc., and that while the more conservative Guild members wished to bargain with the owners along recognized lines, the radical element insisted on a strike regardless of cost. Mr. Kimball joined the strike advocates and was active in attempting to gain the cooperation of the other members to strike. He wrote pamphlets, spoke at meetings and definitely aligned himself with the Communist element.

That was the "strike" that never happened when serious bargaining began in response to the vote by the membership. That was the settlement which was celebrated by red-coated waiters pouring champagne.

This researcher was a woman of strong opinions and total confidence in her own perspectives of the world. And she had a gripe with me. Miss Real World must, at the time of the investigation, have been aware of my complaint to Fuerbringer that she had been making a nuisance of herself. When I read the hatchet job in my file, I was sure who the source was. My suspect, I found out when I inquired, was long gone from *Time*. I determined to track her down. This time it would be my turn to do the checking.

I found an address for Miss Real World in the directory of members of the Time–Life Alumni Society. Janet and I had not belonged before, but joining seemed an easy way to track down some of the characters out of the past who might shed more light on my file. Leafing through the pages was a nostalgic experience besides: there were Otto, Marylois, Paul, Ernie, Dunc, Gilbert. Some, like us, missing: Tom Matthews, who had hired me; Dick Donovan, whose office had been next to mine. Others, lost in the mystery of married names. Still others, sadly, dead and gone. Reliving this short episode of my life, I was struck by what might have been. Suppose I had stayed. Suppose those three who had been interviewed had spoken less harshly of me. It was like reading my own epitaph, out of synch. So much of life was a matter of chance, a decision here, a circumstance there. The *Time* researcher and her companion, the *Time* writer, had been central to Counsel for ACOPS' final decision. All the excellent reports from those who knew me well were

> outweighed by the information which comes from Kimball's present associates on *Time*. . . . The conclusion of the two leading witnesses [Names blacked out], both of *Time*, is the same; it is that while Kimball is not a Communist and while he is extremely able intellectually, he is essentially immature in his political opinions; and this immaturity, coupled with his intellectual skill and ability, push him in the direction which he thinks is "super-liberal", but which ends up with associating himself and his views with Communist-led groups.

Miss Real World had a phone listed at her address, but another female answered the first couple of times I tried to reach her. Miss Real World had a job which kept her pretty busy, I was told. I decided not to leave my name, lest she begin checking around with Gilbert Cant or Otto Fuerbringer. When she finally answered, I gave her a cover explanation—that I was doing research on news magazines after World War II. She was very friendly, but said that making a firm date was difficult. She knew a place near where she worked in the garment center; maybe we could meet there for a drink one afternoon. Could I call her back next week? I asked if she had an office number. No, her home phone number was the best way to reach her.

I tried a couple of times the next week. Once the roommate answered. Once nobody. Strange, I thought. But then I asked myself: why should she be in any hurry to see me? She was an experienced researcher. She must have an inkling of what I was after. Her hesitancy merely confirmed to me my identification of her as Special Agent Clare's confidential source. I could wait.

I decided, however, that when I did reach her, I had better pin her down to a firm date at a convenient place. The Princeton Club would be just right—only a few blocks from Seventh Avenue where she worked, and my turf. (I secretly hoped a couple of stuffy classmates might drop by our table to greet me, the ally of "the Communist element".) When we finally connected, she said she knew where the Princeton Club was. It would be close by her appointment after lunch a few days hence. Noon. In the lobby. (I wondered if my vivid recollection of what she had looked like 33 years ago would serve to identify her now, or for that matter, vice versa.)

To prepare for the encounter, I made a copy of the pages in which testimony from the *Time* researcher had been reported by Clare. I blanked out on the copying machine all the adjacent material, so that Miss Real World's part would stand on its own, with no supporting context. Unlike the data from informants Wechsler and Cant, for this I possessed no independent corroboration confirming the source. I typed her name into the blank space I had created on the document, as though for my own index of my own file. Evilly, I hoped to trap her into the assumption that her name had been revealed. You can see what was happening to me.

Since taking notes was likely to be too threatening, I decided to fall back on a technique I had learned years before in a year as a pollster with Lou Harris. I would pay close and careful attention to everything she said, sit down by myself as soon as possible after our meeting, and then reconstruct in chronological order her part of the conversation on paper. So long as the flow of memory is uninterrupted and written out immediately after an event, such reconstructions are remarkably true to verbatim notes taken on the spot.

I made sure to arrive at the Princeton Club early, taking a seat in the lobby where I had a direct view of the door. I must have watched a hundred persons walk through, without the slightest flicker of resemblance to anyone I had ever seen before. Suddenly, there she was. I would have known her anywhere. The close-cropped hair was gray now. She wore a blue-and-white striped shirt with a gray skirt, tailored and trim. I stood up, and she recognized me instantly, too. We shook hands awkwardly, exchanged pleasantries about our mutual states of preservation and went up in the elevator to the main dining room. Our table was a banquette on the side of the room, and she made a point of taking the place to my right. "The left is my good ear," she explained.

She said she had begun to have ear and throat trouble in 1964. Then her hearing went bad. She retired. "They gave me a very generous settlement."

She mentioned seeing Otto Fuerbringer in Grand Central Station not long ago. She supposed I knew Otto was retired, now, but was occupied cooking up some sort of new magazine. She said she had seen in the paper that I had been appointed a professor at Columbia. Otto had told her about the book review I had done in which I had quarreled with the author's harsh judgment of him.

"Otto always respected you, too," she said, "No matter what. I remember you complained about me once to him and he called me into his office. He said to cool it. You and I, Penn, may have had our differences, but I always had a lot of respect for you. *Time* was full of second-raters and third-raters. Otto would assign me to the young writers to help them along."

We had ordered Bloody Mary's by this time, and the chopped steak. Everything was falling into place nicely. She was practically admitting her role watching over me; she remembered her differences with me without any prompting. I hadn't realized she had been as close to Fuerbringer as she seemed to indicate.

I prompted her to try to remember some more about the old days. "You know I was a Trotskyite," she said, "going back to my days as an organizer for the International Ladies' Garment Workers' Union. I think probably that's where my ear trouble started. I got cuffed around on a picket line up in New Haven. The Commies were as bad as the owners."

When she had gone to work for *Time*, she said, she wrote the State Department for their file of subversive organizations. Then when the magazine wanted to publish anything about fellow-travelers and so forth, she would just check them out against her list. If they belonged to an organization she found on the list, she would tell

Jack Dowd, the libel lawyer, that "left-leaning" or "Red-eyed" was okay.

"I had to fight the Commies in the Guild, too, working on the New York *Post* during the war. They were always screaming about opening up a second front."

Of course, there were people in the Time, Inc., Guild unit who were strictly party-liners, she went on. "Mostly on *Life*. We had a caucus of our own. Gilbert Cant would make the speeches and I would do the research on Robert's Rules of Order, stuff like that.

"But I don't remember exactly about those days. I would have to go back and check my notes. I remember you and Cerf in that office together. I liked Cerf. I contributed money to the education of his kid."

When coffee came, I gave her the three Xeroxed pages from the file. She had confirmed over lunch my every suspicion—an expert on labor, militantly anti-Communist, a list keeper and a watchdog, a self-described antagonist toward my outlook on life back in 1946, a Guild politician working closely with Gilbert Cant, who had already been identified as the other confidential informant among my colleagues at *Time*. Case closed, or about to be closed when I confronted her with the file. Page 1: "A confidential appointment was arranged with [Name blacked out]. [Blank] asked that what [blank] had to say should be held in absolute confidence by the Department." Page 3: "[Name blacked out] maintained that it was [blank] considered and honest opinion that the employment of Mr. Kimball by the Foreign Service would be hazardous to the American Government . . . that it was [blank] conviction that in his present state of mind he was intellectually incapable of adhering with undivided loyalty to the American system of Government."

Her face flushed almost immediately as she began to read. The corners of her mouth twitched. She kept on reading, saying nothing. I watched, watched, watched. Suddenly, she blurted out, "I wasn't even there, you know. When that strike business was going on, I was in Florida."

But it didn't matter whether she had been there or not; she had made it sound as though I had been in favor of a strike because I "became associated with the Communist element."

I said nothing as I watched her follow the testimony in the document all the way to the bottom of the first page. At the top of the second page ("Mr. Kimball has consistently and without exception supported the Communist element, voted for every resolution they proposed, has solicited votes on their behalf, and has battled the conservatives on every issue."), she suddenly looked up at me. Pain was etched into her face, creasing her forehead and stretching her mouth tautly.

"You don't think I had anything to do with this!" she exclaimed. "Why this is terrible. So help me God, it isn't me."

I said nothing, while she went back to reading it through to the end. I had by mistake, I discovered later, included a paragraph at the end from the next witness, Gilbert Cant. Although his name was blacked out, the pronoun obliterated from the preceding testimony had suddenly been restored. But she didn't take notice of the "he's" which appeared instead of the blanks which had eliminated the "she's."

She was in a state. She gave me back the pages of the file, then asked to see it again.

"I want to keep this," she said. "I can't figure it out. Oh, Penn, I might have said things like that in a Guild caucus, or having a couple of drinks with someone. You know, Penn, you and I had our differences. But be an informer to a government agent. Me? Never. I never did anything like that in my life. I spent my whole life fighting against that kind of a state—that KGB stuff.

"I want to get to the bottom of this. Let me keep these papers." (I had picked them up and put them back in my pocket. I said I would send her a copy.) "You know I'm a pretty good researcher. I'll help you get to the bottom of this."

And, then, something else suddenly struck her. What was her name doing on those papers? And what was this investigation all about, anyway?

If she was stonewalling me, I was equally determined to show no quarter. I went over the story, of my applying for the Foreign Service, taking and passing the exams, and then, unbeknownst to me, being investigated and declared a security risk. I bore down on my objections to having something like that hidden away from me in the files all those years, but free to circulate within the government. She could understand, I said, how much it meant to me to clear the record now. I told her about making an appeal to the State Department.

I said the authorities had released to me the name of Eddie Lockett—which was true.

Jimmy Wechsler—also true.

Gilbert Cant—true again, if only by mistake.

And then, uttering her name firmly and confidently—"you!"

The morality of this scenario, which went a step past indexing her name at the top of a page, has given me pause since. I was, of course, fighting to protect my name from considerable past damage, to which I was sure she had contributed. Was it immoral when the prosecutor seeks to trip up a defendant on the stand? Wasn't there a higher interest being served? The trouble with that line of argument was that it merely claimed the end justified the means. How could a college professor live with that? Another price to be charged to the account of that damned file.

I looked her straight in the eye as I repeated her name. The tension, I imagined, must have been nearly unbearable. She had been stripped of her protection. And now this miscreant out of her past was righteously facing her down. What was the use of pretending any longer?

Collapse, she did not. Instead, she protested her innocence even more vehemently. I couldn't believe my ears. She had never talked to a government investigator about me, never. She didn't waver. Did I mind if she talked to Otto to find out what he could recollect? She had never heard the name before of Special Agent Clare.

She said she wanted to go back and see what stories she might have worked on with me in those days. The file had mentioned something about Joe Curran. She couldn't remember exactly. She said she was a Curran fan, herself. "You can see how silly it would be to accuse you of not liking Curran." I didn't follow that logic, but let it go.

"I want you to send me a copy of that file," she insisted. "I want to get to the bottom of this. I swear to you, I never did this to anyone in my life."

She spoke with such feeling that it was difficult to believe she was not telling the truth. At the very least, it was the truth as she remembered it now. Can people blot out reality when its perception is too painful? And yet an incident like that would be likely to stick in one's mind—even for 33 years. Unless there had been too many similar occasions. If the latter, why would she risk such a categorical denial, declaring that she had never in her life spoken to a government investigator about anyone? The lunch was already three hours old. There was little point in pursuing it further. It was her word against my suspicion.

I walked her over to the Time–Life Building, where she had an appointment with a textile firm. I felt emotionally drained, but hastened to write up my notes on the bus ride home.

Could it be, I asked myself, that I had done the same thing to her that the confidential informants and the government had done to me? Guilt by association. Conclusions at second hand. Circumstantial evidence. Biased sources. Had the poison in the file spread into my own head, so that I had leaped to unwarranted conclusions about somebody I didn't happen to like very much? Frightful thought. I had been prepared to record a confession. Instead, my confident expectations had been dashed. More than that, my quarry had fought back so earnestly, so passionately—"So help me God, it isn't me"—that it was impossible for me to believe that a human being could act out such a role so spontaneously, unless it were true.

Who on earth could it be, if not Miss Real World? The maddening thing was that everyone who had ever looked at my file in Washington knew the answer. My case officer in the State Department knew the answer. The members of the Privacy Policy Appeals Board knew the answer. The person who had held up my passport knew the answer. Once I knew the identity of a confidential source, I could persuade a fair-minded person to look at the case against me in the proper context. Wechsler, for what it was worth, had denied the accuracy of the statements attributed to him and cast doubt on the competence of the special agents who had interviewed him. An identified source was there to be judged, even as I was being judged; he could speak to the facts of his true knowledge about me, or about my beliefs, or about the chapter-and-verse of any activity of mine as opposed to the insinuations in the official record. But if I could never be certain of Miss Real World's identity, my defense against her statements would remain irrelevant.

I considered sending her a copy of the document as she had requested, then decided against it. My goal was to repeal the file, not propagate it.

Next morning, Miss Real World was on the phone, not to thank me for lunch, but to offer her own speculations.

16

THE *TIME* WRITER

DURING MY LIFETIME the sin most difficult for me to abide had been hypocrisy. Now I was on a dangerous edge myself. When did confrontation become vindictive? The question was particularly apt when I got to the second "leading witness" whose testimony had been so damaging to me.

That Miss Real World was one of the two "leading witnesses," was only a guess; the name of the other I knew for sure: *Time* writer Gilbert Cant was my National Affairs colleague who had warned the government that I might "turn either way," including toward "outright" Communism. Bureaucratic fatigue had disclosed his identity as well as Jimmy Wechsler's, this time buried within the handwritten notes from which Security Officer Bannerman had composed his final summary to ACOPS.

Cant's testimony about my political unreliability had been particularly noted by the chief security agent of the Department of State. He took pains to point out how a *Time* writer—about whom it could be flatly stated "there is no question as to his Americanism"—had blown the whistle on the *Time* writer under investigation. "He mentioned Mr. Kimball's participation with the leftist movement of the *Time* element of the Newspaper Guild, his sympathy with the Communist side of international questions, and his familiarity with those acknowledged to be Communist party members. [Mr. Cant] . . .

feels that his employment by the United States Government as a Foreign Service officer would be ill-advised; that the danger of Mr. Kimball's making a leap in the wrong direction is ever present."

A fellow employee of comparable rank, working shoulder to shoulder in the same department at the time of the investigation would be a witness worth cross-examining. And I knew his name!

If I succeeded, 33 years later, in persuading the State Department to hold a hearing on this star-chamber verdict, Gilbert Cant might be of paramount importance. If he could now be forced to recant, if you will excuse the expression, I felt it would knock the pins from under the case spelled out in my file. In my dreams of glory as the cross-examiner for my own defense, I could see myself knifing through Cant like the little figure atop a wedding cake, ending with a modest bow to the awe-struck jury.

My animus was less against Cant personally than a system that would permit hearsay from a comparative stranger to brand the unsuspecting innocent a potential traitor—with no opportunity for rebuttal. Someone at some time, I said to myself, should force a showdown over that type of proceeding and remove it as a precedent never to be followed again in the United States of America. By letting slip the name of a confidential source, I dared to hope, the bureaucracy might have undermined some of the sham of claiming to protect the privacy of informants. Let the informant and the accused match credibility before an impartial arbiter. Then let the record show all sides of the case, not just those portions selected at secondhand by a government employee covering his own rear. The protection of human rights should afford nothing less and a good deal more in my own estimation.

I had scarcely known Cant himself, when we worked in the same shop. When his name slipped through the censors of my file, he had retired without ever advancing up the masthead from the rank of contributing editor, the status he and I had shared 33 years before. I noted his byline on a couple of medical stories written for *Look* magazine during its temporary reincarnation. A journeyman journalist continuing to ply his trade.

I tried to locate Gilbert Cant. There was no such listing in the New York City telephone book. Janet and I still had former colleagues at Time, Inc., whom we could call for information about other former colleagues and one of them came up with Gilbert's address on the East Side of Manhattan.

I wrote him an ambiguous letter on Columbia Graduate School of Journalism stationery, saying that I wanted to see him to check out some data of when he and I had worked together at Time, Inc. I explained that I had not been able to find his phone number, noted that he was writing for *Look* and remarked casually that I hoped we might lunch one day when he could spare the time.

When a reasonable period had elapsed with nothing in the mail, I feared the worst. A note from me, out of the blue and vague to the point of flimsiness, was the last thing a Gilbert Cant might expect. It would certainly start him thinking. Undoubtedly, he had put two and two together and was having none of it. I was sure I was in for another frustrating experience in my attempts to retrace the history of the file and to understand key players in it.

Then it came.

Dear Penn:
Your undated note just reached me. You will at once understand why, after a divorce and remarriage, I have an unlisted phone. But why can't the Sch. of Journalism put a phone no. on its letterhead?

I've often wondered what you were up to, but you've moved around so much that whatever my current information told me was already out of date. To trace you through Who's Who, I needed an atlas.

Of course, I'd be delighted to lunch with you, and am free any day except when there's a big medical production or an office lunch. Just give me a ring and we'll set a date.

I may prove to be a dry hole as far as your Time Inc. research is concerned, but if you'll risk that, we can enjoy breaking bread.

allbest,
Gilbert

In the upper-right-hand corner he had typed his unlisted phone number. Friendly enough, from a fellow who had once turned me in as an enemy of the Republic. Had no shadow of that occasion crossed his vision?

I let a decent interval expire before calling the unlisted phone number one Sunday afternoon. A female voice answered. I asked for Gilbert. She asked who was calling, and then left the phone for what seemed to me like ages. She returned to explain that Gilbert was under the weather and unable to come to the phone. Could I leave my own number? Oh, oh, I thought, here we go. I passed on my condolences and swallowed my irritation along with my disappointment. No word from Gilbert the rest of that day, or the next, or the next. Should I call again, or would that betray undue eagerness? I decided to sweat it out.

Finally, "Gilbert Cant here. Sorry, I've had a bout with the flu. Do you know Ho-Ho's, next to the Time–Life Building? Do you like Chinese food? I'm pretty well known there. Say, next Wednesday. About one. See you there. Ta."

On the appointed day I went over in my mind one last time the approach I had worked out. I would say nothing at first about my file. Just keep the conversation going as long as I could through lunch. Perhaps Gilbert would volunteer something. Let him set the stage himself, if he would. That would be the easiest way to reconstruct the whole episode, just as it happened 33 years before, and perhaps he would confirm the identity of the *Time* researcher or the "supervisor" who had also been an informant. Wouldn't it be logical for a visiting special agent to mention others who had been cooperative in case Gilbert felt awkward discussing a colleague behind his back with a government investigator?

In case Gilbert protested innocence, there was a small technical problem about confronting him with the evidence. Since his name had not been officially released to me, the pages containing his testimony continued to show the name of the source blacked out. The passage where his name had been inadvertently revealed was in a summary of the evidence prepared by R. L. Bannerman, a different document. There could be no doubt, but it required a bit of explanation, a putting of pieces together. Not an easy scenario to carry out with a resisting pupil.

I Xeroxed pages 6 and 7 of Document 53, the portion of Special

Agent Daniel H. Clare Jr.'s typewritten report that contained his conversation with [Name blacked out], whose "anti-Communist sentiments" had been "ascertained through [Name blacked out] and others, as well as through an examination of papers relating to the struggle in the New York Newspaper Guild to overcome the dominance of the Communists." I masked out the testimony immediately preceding Cant's so that it showed up as a white space on the top third of page 6. There I typed "Testimony of Gilbert Cant" as a heading over the two paragraphs that followed. The next page completed Cant's testimony, then continued with other informants. On that page, I left in the paragraph immediately following Cant's testimony but eliminated the remainder from the Xerox copy. The extra paragraph was the vote of confidence from James Linen, publisher of *Time*, a touch which I hoped might trigger a flush of shame from Cant as well as adding a note of authenticity to the presentation.

Doctoring the document again—an old Communist trick, I said to myself. But I was actually changing nothing from the copy of Document 53 in my file, merely focusing attention on the relevant parts. And this time I was identifying the blacked-out source on the basis of solid evidence in my possession. If pressed, I was willing to admit the circumstances which had prompted me to add the heading: "Testimony of Gilbert Cant." Wasn't I entitled to add headings to my own file of my own file?

My internal struggle over this question, I thought, illustrated the insidious nature of the whole business. Here was I, the wronged victim, feeling defensive about my efforts to try to flush out a principal confidential informant who had cast doubt on my loyalty to the United States of America. On the sly. With barely a qualm. Now that I had my first chance to fight back—33 years after the secret blow—here was Penn Kimball, feeling guilty over taking unfair advantage.

Armed with my paper weapon folded neatly in my inside coat pocket, I set out for Ho-Ho's. Arriving at Sixth Avenue and 48th Street, I saw pickets strung along at intervals down the block, across the entrance to the Time–Life Building and the restaurant next door. The ultimate irony, I thought with dismay. The Old Guildsman, whose belief in trade unionism had exposed me to all this trouble in the first place, who prided himself still on never crossing a picket line, was about to find himself shut off by his principles from the prospective scene of his own vindication. I was sure a picket line wouldn't faze Gilbert Cant in 1979; but if he were already inside, it would be dreadfully awkward to try to reach him by phone and lure him to another rendezvous. And it would shatter the chummy, casual reunion I had pictured would disarm my quarry. What to do?

As I drew close enough to read the picket signs, my apprehension dissolved. "Time Magazine Unfair to Aesthetic Realism" was the message. "Stop Press Suppression of Eli Siegel" said another being carried by a well-dressed and polite young man. He pressed a leaflet into my hand, explaining how 132 men had changed from homosexuality through study of Aesthetic Realism's philosophy of the mind. I wasn't sure that I fully grasped the issue, but it was clear that the controversy did not include Ho-Ho's. I passed under the marquee and into the restaurant without a twinge.

Not having laid eyes on Gilbert Cant either for 33 years, I wasn't dead sure I would recognize him. There was a shortish man with gray hair standing by the door. I walked up to him and said, "Penn Kimball." With a startled look he waved me on to the reservation desk, apparently thinking I had mistaken him for the maître d'. I pressed on, feeling sheepish. Catching the attention of the head-waiter, I asked "Do you know Mr. Gilbert Cant when you see him?" Sure enough, Gilbert had not made an idle boast. The maître d' replied, "Yes, indeed, he's waiting for you over at the bar," and pointed to a long alcove to the left of the door.

I turned and spotted a bantamlike figure with a black mustache and close-cropped hair, now wholly gray, coming forward to greet me. Gilbert was already drinking a martini on the rocks and, although I was due at a faculty meeting after lunch, I ordered the same. There are some priorities in life. He apologized for our having to wait for a table. He had forgotten it was Wednesday, matinee day, and had neglected to phone ahead. He assured me we would have a table soon since he had "practically supported the place" when he had worked next door.

I had worried about getting a conversation going, picking up after 33 years, especially since he had forewarned me that he might be a "dry hole" as far as my interest in the past at Time, Inc., was concerned. I needn't have worried.

Over the first drink, Gilbert filled me in about his children, about his second marriage, about trying unsuccessfully to swear off smoking, about his prostate operation, about waiting an hour and a half for a doctor's appointment that morning and taking a cab ride to keep our luncheon date through so much traffic that it had cost him five bucks. (I made a mental note to pick up the check.) Only cabdrivers in Chicago, he went on, ever seemed to pick up on his British accent.

How come? I asked, to keep the sluice gates open. Why do you want to know? he replied, eying me with what I conceived to be suspicion. I was about to remind him that I had gone to university in Britain, hoping I was not seeming to express too much curiosity, too early. I needn't have worried about that either.

Gilbert rattled on, uninhibitedly. He had been born a bastard, he said, the son of a Spanish Jew and an English mother from the Midlands. When he was 19, he had gone to Bermuda to work on a newspaper there. He did such a good job revamping the paper, Gilbert explained, that the boss got worried and fired him.

Gilbert came to New York in the 1930s and landed another job there with the London *Daily Express*. I'm 69 now, he allowed. Things didn't work out with the *Express* either, so he took a job at the New York *Post* working as an assistant to Ed Hunter on the foreign desk.

Ed Hunter had been mentioned in my file as a "reliable" informant who had been approached by a State Department security agent to make "discreet" inquiries about my activities in the New York Newspaper Guild. I supposed that this reliable informant might have passed on the investigating agent to Cant, his former assistant and colleague in the "anti-Communist" caucus at the *Post*.

Poor Ed Hunter, Gilbert said. He died not long ago. "Completely off his rocker. He ended up a complete reactionary, somewhere to the right of MacArthur. Too bad. Ed and I were close friends, working together on the *Post* against the Commies in the Guild."

"You know the old cry," Gilbert continued, " 'How can you tell a Commie?' Well, the saying goes, if it looks like a duck, waddles like a duck, quacks like a duck, then it's a duck." Gilbert chuckled and took a swig from his martini.

"The Commies, there's no other word for them, were in complete control of the New York Guild in those days. I ran for President of the New York local in 1940 as the candidate of the anti-Communist caucus." (I had no recollection of that. Gilbert, in any event, conducted his recitation without indicating any awareness of my existence before joining *Time* in 1946. I must confess I had been equally oblivious to his prewar union career.)

"I found out later," Gilbert declared, still wrapped up in his own soliloquy, "that I won that election on the ballots. The Commies stole the election. They just stole it.

"After that I was sort of the titular leader—hind-titular leader, Harry Truman once described the place of the party's defeated candidate for President—of the anti-Communist cause."

Somewhere during this monologue, carried on with very little prompting from me, we were shown to our table and ordered a second drink. Faculty meeting be damned. What a prelude to producing the document burning a hole in my pocket! I had decided beforehand that I would wait until dessert, coffee or whatever before revealing the true nature of my mission. Find out as much as I could about the star witness in my case before the confrontation. It was like writing a play and then waiting for the final scene to write itself.

Gilbert poured water into his martini, asking forgiveness for the barbarous gesture. The prostate, you know. The light at the table from a lamp on the wall was Chinese-restaurant dim, a low pink. When I finally give him my file, he won't be able to read it, the terrible thought struck. What an absurd climax that would be. I lost the thread of the autobiography for a few moments while I contemplated the alternatives. With the glasses he was toying with as he talked, I decided, Gilbert might just be able to make out the typed documents.

I suggested to Gilbert that he order for us both and was relieved to observe that he could read the menu without difficulty. He picked a hot soup, not too much spice, please; lobster with snow peas, and tea, jasmine, please. With relief, I tuned back in.

Gilbert was describing a book he had written on naval warfare. Ed Hunter had goaded him into it. It was in galleys on Pearl Harbor Day. He quickly made a few revisions and got it out fast. Years later, he said, he had received protests from scholars who felt they had been misled by the title: "The U.S. Navy in World War II." The book ended at the battle of Midway; researchers decades later, finding it in the card catalogues, expected to find a definitive account of the Navy for 1941–45. They felt cheated, Gilbert said. Who could have foreseen that?

The book helped him get his job on *Time*. *Time* used it as a reference constantly, Gilbert explained, and someone had said to Roy Alexander, who was in charge of the magazine's war coverage, why not hire the author? Alexander sent an invitation to lunch. Gilbert said he called back and told Alexander's secretary he worked until 3 p.m. and would be glad to stop by after work.

"That flabbergasted them at *Time*. You were supposed to drop everything and come running. Nobody ever turned down an invitation to lunch. Well, I finally did have an interview with Alexander and Dana Tasker. Lots of chitchat, you know those things. Finally, Tasker said 'Why don't we do what we came for? Why don't we hire this guy?' And that's how I became Army & Navy editor for *Time* all through the war."

Army & Navy—the job in which Cerf and I had, unknowingly, replaced Cant when we were first hired. If Cant's nose had been out of joint when Cerf and I were assigned his wartime territory, the incident was gone from the recollections of the man talking to me across the table.

Now Gilbert was telling about shipping overseas as a war correspondent for *Time* on the same boat taking Marine Officer Joseph R. McCarthy to the South Pacific. Gilbert and another correspondent shared a cabin in officers' quarters. McCarthy was in a bay below with 20 other Marines shipping out and had a big footlocker marked "Office Supplies." It was full of booze. Gilbert found McCarthy much more interesting than his fellow correspondent and said he spent the voyage helping him use up his office supplies.

When the ship crossed the Equator, Gilbert recalled, all hands went through the usual hazing ritual. Somehow, McCarthy slipped and broke his ankle. Gilbert had gone to commiserate with him in sickbay and was the first to autograph McCarthy's cast.

"Joe and I were good friends. I stayed in his tent at Guadalcanal.

I was with the 43rd Division when it captured Munda airstrip. Joe's squadron was one of the first to fly off that strip. You know when I was at Munda, Jack Kennedy's PT boat squadron was based on the island. I found out about that and had it all arranged to take a trip with the squadron, but at the last minute I had to cancel out. That was the very trip when Jack's boat went down. I was supposed to be on that trip. I didn't know how to swim then. Missing that trip saved my life. How's that for irony?"

How's that for irony? I, too, had been on Munda at the same time as Joe McCarthy and Jack Kennedy. I, too, drank from Joe McCarthy's "Office Supplies," played poker with him and listened to his plans for postwar politics. I went for Sunday rides on the PT boats in Jack Kennedy's squadron. Gilbert and I never knew each other well enough at the office at *Time* to trade war stories and discover such coincidences. Even now, I didn't mention the coincidences to Gilbert. There weren't that many pauses in any case.

"Joe and I remained friends after the war," Gilbert went on. "He got me tickets in the Senators' family gallery when I took my wife and kids to Washington.

"When he was running against LaFollette in Wisconsin, I remembered his telling me about a scheme he had to send a postcard from the Marines to everybody in his hometown. I went to see Fuerbringer and said, 'Don't underestimate this guy.' Otto, all 6 foot 4 of him, stood up, looked down at me and pooh-poohed the idea that McCarthy had a chance. *Time* knew better, but they found out."

(How's that for irony? Otto assigned me to write the story of McCarthy's 1946 senatorial campaign for the National Affairs section. He never mentioned that Gilbert knew the candidate personally. Assigned to me instead of Gilbert.)

"When Joe made that speech in Wheeling about Communists in the State Department, that finished him with me. It was a moral issue as far as I was concerned. I just couldn't stomach that sort of thing."

I could scarcely believe that this was confidential informant Gilbert Cant testifying—but this was 1979 and in the pink light of Ho-Ho's the past might take on a different look.

"I think I can say that I had a lot to do with bringing Joe McCarthy down. I tipped off the *Milwaukee Journal* on the stuff I knew about Joe—how he had put in for a purple heart for breaking his ankle during the initiation rite going across the Equator, waiting until his squadron commanding officer was missing in action to put through the papers. When I visited him in Washington, I could see that he was in the hands of the real estate lobby and the mink-farm interests in Wisconsin. And then that Wheeling thing was just too much. McCarthy had to go."

Kimball and McCarthy, the Republic saved from each by the identical informant: Gilbert Cant. I swallowed a slug of tea. We were nearly done with our lobster and snow peas. It was almost time to get to my own item on the agenda.

Gilbert brought the lunch back in focus. We hadn't come to hear so much about him, he ventured modestly. What was it I hoped to find out about *Time*?

"I don't know that I can help you much," he warned again. "I never gossip about people. Just not interested in gossip, or people either for that matter. Ideas are what interest me. Always have."

I started by asking him to help me reconstruct what he might remember about *Time* in 1946 and Newspaper Guild affairs there at that time. He recalled that there had been a strike vote. Bread-and-butter issues, as he remembered it. He had supported the strike vote then, he said. Always knew *Time* was trying to break the Guild and keep the commercial employees from joining, he went on. He later became chairman of the *Time* Guild unit himself. Still belonged to the Guild, although since retirement he was a little behind in his dues, he feared.

Lots of Commies in the *Time* Guild unit, he recalled, mostly on *Life* and *Fortune*, although he did remember a "blonde bitch of a researcher who used to crank out Commie propaganda on the mimeo machine. I went into the head researcher and told her never to assign that woman any more stories with me."

(Who could that have been? I thought to myself, ashamed to think that I had complained similarly about Miss Real World, although on quite different grounds.)

Gilbert was saying he found it hard to conjure up the past, though he remembered Janet. "Both beautiful and bright," he recalled. "Are you still married?" Thirty-two years, I said. We had lunched at Tavern-on-the-Green to celebrate just 10 days before. "How nice," said Gilbert. He said he was usually shy these days when it came to asking friends about their marriages. Please convey his best to Janet.

Gilbert was obviously running down and the matinee crowd had left the restaurant. When he had excused himself to go to the men's room during lunch, I had slipped the two pages from my file out of my pocket and balanced it between my knee and the tablecloth. When the time came, I wouldn't have to fumble for it.

The time had come.

I told Gilbert I had brought along something I wanted him to read. I passed it over to him without further comment. He put on his glasses and started to read. I watched him like a hawk as he read to the bottom of the first page. "At this point [Name blacked out] feels that Mr. Kimball is at the cross roads of his political development; that he is completely confused and that his viewpoint is still dominated by his immaturity and his desire to be known as an ultra-liberal. He can turn either way, [Name blacked out] believes."

His face betrayed nothing for the first minute he scanned the copy of the file. Then, he looked up. "What's this got to do with me? Why are you giving me this? Who is this being quoted here?"

I thought he was going to stonewall it.

"Gilbert," I said, "that's you. That's you talking about me." There was an endless interval of silence. Then, "Oh, yes. Some fellow did come in to ask about you. Something like that only happened to me twice. I get the occasions mixed up. Now I remember. Tall guy, with an impassive face."

Gilbert turned to the next page and read the rest of the sentence which had begun "He can turn either way, [Name blacked out] believes, either to outright Communism or towards a more balanced liberal viewpoint. Regardless of the fact that Mr. Kimball is not a Communist party member, [Name blacked out] feels that his employment by the United States Government as a Foreign Service Officer would be ill-advised; that the danger of Mr. Kimball's making a leap in the wrong direction is ever present, and that until he has straightened out his political philosophy he would be in danger of permitting his Communist sympathies to overpower his fundamental

Americanism. [Name blacked out] stated that he could not recommend Mr. Kimball for the position involved, even though he recognized his suitability in every particular except that of political loyalty."

What was he thinking now as his eyes passed over these next words while sitting across the table from an old colleague out of the past who had just picked up the luncheon check? I had anticipated feelings of pure exhilaration when I confronted Cant with his moment of truth. Instead, I found myself torn by compassion for his predicament.

"Look, Gilbert," I said lamely, "I didn't get you here just to hassle you about this."

He shook his head, morosely I thought. "I'm shaken. I'll admit that. You've just hung an albatross around my neck. I won't be able to think of anything else for the rest of the day."

Then he seemed to gather himself. He took the pages in his hand again, flipping them over once more.

"I hope you don't believe I said all those things about your political loyalty. That's just some clunk who doesn't understand what somebody means who talks about an idea such as Jeffersonian democracy and throws in his own interpretations. I thought somebody representing himself as an investigator from the State Department would be a cut above the average cop. I was obviously talking over his head."

He took his pen and started to edit the copy like a professional deskman, crossing out words here ("he is completely confused") and a phrase there ("his viewpoint is still dominated by his immaturity") and, finally, the whole paragraph dealing with the dangers of my "Communist sympathies" and "making a leap in the wrong direction." He handed the edited version to me with the air of a person who had officially corrected the record.

I suppose there should have been some satisfaction in Gilbert's denial that he had ever made the accusations he had crossed out on the copy of my file. I wasn't sure what the State Department, which had made such an issue of his testimony in 1946, would say about such a declaration in 1979.

The trouble was, things weren't as simple as crossing out a few lines in my security file. That document had been kicking around the government for 33 years—without Cant's edits.

I'm afraid I never thought through exactly how I might handle the moment when, at long last, I had the opportunity to confront an informant with his own admission. There was no flush of satisfaction. Watching Gilbert Cant—age 69, author, journalist—deflate was only sad. If my file had become an albatross to this informant, it now weighed still heavier on me. Not only did the heap of documents represent me to be a person I did not recognize, but the actions it engendered in me were making me a stranger to myself.

I bid Gilbert a polite good-bye and returned, late, for the faculty meeting.

17

AFTERMATH

WITH THE CONFRONTATION of Gilbert Cant, my hope to really understand even a few of the mostly nameless villains in my file came to an end as final as had all attempts to correct the file itself. I failed to find in my accusers the sheer meanness of spirit that would have been the simplest explanation of their past behavior. True, Jimmy Wechsler, Miss Real World and Gilbert Cant—perhaps the "*Time* supervisor" too, whoever he was—had been among that group of bitter anti-Communists whose single-minded passion damaged so many. But my accusers seemed now to be rather ordinary, even pathetic, and if their protestations of innocence had moved me to see them with compassion, the experience had also blurred for me the distinction between hypocrisy and self-delusion. Worse, I was treated to a view of myself, an elderly professor handing on the torch of idealism to new generations of journalists, scheming to entrap my victims. I didn't like that view of myself. From this low point, I looked again at my own life.

Perhaps the state of a person's mind is not only none of the State Department's business, but is also beyond inquiry, even to the person whose mind it is. But a person can at least look over what he has done with his life, and see how he likes that. The verdict is, I like it fine; and I don't like the fact that the government took no note whatsoever of the best years of all.

The years between my job at *The Times* and my acceptance of a teaching post at Columbia University were among the most exciting of my life. By the time the FBI launched operation COMINFIL I had left not only the Guild but my job at *The Times*, to join the staff of the experimental television program "Omnibus." Watching national conventions—I had the only TV set on the block during the election year of 1952—had whetted my curiosity about the new field of television. Robert Saudek, the producer of "Omnibus," was looking for a professional newsman to help write and produce fact pieces on the show. My name was suggested to him; he called me up, and I became a member of the TV–Radio Workshop of the Ford Foundation for the upcoming 1954–55 season.

Television at the time was locked into a format of 30-minute shows, minus commercials for which the program had to be interrupted in midstream, come hell or high water. "Omnibus" introduced the revolutionary idea of letting each segment run as long as it was worth, putting the commercials in only where natural breaks occurred in the continuity. Some segments ran only a few minutes, others more than an hour. But each was allowed to play out without a commercial break. This unaccustomed independence was the result of another experimental aspect of "Omnibus"—a private grant.

The Ford Foundation put up sufficient front money to pay the staff of the TV–Radio Workshop, buy 26 weeks of air time—one and one-half hours each Sunday afternoon—from the CBS network and underwrite the costs of production. "Omnibus" then went out and found its own sponsors, selling commercial time in the same way that magazines sell their ad pages. The idea was to free the program from stifling control by either network brass or advertising agencies. The idea worked; the creative juices flowed. I was delighted.

Many on the staff, like me, came to "Omnibus" with little or no television experience. They applied their dramatic or journalistic abilities to program ideas without worrying over the mysterious technology. Saudek hired the best directors around on a free-lance basis, and network cameramen and technicians fought to be assigned to the show. The creative staff thought up ideas, approaches to programs, casting innovations, whatever came into their heads that might make exciting use of a powerful new instrument of communication. It was educational television in its purest sense.

The show was put on live. Videotape, the technological break-through which made it possible for TV to retire to production stages in Hollywood, work over the product and dub in the laughs, had not been perfected. New York in the early 1950s was still an important TV production center with its reservoir of writers and actors trained on the stage. The talent was eager for exposure on the new medium, especially on a show with high standards of artistic excellence, and "Omnibus" had the pick of the best young artists in town.

Saudek hired his own panel of house critics—a professor of communications and a magazine drama critic, among others—who watched each Sunday's broadcast and then fired off their reactions to be circulated among the staff. The whole staff assembled in his office on a regular schedule to brainstorm together. We had 26 weeks to get things rolling for the upcoming season, then we worked seven days a week once the program started on the air—rehearsing next Sunday's show and simultaneously working up ideas for the next month. Everybody went into the studio on Sunday, setting up for the final dress rehearsal at 1 p.m. The show went on the network, live, at 4:30. The dress rehearsal was always a shambles. Then the on-air production through some mystical process went just fine. I still thrill to the recollection of the "Omnibus" musical theme and sunburst logo coming up on the monitor in the control room. It was show business, stop the presses, historic moment, all wrapped into one.

"Omnibus" introduced Alistair Cooke, then American cor-respondent for the *Manchester Guardian*, to the network audience as the urbane, erudite, British-accented host of the show. It was a dar-ing departure, although it is commonplace now to watch Alistair introduce "'Masterpiece Theatre" on public television.

Another "Omnibus" innovation the season I worked there was the idea of having Leonard Bernstein explain about music while conducting the National Symphony Orchestra. In the middle of a Beethoven symphony, Bernstein stopped the music, walked down-stage baton in hand, and explained to the audience the meaning of the music that had just been played and how to appreciate a great composer like Beethoven. As he lectured, he would turn and conduct the orchestra for a few bars to illustrate his points. He made a career out of that idea in the years that followed.

"Omnibus" that season hired Madison Square Garden for a skating exhibition and commentary by Olympic champion Dick Button, thus launching another TV career which is still going. Although broadcasting live from locations remote from the studio was a relatively untested art, "Omnibus" went to the scene as often as it could. It showed for the first time Harry Winston's diamond cutter in his own shop in the act of splitting a million-dollar gem. We put a camera aboard the locomotive of the Twentieth Century and beamed back the engineer's story as he pulled out of Grand Central and went roaring up the Hudson.

Shooting documentaries live on location was fraught with its own perils. I suggested and wrote a segment to be broadcast from Long Island from the underground air command for the Eastern Seaboard, at that time the heart of the air defense for the largest city in the nation. Trained in radar in the Marines, I was familiar with the process by which aircraft were tracked on a huge, lighted, transparent board. The commanding general was away on assignment, but scheduled to return on the Sunday we were to go on the air. So we rehearsed the show without him, figuring he could just be himself when the red light went on above the camera.

Our director was Don Hewitt, later to achieve fame as director for the Nixon–Kennedy TV debate and producer of "Sixty Minutes," another direct descendant of the magazine format originated by "Omnibus." Don and I worked together all week to block out the show, run through the script with the personnel in the underground command showing the viewers what would happen if there were an air attack on New York City. Everything was ready for when the principal character in the show would arrive in person to be fitted into the part reserved for the Defense Commander. He flew in on Sunday morning, right on schedule. Air time was now only hours away and Hewitt and I were ready and waiting. When the general opened his mouth, both of us were ready to commit suicide. He spoke with a lisp you couldn't cut with a knife. Hewitt and I went frantically back to the drawing board. The Defense Commander was suddenly transformed into a tall, remote figure, dramatically stationed on the bridge, peering at the raging battle on the radar board like a silent sentinel from on high. His mike was dead.

For another "Omnibus" episode, drawing on my political background, I wrote a treatment for a play about a young man who sets out to reform politics by running for Governor, but gets caught up in the hard realities of interest-group pressures and party bickering. I could write the story out of my head from my experience watching Chester Bowles transformed from a crusading knight on a white charger into an officeholder appointing local judges on the basis of their standing with party wheels. I called my opus: "Clean Fresh Breeze."

"Omnibus" hired a well-known writer to take my treatment and convert it into a dramatic script, but my collaborator kept hunting for inspiration at the bottoms of bottles. One day he fell down the stairs of his apartment and had to be hospitalized with a broken hip. It was only two weeks to air time. Overnight I became a dramatist. The show went on, beautifully played, I thought, by the young actors in the principal roles—Richard Kiley (who later made *Man of La Mancha* his personal triumph), Eva Marie Saint (star of *Waterfront*) and E. G. Marshall (Mr. Television among actors of our time). That was the way "Omnibus" did things.

The ratings were respectable for a time slot in the Sunday afternoon ghetto, though not sensational. But if you were filling up the tank in Buffalo and told the station attendant you worked for "Omnibus," he would tell you how much he enjoyed the program. Like the readers of *PM*, the viewers of "Omnibus" possessed a loyalty with an intensity that has endured through the years. And like *PM*, "Omnibus" spawned ideas that were picked up and imitated by the orthodox communication enterprises that did not dare to experiment on their own. Television spectaculars, the magazine format, historical recreation, musical education, sports commentary by experts, Alistair Cooke in an armchair—they all trace their roots to "Omnibus." The program, furthermore, was aired within the format of commercial TV, an example of a quality network production which fulfilled some of broadcasting's deeper responsibilities to the public.

Writing of such fond recollections made the picture of me inside my file seem all the more distorted. My exciting days as a young reporter on *PM* had turned to dross when perceived through the filters of bitter informants. The thrill of returning to civilian life as a writer for *Time* had been quashed by disgruntled associates. My glorious times at "Omnibus" never existed at all as far as the official records in Washington ever revealed. The government selected only those parts of my life that suited its purposes—a fragment here, a fragment there, assembled by narrow or craven strangers. The Penn Kimball in the file was strange to me, like some prehistoric specimen of an unknown species frozen in time.

THE 1954–55 SEASON was just drawing to a close when my phone at the TV–Radio Workshop rang one day. It was Paul Smith, an old wartime buddy. I had known Paul, who had been the boy-wonder editor of the San Francisco *Chronicle*, since I was stationed at the Marine training base in Quantico, Virginia. A cocky redhead, Smith was at that time stationed in Washington as chief of Navy public relations. He shared a huge house on Massachusetts Avenue with a cadre of other officers, including Frank Rounds, my old friend from Princeton and *United States News* who was then a Navy Officer and on Smith's staff. Although I was only a Marine private at the time, Rounds invited me to a couple of Saturday night parties along with the admirals and generals. As the evenings wore on, I used to poke the wearers of the gold braid in the chest and explain how they were fouling up the war. Luckily for me, they didn't seem to pay attention.

Smith and I had some long talks about the future of the press after the war, and he used to ask me what I thought of the Marine Corps. I must have laid it on pretty thick, because the next thing I knew he had resigned his cushy Washington post and signed up with the Marines. I never saw him again during the war, but he became an infantry platoon leader in some rough campaigns. He went back to the *Chronicle* after V-J day.

I was still working at *The Times* in the spring of '54 when Smith called to tell me he had just arrived in town to become a twelfth vice president of the Crowell-Collier Publishing Company. He reminded me of our wartime talks. "Get ready," he said. "It will take me about a year to get on top of this outfit. Then I expect you to come aboard to carry out some of those big ideas." I was working on the final shows of the "Omnibus" season a year later when my phone rang again—right on schedule. Paul had become president and chief executive officer of Crowell-Collier. He was ready to move ahead with our old bull-session ideas. *Collier's* magazine needed an infusion of bright ideas. Would I be ready to start June 1?

I had turned 39 the previous October, and I remember thinking about approaching 40, a milestone in anyone's life. Behind me already was a batch of publications, a stint in politics, a short flight in show biz. A rolling stone. My longest job anywhere had been just short of four years in the Marine Corps. Exciting times all, I had to admit. Innovative. Even my job with David Lawrence had entailed launching *United States News* in a new magazine format. A half-dozen starts on the ground floor of promising career opportunities (not counting my abortive connection with the Foreign Service). But it was time, perhaps, to settle down somewhere long enough to make something of myself.

Leaving the fast-developing medium of television to enter the employ of a troubled general magazine was like quitting the automobile business to take a job in a bicycle factory. But Smith was bubbling with enthusiasm for upgrading his firm's editorial product, and talked of buying, when that corner was turned, some broadcasting stations himself. He was assembling talent for *Collier's* from his old *Chronicle* crowd—Pierre Salinger, Bob O'Brien, Dick Trezyvant —plus promising youngsters such as Peter Maas, Raymond Price, Leonard Gross, to beef up an existing stable of able writers such as Bill Davidson, Cornelius Ryan and Vance Packard. My *New Republic* colleague, Theodore H. White, was also coming aboard. Smith planned on installing his own set of top editors to chart a new course on *Collier's*, once one of the great names of American magazine tradition. And he intended to liberate the editors already there— Gordon Manning, David Maness, Jerry Korn, Diana Hirsh—from the stultifying restrictions imposed by the old regime.

The old management at the parent company had starved the editorial budgets of its onetime prime properties—*Collier's*, *Woman's Home Companion*, *American*—while passing out the profits in the form of handsome dividends to stockholders. New entries into the magazine market such as *Life* and *Look* had been quicker to exploit the possibilities of photojournalism and a growing appetite among readers for information and interpretation. All magazines relied on advertising to pay production costs; the selling price was never enough to pay for paper, ink and printing. But TV was soaking up advertising budgets formerly divvied up among magazines. The ad agencies accomplished this reallocation by purchasing space only in the leading magazines and lopping off those third or fourth in their field. *Saturday Evening Post* was still a giant that looked like it would live and prosper forever. *Life* had proved to be a publishing miracle. *Look*, at first a pallid imitation of *Life*, suddenly began to take off, pushing *Collier's* down into fourth place in circulation—lopping-off country.

But Smith had discovered that Crowell-Collier's encyclopedia division was still a gold mine throwing off a cash flow in contrast to the ailing magazines. A former financial writer, he sounded very convincing when he spoke of "hypothecating the assets." In financial-center parlance, that meant pledging the robust future profits from the encyclopedias as security for funds to invest right away in improving the magazines. In addition, Smith was prepared to go public with a stock issue on the American Stock Exchange and to raise additional working capital by borrowing against paper convertible into stock at an attractive price. Stock options would be available for distribution to those valuable employees who came aboard the rocket ship.

Opportunity beckoned: a senior editorship on *Collier's*, at a raise in pay once again; a chance to be a policy-maker on a publication venture dedicated to excellence; a piece of the action in a communications enterprise aiming for a multimedia future—magazines, books, broadcast stations, newspapers, the works; a boss from the Marine old-boy network who had taken a New York corporation by storm in a year; colleagues drawn from the cream of the profession. I couldn't wait.

The year and one-half I was a senior editor at *Collier's* was the best job in my life. I enjoyed every minute of it, with the exception of the last. Paul Smith had a big apartment at 1 East End Avenue, with a smashing view of the East River, and the core group of editors would gather there in the evenings and talk over where we wanted to go with the magazine. Paul was open to ideas, brimming with both enthusiasm and confidence, and seemed to be that rare combination of a publisher whose heart was with the editorial floor but whose head understood the arcane arts of finance and profit-and-loss statements. The financial problems of Crowell-Collier turned out to be monumental, but Paul sounded as if he knew what he was doing. He would throw a lunch in the dining room attached to the test kitchen for *Woman's Home Companion* and invite us to sit down alongside the big stockholders on the board of directors. Paul would tell the board how great we all were. It felt fine.

Collier's, once the voice of muckrakers like Lincoln Steffens and Ida Tarbell, had become stodgy and conservative, heavy with second-rate fiction. The magazine looked as if photojournalism and color printing had never been invented. At the very least, we felt, *Collier's* had to anticipate trends in news, entertainment, life styles, politics, sports, education, health—information and interpretation, well written and attractively displayed, to satisfy growing appetites for actuality relevant to its audience's day-to-day concerns. Escape could be effectively furnished to bigger audiences by television. Our aim was to convince advertisers that there was a deeper involvement between readers and the printed word, especially when they felt a personal relationship with the character of a magazine which came into their home to stay awhile.

Under the old management, *Collier's* had cheapened its former reputation and character with gimmicks, stunts and sensationalism in a vain attempt to stem circulation slippage. That had not only alienated faithful readers, but communicated the smell of death to Madison Avenue. What they needed was some sign that the magazines on their media schedules were communicating with readers who cared. The vital sign of life in the eyes of the advertising fraternity was how well the magazine moved over the counter. We learned an important lesson about what sort of cover made a browser pick up a magazine from the newsstand and buy it almost by accident. Struck by the success of Walter Lord's book on the sinking of the Titanic, the San Francisco contingent had ordered up an article recreating the historic earthquake and fire in their old home town. It was a fine piece, rich with authentic detail, but the question was: would it make a cover, and if so, what sort of a cover? Len Jossell, our talented art director, came up with an old woodcut of the

San Francisco Fire. It was a beautiful and simple work of art, in russet hues. The issue did famously on the newsstands.

The point was that the cover outside expressed perfectly the story inside, an episode of disaster in a Victorian setting. The passing buyers had been drawn to expect exactly what they found—dramatic history, recreated in detail, exactly as it happened. We began billboarding our covers with inviting descriptions of other features to be found inside, a time-honored function of newspaper headlines but up to then rarely used in general magazines.

Newspapers were gray and television in those days was mostly black-and-white. Magazines could pick up and orchestrate popular interests and present them attractively in full color. Jossell and the article editors would sit down together to lay out an issue, as opposed to the system on many general magazines where responsibility was divided and the art staff would fill up the holes with their own concepts of appropriate illustrations. Some facts were best reported with photographs. White space—mortally feared by newspaper editors—could add drama and ease of reading to the printed word. When the art director and an articles editor sat down together to focus on the main ideas in a story, the creative result was often better than that which either might have come up with on his own. And new color presses in the company-owned plant could produce smashing effects.

When the ocean liner *Andrea Doria* went down after a collision with the *Stockholm*, Cornelius Ryan was rushed to interview survivors, and Ryan's story and an aerial photo of the sinking made the very next issue of *Collier's*. The newsstand sale was phenomenal.

Collier's worked out an arrangement with Howell Conant, a gifted photographer who enjoyed exclusive access to the inner sanctum inhabited by Grace Kelly, the beautiful Princess of Monaco. Grace Kelly was the incarnation of the American Dream, male and female alike, but had very special feelings for her personal privacy. Conant was a professional with perfect taste and exquisite skill. The combination was dynamite. Grace Kelly on the cover and Conant's photo series of Grace Kelly's private world sold sensationally, too.

Arthur Schlesinger came by with the manuscript of his new book on Roosevelt. I bought the rights to a chapter on the spot (forgiving him temporarily for the phone call he had made about me to Benton, which was not mentioned between us). I asked Jossell to dig out from the files the famous picture of Roosevelt in a fedora riding in an open car on the streets of New York with his cigarette holder sticking jauntily in the air. We planned to run it as a cover in January to coincide with F. D. R.'s birthday. On the working editorial floors there was a growing feeling of excitement. We could feel the product moving. Three out of four issues in November and early December had outsold both *Life* and *Look* on the newsstands. The book was catching on.

The esprit of the editorial staff was as high as winning the World Series. (As editor for sports, as well as entertainment and politics, I received a free ticket to the 1956 game in which Don Larsen pitched a perfect no-hitter for the Yankees, the first in Series history. I regarded it as an omen.) Smith was full of plans to take Crowell-Collier into television as soon as he succeeded in turning the magazine around. TV news would whet appetites for information it lacked the air time to supply. We were to ride the wave of the future, launch the age of the multimedia conglomerate.

But there were developing problems. Smith seemed to be spending more and more of his own time working out new financial arrangements. He had already had to close down *American* magazine, the weakest in advertising of the Crowell-Collier three, to conserve resources for *Woman's Home Companion* and *Collier's*. The word from Wall Street was that they considered the redhead from the West Coast too big for his britches. Although Crowell-Collier stock did go public—and Smith dazzled the hired hands with promises of generous options down the line—Smith was forced to go to a Chicago group headed by Patrick Lanan, who had made millions taking over the Chicago/Milwaukee Railroad, for working cash. The company gave out debentures to the group with the privilege of conversion into stock at a very cheap price and Lanan was given a place on the Crowell-Collier board. In addition, Smith reported that he had assembled a package of radio and television stations and was only a million or two short of swinging the deal. The broadcasting outlets, he explained, would produce an instant cash flow which would tide the magazine over until next year's advertising schedules came through.

We knew, hoped, prayed, that Smith could bring off his financial juggling act to keep the team alive. We were working together smoothly, enjoying the kicks from the big play. In our joy over the newsstand averages, however, we underestimated one basic fact of life. Without generous support from advertising—all of which had been pledged the year previously when the magazine was at its lowest point—the more copies *Collier's* was selling, the bigger its losses. The magazine could claim a circulation in excess of 4 million, but readers weren't paying the freight for the additional production and distribution costs. Thanks to a crazy, upside-down logic, we had been cutting our own throats.

The decade ahead would mark the end, or the beginning of the end, not only for the Crowell-Collier magazines, but for the seemingly unassailable leaders—*Saturday Evening Post, Look, Life*. They all had millions of readers, but TV could deliver even more millions at a better cost-per-million. The general magazine was giving way to the specialty magazine, appealing to readers with particular interests and advertisers with products catering to those readers. We had been, without realizing it, living on the knife edge of revolutionary changes in mass communications.

When it came, the collapse of *Collier's* in December, 1956, came quickly. (Janet and I felt fated to spend our Christmases in dire financial straits.) The news from Paul Smith's office suddenly turned bearish. While he was still trying to get cash for the television deal, a majority of the board of directors insisted that Smith staunch the flow of the company's assets to cover the huge magazine losses. Stripped of its periodicals, Crowell-Collier was a viable book company with such valuable assets as its favorable lease on our Fifth Avenue headquarters and its printing plant in Ohio. The Lanan crowd that had bought the debentures with favorable stock options was in a position to call its loans, take over the company, liquidate the magazine assets and greatly increase the value of their stock.

The last days of *Collier's* reaffirmed every instinct I ever possessed about the importance of sound collective bargaining for the best interests of the rank and file who work for the mass media. That idea was translated with scorn in my file when I was characterized as one who "unwaveringly espouses the cause of labor in any dispute." The State Department had never been able—had never even tried—to separate my own attitudes from the stew of ideologies that inflamed the Guild in its early years. There were no unions on the editorial floors of Crowell-Collier; here was a test in which, undressed of Guild politics, anyone might have seen the naked purpose of my actions. Yet the saga of *Collier's* is a part of my life which was ignored by government investigators. The ending was sad, but I want to tell the story because I am proud of the effort I made and believe my role in that crisis to be a better measure of what to expect of me than the peculiar indicators our government uses.

The collapse of *Collier's* approached a state of anarchy. When the senior editors held a council of war to assess the situation, it was decided to set up a staff committee headed by Theodore White and me. Teddy thought that he knew where some money might be raised to take over the magazines and continue publishing them. He took charge of what the staff committee characterized as Operation Save. In the event that White's efforts should fail, I was designated to take charge of what the staff committee called Operation Fold. Operation Fold was concerned with the very serious question of the fate of the company's thousands of employees who would suddenly be thrown on the streets. Without editorial unions, pay scales for secretaries and filing clerks had been kept miserably low. The pension plan was not only inadequate, but it was not funded. In the event of a financial reorganization there would be no money to pay pensions, even to those already retired. Operation Fold couldn't be expected to do much for those of us who had taken the gamble with *Collier's* with our eyes wide open, but it was all that those who had spent a lifetime in the company had going for them.

The most severe threat hanging over the corporation, one which might ruin things for all parties, was bankruptcy. To ward off the creditors soon enough to avert bankruptcy, the board of directors might have to move precipitously. I knew from my Guild experience that it would be critical to be in communication with top management, whoever that might be, in the weeks to come. I went to Paul Smith. He was a beleaguered man, his whole scheme tumbling around his ears, but he was totally sympathetic to the idea of trying to salvage something out of the wreckage to tide over the rank-and-file employees. We made an agreement that if the time came that

Smith found himself in the bunker, he, while still president and chief executive officer of Crowell-Collier, would let a committee of employee representatives into a meeting of the board of directors, even if it were the last one over which he was permitted to preside.

Thus Operation Fold became operative in a hurry. We sent a note one afternoon in to Smith, who was in seemingly perpetual session in the boardroom, telling him that the employees' committee was standing by in the corridor. His reply came out: continue to stand by. As night approached, Smith invited us in. He sat haggard at one end and Lanan at the other of a table heaped with papers, half-eaten sandwiches, cold cups of coffee. In our salad days we had been invited to that same boardroom to dazzle the directors with our bright ideas. Some of the same faces were there, not quite looking us in the eye. Patrick Lanan looked us in the eye with the steely glint of a shark. Smith introduced us, as he had promised us he would. I made our pitch about the responsibilities of management to the widows and orphans of pensioners, to aging men and women who had given a lifetime of loyal service and now would be too old to land another job and, with just a show of oldtime Guild bargaining, warned that Crowell-Collier's future management should think twice before giving a group of highly skilled, articulate communicators reason to spread the angry word to the marketplace that Crowell-Collier had not done right by its employees. The shark's eye did not shed a tear, nor even blink. But Lanan said that if it came to that, the board would be willing to sit down for one last meeting with a group from the staff. We were not at all sure that it would do any good, but at least we had a foot in the door.

Lanan and the board voted one Friday afternoon to kill the magazines. There was not even a notice posted on the bulletin board. Telegrams went out over the weekend to all but a handful of employees to tell them to come in on Monday to clean out their desks.

Operation Fold needed immediate help, and the help we needed most was that of a good lawyer. We called upon General Telford Taylor, a prosecutor at the Nuremberg trials, an adjunct professor at Columbia Law and a liberal author in his own right. General Taylor and his firm came up with a handle for negotiating with management. Since Smith had voluntarily awarded severance settlements following Guild patterns when he closed down *American* magazine, the employees on *Collier's* and *Woman's Home Companion* had a "reasonable expectation" to be treated the same when and if the same thing happened to the other two magazines. They had continued their employment under that implied contract. Lawyer talk, but it sounded plausible. To proceed toward a court case the lawyers had to be authorized to represent Crowell-Collier employees and, if the case were ever prosecuted successfully, the lawyers would have to be reimbursed for their time and expense. We needed to obtain a signed form from at least a majority. This meant the equivalent of a Labor Board election among traditionally nonunion, white-collar workers in the corporation.

I remember Diana Hirsh, officially senior editor and unofficially a sort of earth mother within the organization, taking me from floor to floor to vouch for me before crowds gathered in the office bullpens. I would stand on a desk and explain what would be needed if they ever hoped to see a red cent from their erstwhile superiors. The state of anarchy in which the corporation was changing hands helped us to ride circuit throughout the building. There was no one representing management to order us out. Sympathetic employees emptied their files to provide research for the lawyers' brief, and payroll turned over the complete list of corporate personnel.

We rounded up all the manuscripts we had bought from outside authors, and made sure that checks went out immediately in full payment. I called Arthur Schlesinger's agent and told him that the check was on the way, and asked him whether it was okay to send the excerpt from the book on Roosevelt over to *Esquire*, which had expressed interest in the article when I had told them about it. *Esquire* did indeed publish what was to have been the January cover story for *Collier's* and paid Schlesinger all over again. I thought I might receive a note. Still waiting.

Backed by affidavits and an argument fashioned in law, General Taylor accompanied the rest of the high command of Operation Fold to one last meeting in the Crowell-Collier boardroom. Lanan did not attend; he was represented by Wilton D. Cole, whom he had brought in to be the new operating head of the company. Cole heard the General out politely. The corporation intended to honor the pensions of those already in retirement. It was in the process of completing a satisfactory settlement with the printing unions in Springfield. As for those laid off upon the demise of the magazines, sorry.

We all cleared out of our offices before Christmas, but not before the usual last rites attended by the visiting press. For a few years the alumni around New York City would gather every year on the anniversary and drink a toast to the great days on *Collier's*. That petered out pretty soon. I have students now who never heard of *Collier's*, much less "Omnibus," much less *PM*. Where have all the flowers gone?

While the staff dispersed to look for jobs, Operation Fold carried on with our lawyers toward a court test of Crowell-Collier's position. I recruited as complainant Eleanor McAvoy, a secretary who had devoted over 30 years to the service of the company: *Eleanor McAvoy et al vs. Crowell-Collier, Inc.* Eleanor looked like the gray-haired mother in the ads for All-American baking goods: Irish, churchgoing, with a sweet smile. The most profitable division left in the truncated corporation was Collier's Encyclopedia, sold largely door to door, directly to the public. Many of the potential purchasers were housewives who were the spitting image of Eleanor McAvoy. When the case reached court, it promised to be a media event, with every covering reporter a sentimentalist over the disappearance of a publication he had been brought up on. It was not hard to imagine Eleanor McAvoy on the stand, holding a handkerchief in her clenched fingers, occasionally wiping a tear as she told the jury how she had been thrown out into the winter streets without so much as a nickel. Crowell-Collier, on second thought, allowed as how they might be willing to dicker.

The week before the scheduled beginning of the trial, a settlement was reached—the laid-off employees received on average about a week's severance for each year of service with the company. The total came to $750,000. As we left Crowell-Collier's office with our lawyers, I thought to myself, that's the most money I ever expect to earn in one day. It wasn't much compared to the millions realized by Lanan's group. Crowell-Collier merged into Macmillan. Time, Inc., picked up the package of radio and television stations which Smith had put together and just missed financing; in a couple of years they earned more in a single year than *Time*, *Life*, *Fortune* and *Sports Illustrated* put together.

Paul Smith suffered a stroke and ended his days penniless in a Veterans Hospital in Palo Alto. I paid him a surprise visit one day several years later with Pete Steffens, Lincoln Steffens' son who was teaching journalism at Berkeley. We walked together through a huge ward of paraplegics, a depressing experience, to a bed in the corner where a wan figure with graying reddish hair was flat on his back. Pete called out to him. Smith propped himself up painfully on the elbow of his working side. When he caught sight of me, his face broke into a crooked grin. "What in the hell are you doing here, Kimball," cracked Smith, "looking for your severance pay?"

If the best year of my life failed to draw attention from Washington, so did the next year, 1957, but the respite was brief. I had continued to work on my PhD since taking on the *Times* job, but at Columbia University in New York City instead of at Yale, and part time at night instead of as a full-time day student. In the course of my studies, I had run across and admired a book on public opinion research in politics by Louis Harris, a junior member of the firm of Elmo Roper Associates.

What Harris had to say about voters' attitudes toward politics made total sense to me in the context of my own exposure. As political editor at *Collier's*, I sought Harris out to test whether the science of public opinion surveys and the art of political reporting might not be suited to magazines. Harris turned out to be a frustrated newspaper reporter, having worked on the North Carolina *Tarheel* while in college. Although he could handle a sliderule, the meaning of numbers fascinated him more than bare statistics. He liked to play with the data, he said, until he could see the numbers dance. Roper, and his archrival George Gallup, delivered their reports mostly in the form of long sets of tables, with a minimum of interpretation. Harris thought the ratio should be reversed. The trained analyst was most qualified to draw the significant conclusions, and if the methodology was reliable, shouldn't be afraid to stick his neck out, said Harris. He had tested that approach with some of the Roper organization clients —a West Coast brewery, a private power company, a cigarette manufacturer—and they had liked and used his reports.

Lou insisted on doing part of the polling himself whenever he was to write up the results. He had a marvelous way of disappearing into the woodwork while respondents went on and on. He took me with him on a few scouting expeditions and taught me one thing reporters seem never to learn: if the questioner will only shut up, it is the respondent who feels the social pressure of silence and will fill the void. Some reporters end up interviewing themselves with their introductory remarks and leading questions. Lou would ask the touchy question—and wait.

Harris was also a politics buff. The Roper firm did private political surveys such as the one I knew about from Bowles' campaign, and Lou worked on several, but the senior principal insisted on dealing with the clients personally. He was thinking about leaving Roper and striking out on his own.

We talked about the potential of television for reporting elections more swiftly and accurately than the old methods of collecting voting returns that sometimes left the issue in doubt for days after the event. The election was over the moment that the polls were closed, and all the suspense was created by the long count of the ballots. I remembered the night in 1948 when the group at Bowles' house had waited until after midnight for the trend in his favor to be certified, and had pooh-poohed the thought that Harry Truman might be carrying the country. To sit with John Bailey on election night in Connecticut was a different experience. He would phone for the results from Torrington; Torrington was a swing district which usually went with the eventual statewide winner. He would compare the Democratic plurality from Hartford County with the Republican plurality from Fairfield County and predict within a whisker the popular vote in the whole state. Politicians like Bailey were simply human computers, programmed to understand voting trends from long experience watching the returns.

Harris knew how to refine the process more accurately: Democratic strongholds behaved that way because they were in the South, or heavy with Polish-American voters, or Jews, or factory workers or blacks. Republican strongholds behaved that way because they were in the Middle West, or heavy with Swedish-American voters, or Protestants, or farmers or suburbanites. By finding election precincts that reflected such factors, by establishing the percentages of their votes for either party in past elections, then finding out as soon as the polls had closed how the votes had gone this year, Harris could tell instantly on election night how American voters in key precincts were conforming to their norms. Seeing the possibilities for television —it's all so routine now that it's hard to realize such "projections" were ever invented—I was fascinated. Harris and I tested the idea in November, 1956, on the ABC network with a scoresheet for the viewers in that week's issue of *Collier's*.

When Lou Harris finally did go out on his own as Louis Harris & Associates, he asked me if I would like to try my hand as his partner in the public-opinion survey business. I agreed to give it a trial for a year. Our first project together was to design a study under the sponsorship of the Maxwell School of Public Affairs at Syracuse, New York, to try to figure out which factors led to success for Americans working overseas. Lou and I went to Mexico to conduct pilot interviews there among American personnel at the embassy and at General Motors and Du Pont plants, public health employees of the Rockefeller Foundation and a United Nations mission. It was the first time I had been outside the country since the war, but no passport was required, so the trip was never logged in the State Department files.

Lou and I conducted our interviewing in March and then sent for our wives to join us in Mexico City for a week in April. That was a vacation I was to hear about years later.

My job with Lou took me to the tenements of Altoona, Pennsylvania, the neighborhoods of Rockford, Illinois, and the watery lawns of Portland, Oregon. (We had a beer client there and I learned that in Oregon you couldn't just ring a doorbell and ask which brand was preferred; the place was full of teetotalers.) I distributed test packages of baby shampoo in the process of finding out that adults liked the one without any tears. We had a few political clients, and Theodore Sorensen came to call to see if the firm would be interested in doing some work for Senator John F. Kennedy come next year. I rather liked private business, and the political polling was exciting. Lou had formal partnership papers drawn up which would probably have made me rich, if not famous. My name was not to be included in the name of the firm. Proud and foolish Yankee, I moved on.

But I hadn't the stomach to look around for a new permanent job—the fourth in four years. A full-time job for me was anyway not possible if I were to complete my PhD. I had run out of courses which could be taken at night. I needed a job where I could earn a living and still make time for daylight classes.

THUS IT WAS that I was "at liberty" once more when Averell Harriman, a liberal Governor and presidential aspirant, asked me to help out with his 1958 campaign for re-election. The offer stirred in me the beginnings of a plan for my future.

At 42, I was out of work, with a brilliant future behind me. A good prospect for all sorts of political staff operations—excellent education, here and abroad, broad journalistic experience, a recent polling expert, past administrative aide to a Governor and U.S. Senator. I had seen academics move easily in and out of their posts to participate in politics and government. The next presidential election was only two years off; the Democrats seemed due. If I could finish my PhD, I might find for myself an academic perch from which I might take flights into politics as occasions arose.

Harriman, then a vigorous 66, invited me to lunch with him at his elegant townhouse on East 81st Street. We dined alone on light lunches served on TV tables. He wanted another hand to work with him on his television and press relations for the campaign, since his regular staff would be tied up at the Capitol in Albany. There was tension, too, between the regular organization headed by Carmine DeSapio and the reform Democrats led by Senator Herbert Lehman and Eleanor Roosevelt. There was something to be said for an out-of-stater, although he dangled the prospect of a post in Albany if, as expected, he were re-elected. I mentioned my desire for time off to take courses at Columbia, and we struck a deal.

The Republican candidate, a newcomer to elective politics, was Nelson A. Rockefeller. Rockefeller had been coordinator for Latin America for Roosevelt and a foreign policy adviser to President Dwight Eisenhower. He came out swinging from the start. He hired Pat Weaver, former president of NBC, to produce his TV commercials. Rockefeller, carefully rehearsed, would stroll around a book-lined study, perch himself on the corner of a desk and talk heart to heart with the people.

In contrast to Rockefeller's slick commercials, produced with the new and expensive methodology of tape which had the look and feel of a live broadcast, the older, stiff and aristocratic Harriman stuck mostly to film. The trade unions were contributing most of the Democratic commercials, and film was what they were used to. They also favored political broadcasts in which the union leader played a prominent role. Mike Quill of the Transport Workers Union would roar his head off at the audience while Harriman stared at the camera like a zombie transfixed.

One day Rockefeller went on a tour of New York City's Lower East Side, territory on which no Rockefeller had set foot before. *The Times* assigned one of its ace reporters, Ira Henry Freeman, to follow him around, as Rockefeller cruised in and out of delis, gnawing on lox and knishes. I had known Ira on *The Times*. He told me later that in his story that day of the millionaire Rockefeller trying to mingle with the poor he imagined he had been writing satire. He picked up snatches of dialect as the East Siders commented on the way the visitor from uptown mishandled blintzes and the paucity of the tip he left behind. Freeman felt it was devastating. Instead, the piece converted Rockefeller overnight from a rich outsider into a folksy human being, not too proud to rub elbows with the masses. The *Daily News* began fondly calling him "Rocky" in its headlines.

Things seemed to go from bad to worse in this popularity contest. Averell Harriman, after a lifetime of public service, was stung to hear himself accused of harboring criminals, bankrupting the state treasury, capitulating to the denizens of Tammany Hall. Harriman had never mastered the trick of fending off a reporter's needle. Invariably, the lines would deepen on the patrician countenance, the painful struggle with words would begin (half caused by almost total concentration, half by almost total shyness), and the reporter would have his quote for the day. This old-fashioned instinct for saying what was on his mind—not what more sophisticated advisers thought might better serve the occasion—cost Harriman dearly. There was no guile to the man in an era of beguilingness.

The Rockefeller family philanthropy in behalf of black and Jewish charities raised problems within those traditionally Democratic ethnic groups; these and other traditional supporters of the liberal Democrats in New York State began to defect. At a press conference seven days before the election, Harriman took a fatal stumble. In answer to a New York *Post* reporter's planted question, he criticized the Eisenhower–Dulles policy in the Middle East as a "change from Truman's strong support of Israel to one of appeasement of Nasser and the Kremlin." The reporter closed in to ask if the Governor believed Mr. Rockefeller had had a hand in shaping that policy.

"As far as I know," Mr. Harriman's reply was quoted in *The Times*, "Mr. Rockefeller was in the White House when we supported Nasser and the Arab nations." Almost the same exchange was repeated live over radio on the Barry Gray show only four days before the election.

The final blow fell on Election Day eve: the Big Switch by the New York *Post*. Its editor was James A. Wechsler, my fellow reporter at *PM*, and the FBI's old informant who had worried so about the state of my mind. We had reason to be grateful to Jimmy, since he had written the editorial endorsing Harriman for Governor over Rockefeller.

Jimmy Wechsler deserved sympathy, working as he did under the direction of the paper's unpredictable owner, Dorothy Schiff. Dolly Schiff, who shed editors with almost as much regularity as she shed husbands, was susceptible to crushes, and Nelson Rockefeller was still young and dashing compared to Ave. "Lovable Nelson Rockefeller" she had described him only a week earlier in her "Dear Reader" column, and had gone on to discuss "his very attractive personality and amazingly liberal views." But Wechsler had prevailed with this publisher who was not averse to asserting her prerogatives. Five days before the election, the regular editorial page of Mrs. Schiff's paper announced: "We favor Harriman's reelection."

The first inkling at Harriman campaign headquarters that the paper had changed its mind about our candidate came late in the afternoon of election eve.

The polls were scheduled to open in less than 18 hours. The last television show had been taped the day before; the last scheduled speaking engagement had been filled. The morning had brought a clammy mixture of snow and rain. Another person might have pulled a chair up in front of a blazing fire, poured himself a drink and prayed for continued snow in upstate Republican strongholds.

309

Not Harriman. When, around noon, the weather broke slightly, he had sent word for the sound truck, called for the leaflet corps, the press car and his own "Number One" Cadillac to assemble outside the library at 42d Street and Fifth Avenue. "We'll go as long as the weather holds out," snapped the Governor, "no use wasting time around here," and he took off down the avenue with those long, loping strides that left men half his age gasping for breath.

"We'll make for Union Square and then Queens," said the Governor, signaling the motorcade to follow while he proceeded on foot. I peeled off at that point.

Back in the warmth of my office in Room 831 of the Hotel Shelton I gazed out the window into the murk of a raw November twilight. The phone on my desk rang.

"I'm calling from the New York *Post*," a hushed voice said. "I've got something important to tell you. Forget who this is, or I'm likely to get canned. Now listen. The publisher has ordered the presses stopped. The *Post* is withdrawing its support of Harriman. That's all I can tell you, but it's for real. We thought you ought to know."

The paper's Election Day editorial read:

To *Post* Readers:

Govenor Harriman's recent snide insinuation that Nelson Rockefeller is pro-Arab and anti-Israel should not be condoned by any fair-minded person. Rockefeller, far from being anti-Israel, has been a liberal contributor to the United Jewish Appeal for a 12-year period. It is deplorable but true that in political campaigns lower echelons on both sides indulge in vile demogoguery. But when the head of the ticket repeats such libels, he should be punished by the voters. If you agree with me, do not vote for Averell Harriman tomorrow.

Dorothy Schiff

The effect on me was like the feeling I remembered having once when, as a student in Europe, I saw a frenzied mob suddenly turn on an old man watching a political demonstration in Vienna. For apparently no reason, the young toughs in the crowd had begun pushing and beating the old man, and when he fell to the pavement, a shouting girl from the pack had kicked him in the stomach, then spat. I had stood frozen by the monstrous sight, unbelieving, temporarily detached from the scene by some inner block which refused to concede that what I was watching was really there.

When the blow fell on Averell Harriman, still campaigning in Queens, the *Herald-Tribune* reported, "the Governor appeared stunned, and had difficulty in making immediate comment."

I had retired from New York politics by the time Dolly's version of the switch appeared the Friday after the votes were counted. "Overwhelmed for inspiration," she wrote, "I looked at the large portrait of my forceful, outspoken grandfather, Jacob H. Schiff, hanging opposite my desk. I was sure I knew what he would have done. . . ." Editor James A. Wechsler added his own postscript:

"I voted for Harriman. To all those who have called, wired or written to inquire about the editor's whereabouts in these difficult moments, the answer is that he is at his desk, and that what the *Post* stands for in the battle for decency, justice and freedom is as clear today as it was a week ago."

The battle for "decency, justice and freedom" seemed in bad shape even in 1958, as I stood back from Harriman's defeat and wondered about my propensity for backing the right causes and the bruises that entailed.

To me, what I have stood for seems obvious—and innocent. I admit to optimism. I always thought the next experiment in journalism or the next liberal political campaign would reach more people with better answers than what had come before. I still think an individual like me can do some good in the world. That such do-gooders, however cynically one might view their efforts, should be perceived with suspicion as to their subversive potential remains alarming to me. Even more alarming is the subjective nature of such judgments. For in the end, the qualities that marked me for suspicion within the State Department singled me out for attention from the CIA as well—but in an entirely different way.

AT JUST THIS POINT in my life, the fall of 1958, a dozen years after the assembling of my original files in the State Department and the FBI, a brand-new file on SUBJECT: Penn Townsend Kimball was aborning—this time within the Central Intelligence Agency. The first hint to me that such a file even existed was a covering letter among my FBI documents dated May, 1959, and attached to an updated summary of my case that included a rehash of the FBI's 1955 COMINFIL report on *The New York Times* and other reports. The covering letter was from J. Edgar Hoover to Colonel Sheffield Edwards, director of security of the Central Intelligence Agency. (Edwards later headed the CIA task force formed to plan the assassination of Castro.) Everything in that letter was blacked out except one sentence: "There are enclosed two copies of a memorandum containing information regarding Penn Townsend Kimball." The FBI contends still that it cannot reveal the contents of Hoover's letter without CIA permission. The CIA claims the exchange between Hoover and Edwards about me a quarter of a century ago is still unreleasable on the ground of national security. But I have since discovered that the request for an FBI update originated with the CIA, which had begun its own investigation of me just prior to Election Day in 1958.

On the Columbia campus to attend a class one afternoon that fall some weeks before Election Day, I ran into Edward W. Barrett, whom I had last seen when I was executive secretary for Senator William Benton and Barrett had been Assistant Secretary of State for Public Affairs. Barrett was now a recently appointed dean of the Graduate School of Journalism. We had been comrades in arms in Washington in the battle for right and justice. Barrett asked me what I was up to and invited me to drop around when the election was over.

When I wrote him a note in November, 1958, saying that I had single-handedly stemmed the national Democratic tide inside New York State, he invited me to his office. He said he could use a hand helping him teach a course in news magazine writing and needed a co-author for a piece on press coverage of Latin America he had been commissioned to write for the American Assembly, the Columbia-sponsored think-tank founded by Dwight Eisenhower when he was president of Columbia and which met at Arden House, Averell Harriman's former family estate.

I arrived at Columbia at an age, 43, when it is said individuals should begin to reconcile themselves to the realities of what they are actually going to achieve in life. I had tasted the full range of exciting media innovations—on newspapers, magazines and television. I had intensively shared the power centers of politics. I felt capable and ready to hold down a position of top responsibility in any of these spheres, but too many such opportunities had been dashed by forces beyond my control. These ventures had made me something of a rolling stone—spoiled perhaps by too many choices in my tender years. I needed time to regather my aspirations.

In May, 1959, I was nominated to a full professorship at the Graduate School of Journalism. That May was, it turned out, the very month J. Edgar Hoover wrote the mystery memo to Colonel Sheffield Edwards.

When I called up the Freedom of Information section in the FBI to discuss Hoover's letter, the agent who answered explained that only the CIA could declassify it.

"I shouldn't tell you this," he went on, apparently looking at an unexpurgated copy of the document on his own desk, "but the memo involved references to CIA operations about which the bureau had previously been informed. This information involves methods by which the CIA obtained information about you, something which you would immediately recognize if it were disclosed to you. And since the method is still used by the CIA, the CIA insists that it be classified."

Not only did the letter that let me know the CIA had been messing into my life remain classified, but it was only as this book was in its final stages, in the summer of 1982, that I received any clues from the CIA itself. Meanwhile, I did not know in what context my activities had been monitored, when the inquiry had begun—or even whether it had ended. This was perhaps the most astounding revelation in my file. What methods was the CIA using to collect information in which my name might have cropped up? Wiretaps? Opening mail? Imagine my being the topic of a letter from J. Edgar Hoover himself to Colonel Edwards, director of spooks for the whole CIA!

18

A VISIT FROM THE COMPANY

I WROTE TO Admiral Stansfield Turner, director of the Central Intelligence Agency in Washington, D.C., on May 29, 1979. A year had passed since my FBI file had revealed to me the CIA's unexplained entry into my life, and so far the FBI had not been cleared to show me what J. Edgar Hoover and Colonel Sheffield Edwards had had to say to one another about Penn Townsend Kimball 20 years before. I asked specifically for that memo. Because it had dawned on me that State and FBI are not necessarily privy to everything the CIA is up to, I also requested from the CIA any other files they might be holding indexed under my name.

The story that came to light was by far the most bizarre turn in my case, and the least amusing. But the CIA seemed determined to keep me in suspense. The elapsed time came to three years, two months and six days from my May 29, 1979, letter to Admiral Turner, who was long gone from the post before this final plain brown wrapper arrived on August 6, 1982.

June 12, 1979: "We are processing your request and will provide you with the results as soon as possible."

September 13, 1979: "One of our most heavily backlogged components has indicated that there are approximately 998 cases ahead of yours. . . . requests currently being processed by the Agency number in excess of 2400 . . ."

May 13, 1980: "Please be assured that we are continuing to process your request. . . . requests currently being processed by the Agency number in excess of 2800, which has resulted in significant processing backlogs."

And on July 3, 1980:

> We have checked our records and find that your request was indeed received one year ago. It was promptly sent to the various components for a file search. . . . To date, three of the components have reported finding no record, one has located records and one—our most heavily backlogged unit—has not yet reported. Until such time as this last unit has reported, we cannot respond to your request. We cannot say how soon that will be, since there is no way of knowing how many previous requesters are in that backlog ahead of you, or how complex some of those requests are. . . . We regret that we cannot respond more promptly, but we are constrained by circumstances beyond our control.

The picture of the CIA paralyzed by backlogs so deep that it didn't even know what was going on in its own shop might have brought solace to the KGB. Of course, I had already provided them with the name and number of at least the one specific document which required no search whatsoever.

> If we may refer to the FBI document which you say that we have refused to process. . . . We informed the FBI that our information was not releasable. . . . We did not refuse to process that document.

Then on July 22, 1980:

> In reviewing your request file, we note that your original 29 May 1979 request to this Agency enclosed a copy of a document previously released to you by the Federal Bureau of Investigation. Although not specifically stated, your letter made it apparent that your intent was to appeal the determination

of this Agency to deny portions of that FBI document. We apologize for not having recognized your intent earlier, and will now proceed with the processing of your appeals of the denials in this one document. . . .

The remainder of your 29 May letter requested a copy of any documents which might be indexed or maintained by this Agency under your name. This portion of your request will be processed as an appeal based upon the lack of a timely response, and will be placed in our backlog queue for processing at the earliest possible time. As you may be aware, we have a backlog of about 400 appeals. . . .

Just in time for the New Year, I received a small packet from the State Department and a covering letter dated December 24, 1981—Christmas Eve.

The letter informed me that three documents that had originated with the State Department had been located by the CIA. Two had to be forwarded to—I could hardly believe it—the Privacy staff for "final determination regarding release of this information." One of these, what's more, had to be cleared by the FBI as well. A third document enclosed originated in the Office of Passport Services.

This initial result of CIA sleuthing turned out to be requests from or to the department's Office of Passport Services, most of which I had seen before. A REFUSAL form had been filed under my name by the chief of the Passport Office on August 2, 1951, when Senator Joseph R. McCarthy's witch hunt was in full cry. Under "Reason for refusal" the form stated: "Subject of security report. Check SY files before granting passport facilities." There it had slumbered for 12 years until I sought to embark on my first postwar trip overseas, thus explaining that passport delay in the year of my Balliol reunion. There was also a new item of intelligence.

In 1967, I had participated in the Salzburg Seminar in American Studies in Austria. At the time I applied for a passport to make the trip, a document now returned to me showed that Francis G. Knight, director of the Passport Office, had written a letter to a Mr. A. P. Flynn, Deputy Director Plans, Central Intelligence Agency.

Dear Sir:

The Passport Office would be interested in any information of a security nature which may come to your attention
concerning the individuals mentioned in the attached memoranda.

Enclosures: 14 Memos

The request, dated January 13, 1967, gave no hint of what, if
anything, the 14 individuals had in common. Perhaps it is routine for
the Passport Office to keep tabs with the CIA on citizens going
abroad.

Having learned from my trials by Postal Service in the State
Department and the Justice Department the value of a word from
the Hill, I enlisted the support of the Congressman who represented
Martha's Vineyard, Gerry E. Studds, a member of the House Foreign Affairs Committee, in my battle to wrest my file from the CIA.
That elicited this explanation on July 16, 1980, from the legislative
counsel for the director of the Central Intelligence Agency: "We
must hold to our long-standing policy of first-in, first-out. . . . I wish
to assure you that Mr. Kimball's request is in the proper channels."
A letter to the Congressman more than a year later, from J. William
Doswell, Director, External Affairs, CIA, September 14, 1981: "I
certainly understand Mr. Kimball's concern. . . . We are awaiting
coordination from two other Government agencies." A year following that, on February 4, 1982: "We are hopeful of having it completed in the not too distant future."

In March, 1982, I received a phone call from Congressman
Studd's office. They had been told my CIA file was on the verge of
release. I thanked the Congressman's staff for its noble efforts. When
I called them back in June, they reported that the file was still sitting
on a desk within the CIA, waiting for somebody to sign off. The CIA
is not an agency to be stampeded by the people's representatives on
Capitol Hill.

The long process was wearing, and I had other things on my
mind. Janet had fallen ill with cancer in 1980, then a brain tumor in
the summer of 1981, and was back in the hospital once more as I

continued to wage the battle for whatever else might be in my CIA file.

That file was ultimately delivered to me in the morning mail on August 6, 1982. I had just returned from the hospital where Janet had died two hours before. I didn't feel much like opening it and finally did so with a feeling that this was simply too much.

It was. My eye lit on a note written in 1958: "Also, the fact that the subject's spouse is probably connected with the [Name blacked out] case, questions the loyalty of the family on a present-day basis." For nearly 25 of our 35 years of marriage, the CIA without her knowing it had been questioning the loyalty of Janet Fraser Kimball, daughter of a Republican, stepdaughter of a district attorney, fiercely independent and free. And now it was too late for her to defend herself.

The CIA file—Case No. 177145—released to me at long last, consisted of 14 documents, numbered in red in chronological order, exactly the opposite of the numbering system followed by the Department of State. Document 1 was only a single page, a summary of "Biographical Data" on me from my birth in New Britain, Connecticut, to 1958, the year when the CIA initiated its record-keeping on Kimball, Penn Townsend.

Except for the biographical data sheet all the other documents were released only "in part." Document 15, the covering letter disclosed, was "Denied in entirety" by Mr. John H. Stein, deputy director for operations, on the ground that it "encompasses matters which are specifically authorized under criteria established by Executive Order 12065 to be kept secret in the interest of national defense or foreign policy." Heavy stuff.

As a result, my CIA file was blotted by the long familiar black brushstrokes, deleting whole sentences and paragraphs so that it was impossible in places to understand the gist of what the CIA investigators were trying to find out about whom. Furthermore, the reproductions were of such poor quality that it required a magnifying glass and some guesswork to figure out the contents of the blurred and dirty pages. The office machinery in the superpower's central nerve center worked as if it had been purchased at a tag sale.

The CIA investigator started out like a journeyman reporter, checking out what was in the clip files of the local press. The first few documents put together in October of 1958 read like a resume. Document 1 included a description of my employment record from 1951, when I went to work for *The New York Times*, to "1958-Pres: Public Relations Director for Gov. Harriman, 16 East 81st St., New York City."

This was followed with information from the files of *The Times* and *The New York World Telegram and Sun*. It simply quoted from whatever had been printed about me over the years—and even noted that Janet "was graduated from Syracuse University and subsequently was on the reportorial staff of the Syracuse Post-Standard. She is with the Affairs [sic] Section of Time Magazine."

The material in the *Times* morgue on Janet sounded like it had come from the report of our wedding, and sure enough, on 29 October, 1958, the CIA agent went to the Marriage Bureau in the Office of the City Clerk at the Municipal Building, Chambers and Center Streets, and located Marriage Certificate No. 9715, dated April 2, 1947, for Penn Townsend K——, 2nd, and Janet E. Fraser. (CIA style used only the first initial of my last name followed by a line, for what secret purpose I could not divine.)

The record shows that a CIA representative interviewed "Confidential Informant R-1, a source of known reliability" on November 5, 1958, the day after Election Day. ("R", apparently, stood for reference, or at least REFERENCES was the subheading on this portion of my CIA file.) R-1 confirmed my employment record as I sat around licking my wounds from Governor Harriman's lost campaign.

Subject was simultaneously being run through both an "H" and a "K" name check. (I don't know what those letters of the alphabet stand for.) Not only was my marriage license in order, the New York City Police Department had assigned me Press Pass No. 543 in 1940. Neither the Princeton nor the New Jersey State Police had anything on me. Same with Westport and the Connecticut State Police. Dun & Bradstreet reported my partnership with Lou Harris. Credit bureaus were checked too. From New York City came the report of no litigation on file, favorable past accounts with payment in 30 days and high credit of $50.00 (this was still pre-inflation

1958). Other credit bureaus had nothing more interesting to say. The Princeton Bureau of Alumni Records noted that I had traveled through prewar Europe in 1938, with Jack Irwin, and the CIA here inserted into their routine check: "AGENT'S NOTE: The same clipping lists one Jack IRWIN, who apparently is the individual who travelled through Europe with SUBJECT in 1938, as a Deputy Assistant Secretary of Defense for International Security Affairs."

In Washington, the dragnet included a system for canvassing the files of government agencies and committees of Congress. Document 6 was a "Name Check Report" sheet listing the name or initials of government sources in one column, next to a "return" column and a third column for the date of the reply, almost all of which were in December. It was headed by a box labeled "Subject 177145—P.T.K. [additional area blacked out]." "NR" in the return column meant "No Record." Where something had turned up, the code initials "SA" appeared next to the designated source. It took me a while to figure out that stood for "See Attached." Most of the initials describing sources were familiar to me. Four sources reported no record: HCUA (House Committee on Un-American Activities), ACSI (I didn't recognize that one), ONI (Office of Naval Intelligence) and OSI (Office of Security Information?). Marked "SA" were CSC (Civil Service Commission), MARINES (initials would never do), PASSPORT and STATE. The column labeled FBI was blank. Marine Personnel forwarded fitness Reports (Excellent) and Proficiency and Conduct Reports (Excellent, Excellent). The "See Attached" return from the Civil Service Commission—Document 4—was a cloud no bigger than an anonymous hand.

> Security Investigations Index, CSC, searched 12 December 1958, disclosed Form 79 which indicated that the Department of State initiated an investigation of Subject, 14 January 1947 [sic] for an FP Career with the Department of State. Reports will be available at the Division of Security, Department of State.

No chance the CIA was going to miss that. But it took a while.

The first more personal source of information about me was

approached December 9, six weeks after the start of the CIA investigation. From the beginning, the CIA interview material had a pleasant tone, as though that agency was purposely looking on the bright side of SUBJECT P.T.K.

"On 9 December 1958, [Name blacked out] was interviewed by telephone by Assistant [one-half line blacked out]." Assistant who of what? Assistants with a capital A in Washington are usually Assistant Secretary or Assistant Director of something pretty important. Whoever Assistant Blank was, his confidential source guessed, on the basis of my once working for *PM*, that I was "an extreme liberal."

[Name blacked out] said one informant had advised him that when SUBJECT was on the staff of PM, SUBJECT was opposed to the Communist faction on that paper. Another informant, who was familiar with one of the campaigns of Senator Benton, told [Name blacked out] that before SUBJECT went to work on BENTON'S campaign, they had to "check him out", as the word was around that he (SUBJECT) was a fellow traveler.

This same informant seemed to know me in a more present context, evidently as an insider in the Harriman campaign.

While working in the campaign, SUBJECT had a difficult job as there was quite a bit of friction between the HARRIMAN HOGAN group at the SHELTON TOWERS and the regular Democratic State Committee, which was at the BILTMORE HOTEL. SUBJECT spent a good deal of time trying to act as a mediator between the warring factions.

He did an acceptable job on the campaign—was liked by some—disliked by others. . . .

[Name blacked out] said that SUBJECT had just started or was about to start in a new job as assistant to BARRETT, the Dean of COLUMBIA UNIVERSITY, School of Journalism.

On December 11, R-2 was heard from. R-2 called me "a personable individual, whose personal and moral standards were entirely proper and acceptable. SUBJECT has a good home life, a nice wife and gets along well with others." He then went on to call me an "egghead," but explained,

> He is highly intelligent, well educated and well informed on world problems. SUBJECT is professionally associated with HARRIS ASSOCIATES, a New York firm of public opinion researchers. In this connection, informant was of the opinion that sometime in the spring of 1957, SUBJECT went to Mexico. Informant said he could not be certain as to the exact time of SUBJECT's stay in Mexico, but, to the best of his recollection, SUBJECT went to Mexico on business and SUBJECT's wife remained at home. [Actually, Janet had joined us for that week's vacation in Mexico City in April.]

Outside of the fact that I had parted company with Lou Harris six months before, the CIA's confidential informant had come up with a piece of information which might well catch the eye of a CIA evaluator—my 1957 trip to Mexico with Lou Harris to interview members of the embassy staff and others in our pilot study on overseas Americans for Syracuse University's Maxwell School.

Unfortunately, the censorship technique practiced by the brush artists at CIA went a step further than the protective coloring provided by the State Department and FBI. Not only were the names of all informants eliminated, but the context in which their path might have crossed with mine was also carefully concealed. R-2, for example, ". . . knew SUBJECT for [approximately six and one-quarter lines blacked out]." This personal acquaintance, as I imagine he must have been, also assured the CIA investigator that

> SUBJECT has a good working knowledge of Government . . . , has considerable experience as a newsman and is a competent writer.

> Informant volunteered that SUBJECT is decidedly liberal, and he is firm in his convictions, which are clearly New Deal and Democratic. Informant said he favored SUBJECT from

a standpoint of security, because he, informant, knew of
nothing that would cause him to have reservations concerning SUBJECT's loyalty to the United States.

Confidential informant R-3 mentioned that I had had a "high
ranking position" on *Collier's*, and described me as "a likable fellow
who got along well with [one-half line blacked out]. There was
never any criticism of his personal conduct or his moral standards,
everything in those categories was satisfactory. There was nothing to
indicate that the SUBJECT had off color political leanings nor was
there anything to indicate that SUBJECT was disloyal to the United
States."

Confidential Informant R-4 recalled me as a "brilliant student"
at college and a member of the football team—

. . . a likable individual with a pleasant personality, who
would never hesitate to have a sociable beer with a classmate.
    Informant advised that he could not recall any irregular-
ities in SUBJECT's political thinking before or after college
days. Informant volunteered that on the basis of [one-half
line blacked out] he would describe him as a "middle of the
road Democrat."
    Informant indicated that he could rate SUBJECT as "A-1"
and recommended him highly to a position of trust.

What "position of trust"?
When I first got wind of my CIA file, I assumed the worst. Another part of the package of lies, accusations and secret proceedings
that had haunted my life. As I thumbed through the pages of the 14
documents released to me in 1982, a new thought began to dawn.
There was no plausible explanation for a security check of my private life by yet a third government agency in the year 1958. I had
not belonged to the American Newspaper Guild, the source of so
many suspicions from the security apparatus, for over four years. I
had most recently worked for such benign enterprises as "Omnibus,"
Collier's, Louis Harris & Associates, Governor Averell Harriman
and, now, the dean of the Columbia Graduate School of Journalism;

Janet and I were living the life of typical suburbanites. As far as the world knew, as far as I knew, as far as the CIA knew, I was a more or less model citizen.

A perfect prospect to be tapped for membership in the secret society of the nation's elite—The Company.

The Central Intelligence Agency is another one of those instances where things take on a different light as the years pass. World War II had been an occasion for utilizing the best and the brightest in all sorts of clandestine activity to help win a war about which there was a national unity. There were bravery and romance in the exploits of our wartime intelligence operators. My old roommate Ricardo had been parachuted into Spain to cut off German communications with their U-boats. Others joined the partisans in Yugoslavia or the resistance inside France. My contemporaries at Princeton and Oxford cracked codes, assessed bomb damage and landed on the beaches at night with commandos. When the war was over, some stayed on in the CIA, the peacetime successor to these wartime units. It was considered honorable, if sometimes dangerous, duty in defense of freedom in the civilized world. Only when time wore on did the doubts begin to surface about secret policies and covert operations that took on a life of their own. A government within the government, choosing sides in the internal affairs of other countries, infiltrating the institutions of our own society. In 1958, the country had not yet been awakened by the Bay of Pigs, Vietnam or the exposure of CIA subsidies to supposedly private endeavors.

Some of my closest friends in journalism had worked in Europe in behalf of our government's idealistic and generous effort to rebuild war-ravaged countries. We used to joke at parties in Westport about their possible connection with the CIA. There was nothing sinister then about The Company, as it was called in fiction and fact alike.

Document 5 reveals that the investigating agents looked for sources of "known reliability" in my hometown of Westport, Connecticut.

When the Central Intelligence Agency came looking for information about us, Janet, Lisa and I had been living in Westport for six years—from the time we had rented a house there in 1952 while I worked on Senator William Benton's unsuccessful campaign for re-election. We had stayed on, bought a ranch house on an acre of land, put Lisa in kindergarten in a brand-new public school and entered into the life sought by millions of others in the '50s. Westport had a population then of just over 10,000, small enough to give you the feeling of being part of a community.

Westport, a Republican town, was going through all the growing pains of postwar suburbia; not enough schools, not enough sewers, no zoning controls and a resident core of old-timers determined to keep taxes from growing through the roof to pay for all the services demanded by newcomers. It was a place where an interested citizen could make a difference. I longed to practice all the ideals I had been writing about for political candidates and officeholders on a larger stage.

I became a member of the Board of Finance, which drew up the town budget and enjoyed the power of veto over increases by the legislative body, the Representative Town Meeting. I served on the Charter Committee, sponsored by the League of Women Voters, to draft changes to bring the forms of local government into the twentieth century. Running for the Representative Town Meeting, I finished first in a field of a dozen candidates. (I couldn't resist writing John Bailey that he needn't think of me any more as "the appointive type" in politics.)

Janet and I taught Sunday school at the Greens Farms Congregational Church, and Janet was the leader of a Brownie troop there. She served on all those committees which women in the suburbs form to keep things going. When Lisa was 8, Janet found a job that would enable her to be home when school was out for the day, as part-time secretary to the owner of a real estate office, Nat Greenberg. He encouraged her to study for a real estate broker's license herself so as to earn a piece of the action. The whole scene was the American Dream.

All this and then some, confidential informants in Westport affirmed. ". . . They enjoy a good reputation in this community," R-5 claimed, "and have been active in local civic affairs." He mentioned the Finance Committee and the Charter Committee, and thought I possessed

. . . a highly intelligent and keen mind, was quite conversant on financial matters and served very satisfactorily on the two aforementioned committees.

Informant recalled that SUBJECT's spouse had been employed with a local real estate firm, namely the COUNTRY AGENCY in town . . .

He indicated that he knew of nothing derogatory regarding the SUBJECT or his spouse, believes they are happily married and is under the impression that they have three children.

With regard to the SUBJECT's loyalty and patriotism to the United States, informant was of the conviction that SUBJECT is a loyal American and volunteered the fact that he is a Democrat by chose [sic] and liberal in his political views. It was informant's considered opinion that SUBJECT is not radical and, to his knowledge, is definitely not Communistic.

Informant also stated that he has been informed by [Name blacked out] that SUBJECT is not employed at the present time, has been accepting short special assignments and reportedly has a "promising connection lined up". He further disclosed that SUBJECT has a number of influential business and social contacts and in the opinion of informant, will certainly make a business connection very shortly.

Not bad, although R-5 didn't know me well enough to be sure how many children spouse and I had. But he knew that I was still available for a promising connection, and that might be interesting to the folks searching for new talent to join The Company. Had they specifically asked about my availability?

R-6 corroborated R-5's knowledge and opinion, and added a touch of his own. He recalled that "not long ago, SUBJECT acted as one of the judges in connection with an oratorical contest conducted by the AMERICAN LEGION, and gave this as an indication of SUBJECT's good citizenship." "The American Legion," this informant added, "is one of the foremost fighters against Communism and in selecting a judge for their contest, is very particular and careful to appoint only such individuals who are considered to be good, solid citizens.

"With regard to SUBJECT's loyalty and patriotism to the United States, informant stated that there is no question [11 spaces blacked out] regarding either his or his spouse's loyalty, considering them both to be 'good, solid citizens'. . . . definitely not Communistic nor subversive in any degree."

On the whole, I was doing pretty well in this investigation, even though its purpose was obscure.

As of 11 December 1958, Confidential Informants R-1 through R-6 had given me a clean bill of health. A SYNOPSIS on File No. 177145, dated 15 December 1958, reported my education and employment history, the favorable credit checks, the absence of my name in police files. In a one-page summary of the 21 single-spaced pages of security investigation in Document 5, the CIA tentatively concluded:

> SUBJECT, public relations director, 1958, New York State Harriman-Hogan campaign. Subject is said to be a competent writer. During World War II, SUBJECT was an officer, United States Marine Corps, combat duty in Pacific. SUBJECT has a good working knowledge of Government at the State level. He served on staff of former Governor Chester BOWLES and with former United States Senator William BENTON. SUBJECT is an "egghead", an intellectual, firm in his political connections [sic] which are decidedly liberal and New Deal, Democratic. Informants had no knowledge of any questionable political associations by the SUBJECT and has [sic] no reservations concerning SUBJECT's loyalty to the United States. SUBJECT's personal and moral standards are entirely acceptable. He attends church in his community where he and his wife are favorably regarded. . . . Recorded information New York area does not disclose [two lines blacked out]. It is reported that SUBJECT was in Mexico in May [sic] 1957 on HARRIS ASSOCIATES business.

Except for some secretarial slippage and the gnawing gap linked, apparently, with something or someone in Mexico, the SYNOPSIS sounded like what the CIA would want to know before opening negotiations.

All this, however, was early-vintage SUBJECT.

The State Department file under my name that had been flagged by the Civil Service Commission made its way to the CIA on 22 December 1958, exactly a week after the largely glowing synopsis.

"On 18 December 1958 Subject's file was reviewed at the Office of Security, Department of State, and revealed the following information:"

There followed 14 pages of single-spaced summary of the worst of the 99 documents in that old 1946 State Department file: ". . . teetered for a while . . . a telegram of protest . . . preferred the society of known Communists . . . if someone could authoritatively clear up how far to the Left Subject went . . . informant ejaculated 'My God, no! Never!' "

Then the killer paragraph:

Subject's file contained a memorandum dated 1 November 1946 from the chairman, Security Committee, Department of State, which revealed that after a review of all the information available, Subject's application for appointment as a Foreign Service officer was disapproved.

A thunderous silence descended upon CIA File No. 177145 for nearly a year after that, during which, on May 20, 1959, J. Edgar Hoover sent his entirely blacked-out memorandum to the Director of Security, CIA, Colonel Sheffield Edwards. CIA Document 9, dated 25 September 1959, explains what was going on:

An investigation was conducted on Subject during 1958 by [3 spaces blacked out] which included National Agencies Checks, H&K searches, an OS indices check, and a field investigation [one-half line blacked out] conducted in Washington, D.C. and New York, N.Y. Following a review of the material obtained from this investigation, it was felt that additional inquiries should be conducted [17 spaces blacked out] and that the FBI should be recontacted in this regard. The [23 spaces blacked out] requested in February 1959 that it handle the matter with the FBI since it had an interest in [three-quarters of a line blacked out]. In March 1959 the FBI advised [3 spaces blacked out] that it was conducting further checks in this matter; and in June 1959 it forwarded a memorandum dated 20 May concerning subject. During July and August [3 spaces blacked out] has all the information that [3 spaces blacked out] has in this matter.

CIA Document 9 goes on to summarize once again my State Department file, including portions from the FBI, and also the 1955 FBI report on *The Times*. It adds, however, a novel item picked up by a CIA field agent:

Field inquiries in Washington by this Division resulted in the interview with one Confidential Informant who has known Subject and his family for years. Subject was described as being "slightly left of Khrushchev", politically dangerous and in all probability, a Communist Party member. Subject reportedly presided over the Communist section of the Staff of PM, the informant said.

This informant had thus outdone all the competitors, promoting me not only to Communist Party member, but in charge of the Communist cell on *PM*.

Confidential Informants R-1, 2, 3, 4, 5, and 6 were summarized in two sentences: ". . . all recommended him. . . . One of the informants stated that Subject opposed the Communist faction at *PM*."

The next eight lines—a whole paragraph—were completely blacked out.

Additional information in this matter [meaning the blacked-out matter, I assumed] was developed during March–June by the FBI and forwarded to [3 spaces blacked out]. The FBI stated that although it could not be established definitely, it appears very likely that [Name blacked out] is identical with the person who [line blacked out] . . . a review of the information on Subject indicates that Subject should be security disapproved for any utilization by the Agency. (Attached is a copy of [6 spaces blacked out] comments concerning Subject.)

[One-half line blacked out] has a personal interest in Subject. On recent trips to Washington, D.C., he has discussed the progress of Subject's case with [line blacked out] is very interested in obtaining approval for subject.

Who was this individual with a personal interest in my case? What was contained in the blacked-out paragraph which required additional information from the FBI? My head reeled with new mysteries.

The [one-quarter line blacked out] has been advised generally of the derogatory information concerning Subject with the exception of the data concerning the [5 spaces blacked out] case. [3 spaces blacked out] has requested that such information not be disseminated at this time.

Now I was completely at sea. Something had supposedly linked my name with the [5 spaces blacked out] case, whatever that was. It sure sounded like something to do with the law. That was another first. So secret that it was being withheld from being circulated even within the government.

And it was not I alone who was suspect. "The fact that Subject's [6 spaces blacked out] is probably connected with the [5 spaces blacked out] case, questions the loyalty of the family on a present-day basis."

There it was. Janet was being linked with the [5 spaces blacked out] case, and in spite of the unanimously favorable comments on my spouse from the confidential informants in Westport, she had joined her husband as a security suspect.

Document 9 includes this as one of seven items "unfavorable to Subject," but then continues:

In spite of the derogatory data, [3 spaces blacked out] has requested that a Security determination be rendered in this case.

Somebody was pressing for a ruling on me.

I wondered about my former dean, Ed Barrett. He was now in his 70s, with no need any longer to dissemble. Barrett said he had sat on a Psychological Strategy board with Allen Dulles and others in the CIA, but had severed all connections when he returned to civilian life from the post of Assistant Secretary of State for Public Affairs. "You're the kind of a guy they would have recruited," he said. "The CIA always had to ask for a security check before they began negotiating with a prospect. After all, you couldn't hire a guy for a job you couldn't discuss with him."

The memoranda kept flowing: Document 10, 10 October 1959; Documents 11 and 12, 18 November 1959; Document 13, 24 March 1960. All rehashed the same old data. And in each of them, one whole paragraph was blacked out. Document 11 concluded that the information

> appears to raise such a serious question of an operational security nature that it is the recommendation of this Office that Subject not be utilized in any capacity for this agency....
>
> In view of the nature of the above data, plus the fact that Subject has been connected with Messrs. HARRIMAN, BENTON, BOWLES AND HOGAN, the information contained herein should be carefully controlled and protected and should be disseminated only to those Senior CIA Headquarters officials who have a definite need to know.

Document 14, dated 1 July 1960, said simply:

> SUBJECT: Kimball, Penn Townsend
> Subject is no longer of interest to Project [Name blacked out]. It is requested, therefore, that all security processing of Subject be cancelled.
>
> [Name blacked out]
Security Officer
> [The word CANCELLED was stamped in large block letters across the bottom.]

Document 15, 6 July 1960—the final document in my CIA file —was and still remains "Denied in entirety."

19

THE PLOT THICKENS

THERE WAS A single clue to the [five spaces blacked out] case, on which so much energy had been spent to link even poor Janet. In its sweep into the suburbs, the CIA's investigatory arm had made three puzzling, additional stops: White Plains, New York; Ridgefield, Connecticut, and South Salem, New York. None of those places had ever figured in our lives.

The White Plains report informed me that:

[One-half line blacked out] formerly owned real property in [one-half line blacked out]. In April of 1957, negotiations were undertaken by one [five spaces blacked out] to sell a portion of this property to one [18 spaces blacked out], the latter is currently a Justice of the Peace in [20 spaces blacked out]. In connection with the sale one [Name blacked out] a New York attorney, with offices at 1501 Broadway, acted as representative of the [six spaces blacked out]. The purchaser was represented by [Name blacked out], a New York attorney with offices at 15 East Main Street, in [Name blacked out] New York.

It was reliably established that there were no real estate taxes involved in connection with the sale of this real property. The closing transaction took place in the offices of [Name blacked out] at 1501 Broadway on 5 April 1957.

The sale of the property is recorded in the County Clerk's Office at Westchester County, White Plains, New York in [one-half line blacked out]. The recording is dated [blacked out] . . .

AGENT'S NOTE: From available records in this area, it could not be established whether [line blacked out].

I called up the County Clerk's Office in White Plains, only to discover that deeds were not filed in the county records in chronological order, but according to the description of the property by lot numbers in huge books of land records for the whole county. No way to go through 25 years of such records hunting for the needle in the haystack. According to the AGENT'S NOTE, moreover, public records were not going to help me discover what had linked Janet or me with the mysterious transaction. There was no way to trace the closing through the lawyer at 1501 Broadway, where, in the lobby of the old Paramount Building on Times Square, the directory listed not one or two, but scores of lawyers a quarter of a century after the event.

The field report from Ridgefield, Connecticut, said that "the files of the Town Clerk and Assessors Office, located in the Town Hall Building, disclosed no record of any real estate owned by [one-half line blacked out]. Inquiries there elicited the fact that [paragraph blacked out].

"The Town Clerk, namely Mrs. Margaret MC GLYNN, disclosed that she was familiar with the [five spaces blacked out] case after reading numerous accounts in the newspapers, etc., and called attention to the fact that the [six spaces blacked out] during the time they owned their estate in [six lines blacked out]."

Now I was sure I was onto something big. Mrs. McGlynn had passed away several years ago, but the present town clerk in Ridgefield explained why the FBI investigating a real estate transaction in neighboring New York had visited a town clerk in Connecticut. Property owners across the New York State line in South Salem, adjacent to Ridgefield, once used the Ridgefield post office as a more convenient mailing address. That also placed the [five spaces blacked out] case in Fairfield County, Connecticut, where Subject and spouse made their home and spouse worked in a Westport real estate office.

I got in touch with everybody I knew who had ever worked with Janet back then. None had ever heard of or been questioned about a real estate transaction in Westchester County that had attracted the attention of wandering investigators.

The report from South Salem gave me more clues to work with.

A review of the Town Clerk's Records by [half-line blacked out] disclosed the following information relative to the estate formerly owned by [9 spaces blacked out] and [three-quarters of a line blacked out].

The entire property consisted of approximately fifty acres with large residence. The Town Clerk, namely Mr. Cyrus RUSSELL, produced photostatic copies of two deeds filed at the County Seat in White Plains, New York. One deed, filed in [one-half line blacked out] disclosed that on the [five lines blacked out]. This property included Lots No. [blacked out]. The other deed, filed in Liber [half-line blacked out] at the above-mentioned address, sold and deeded land listed on Lot No. [one and one-half lines blacked out].

Mr. Russell disclosed that the above-mentioned [11 spaces blacked out] is a real-estate broker, who operates his own real estate brokerage at [11 spaces blacked out] and is also a Justice of the Peace of that town.

I knew from the White Plains report that the transaction had been consummated the first week of April, 1957. How many 50-acre deals could there have been in a small place like South Salem during a given week in a given month in a given year? Even in the absence of lot and liber numbers, there was a chance of hitting pay dirt there. I tried to reach the South Salem town clerk by phone, and discovered that South Salem was only a hamlet in the town of Lewisboro under New York State's arcane organization of local government. Cyrus Russell, too, had passed away, and the current town clerk couldn't help me, she said, find anything at all without lot and liber numbers. Try the tax assessor's office, she suggested.

The assessor, Gordon G. Washburn, said that his office filed tax changes on a year-by-year basis and that if I wanted to come up to his office and take a look for myself, that was okay with him. He gave me very complicated directions over the back roads of Lewisboro to the old farmhouse in which he kept his office.

Washburn turned out to be a young man who looked as if he had barely been born on that date in April 25 years before when somebody worthy of interest to the CIA had sold 50 acres in a tiny hamlet in the far reaches of Westchester County. It was a beautiful fall day, the leaves turning gloriously on the trees along the way to the farmhouse where I hoped to unravel at least part of the mystery that had so upset The Company in its talent search for new blood among the elite. I was driven as well by an urgent desire to clear the record on Janet, so unfairly deprived by bureaucratic sloth of the opportunity to speak for herself in answer to anonymous charges concerning blacked-out events.

The assessor sat me at a table in the corner of his office with a stack of tax records for the year 1957. I riffled through them until I hit the first week in April. And there it was, unmistakable, 50 acres more or less, sold on deeds recorded in the County Clerk's Office in White Plains, the information forwarded to the tax assessor in Lewisboro.

The sellers of their South Salem estate were one Alfred K. and Martha Dodd Stern (five spaces).

The buyer was J. Ruggles Barnard (18 spaces), Justice of the Peace and real estate broker in Pound Ridge, New York (20 spaces). Everything fitted the blacked-out pieces of the puzzle. There was one very odd feature of the deal: the selling price of the 50 acres more or less had been only $100. I searched through the records for the following year. There I found that J. Ruggles Barnard had sold off an 8-acre piece of his $100 buy in 1958 for $18,000 in 1959. The name Barnard meant nothing to me, and unfortunately he was long since gone, too, though his local reputation was impeccable.

The names Alfred K. and Martha Dodd Stern did ring a bell. I checked them out in the index of *The New York Times* for the year

1957; the names had appeared in numerous accounts. I took out the microfilms and fed them into the optical viewer, just like a world-class operative. The Sterns were alleged Soviet spies. The Stern case was one of espionage.

Martha Dodd Stern was the daughter of William E. Dodd, our Ambassador to Germany during the heyday of Hitler. She was the second wife of a New York investment banker, Alfred K. Stern, whose first wife had been a wealthy Rosenwald, heiress to a fortune made from Sears Roebuck. They owned extensive real estate, *The Times* reported inaccurately, in Ridgefield. The House Committee on Un-American Activities had named them both as supporters of causes linked to the Soviet Union, but more sensationally they had been named by Boris Morros, a Hollywood producer, as Soviet agents in a spy ring Morros himself had infiltrated as a counterspy for the FBI. Although the couple had lived on their South Salem estate, they had fled the country before being subpoenaed to appear in New York City before a Federal Grand Jury investigating espionage in 1957.

Where had the Sterns fled to? Mexico City—and had been selling off their assets in South Salem in the same week in April when SUBJECT Kimball was there with Lou Harris to conduct depth interviews among American government and other employees overseas, and had been joined in Mexico City by spouse, who worked in a real estate office back in Westport. I could see the CIA types chewing their pipe stems.

In May, 1957, the Sterns were convicted of contempt and fined $50,000. Meanwhile, *Times* microfilms showed, the couple was reported to be selling off their remaining assets in the United States, prior to fleeing from Mexico to Switzerland in July, 1957, and thence to Czechoslovakia. A grand jury indicted the absentee Sterns for espionage on September 9, 1957. The couple turned up in Moscow in 1958 just before the time when the CIA commenced its inquiries into my life.

Thinking that even the FBI and The Company put together might have found coincidence a tenuous link to an international spy ring, I looked for other clues to the blacked-out paragraphs of my file.

In 1959—the year when the CIA asked the FBI to update its investigation of me—Boris Morros had written a book, *My Ten Years as a Counterspy*. In 1983, only months after I received my CIA file, Michael Straight, my old boss at *New Republic*, published a book called *After Long Silence* in which he confessed to being a Communist while a student at Cambridge. Both books were a revelation.

In December, 1943, four years before Boris Morros became a double agent, Vassali Mikhaelivich Zubilin, the chief Soviet agent in the United States, took him to a Western Union office in Ridgefield, made a phone call, and soon they were were both picked up in a station wagon driven by Alfred K. Stern. They drove to a large residence in South Salem, where Martha Dodd Stern greeted them at the door and "threw her arms lovingly" around Zubilin. They had been lovers, Morros said, in Berlin. A deal was struck by which Stern invested $130,000 in Boris Morros Productions, which was to serve as a front for Soviet "talent scouts" roaming the United States and Latin America.

In 1944, Morros and Stern went to call on William Benton, my future employer, hoping to buy Muzak from him for $400,000. Benton wanted $600,000 and the deal fell through.

So far so good. The scenario was worthy of Hollywood, but in 1944 Janet was a student at Syracuse University and I was a Marine in the Solomon Islands. But in 1947, when Janet and I were able to enjoy our honeymoon at Beatrice Straight's apartment during Henry Wallace's ill-fated journey abroad, Michael Straight reported that Alfred K. and Martha Dodd Stern helped arrange the welcoming committee for Wallace in Europe.

In January, 1950, Morros was in Moscow, meeting with one Petrov, the NKVD deputy in charge of espionage activities in the United States. Petrov instructed Morros to try to infiltrate the Senate staff of Senator William Benton. Morros claimed nothing came of that idea, but the man in charge of Benton's staff at the time was Penn Kimball, who, a CIA source had reported, had to be checked out as a "fellow traveler."

In the funhouse mirror of my file, the true story of my life as a journalist and citizen had singled me out for recruitment by the CIA.

Yet in the end my sterling resume as a potential Company man had been turned upside down by the investigators and evaluators once again. This time my government's classification of me had escalated from national security risk to—spy!

But is that what my government really thinks of me? There is at this point no way to be sure. J. Edgar Hoover's memorandum, CIA Document 15 and innumerable paragraphs, lines and spaces in the hundreds of pages of my file remain black to me, SUBJECT PENN TOWNSEND KIMBALL.

From the tiniest of beginnings—an offhand remark by David Lawrence—the case against me in the file had been constructed, layer by layer, one presumption leading to the next, to an absurdity of monstrous proportions. The file took on a life of its own which I seemed powerless to influence. How could an individual citizen bring such a wild process to a halt?

20

THE FUTURE IS
NOW

WHEN I BEGAN to write this book, it was in a tone of outrage spiced with some levity and a feeling of self-assurance. I was sure the absurdity and the danger of my file would be evident by placing its nonsense side by side with the real story of my own broad-ranging and rewarding years. I wanted to provide an object lesson to those who, like myself, have dared to hope that our concepts of justice penetrate everywhere within our government, and protect the common man from false accusations, wrongful verdicts and lasting damage to reputation. But that beginning was years ago, and all I had in hand then were copies of the original file the State Department had compiled 30 years before.

By now, more than five years after that first plain brown wrapper arrived on my doorstep, I have been forced to confront the devious ways in which the Federal Bureau of Investigation messes with the lives of ordinary people, and with the odd interests and suspicious ways of thinking in which the CIA conducts its business even on the home front. Those revelations alone are enough, perhaps, to unhinge one's sense of reality. More unhinging, however, was the very process of making such discoveries, and of simultaneously discovering how greatly one's understanding is limited by censorship and how helpless a citizen is to obtain redress. Helplessness breeds changes in even the sturdiest of personalities. As I exhausted one appeal after another—with the State Department, with the Justice Department, and with the Central Intelligence Agency—my feelings grew more and more personal. There must be, I felt, a court in which I could clear my name for posterity if not for the many years of my life in which I had stood indicted of crimes I was not guilty of. I exercised every avenue of appeal available to me within the agencies themselves, and although their replies were slow in coming and consistently negative, I persisted until every possibility was exhausted. I took care to preserve the one last option of taking my case to the federal courts by new rounds of letters keeping my case open against the ticking clock of the statute of limitations, three years from the date of each denial. My correspondence with the United States Government fills a file drawer of its own to overflowing, evidence enough of how obsessive—and, I suppose, how much of a pain in the neck—I had become.

I began to entertain elaborate fantasies, especially of a State Department hearing in which I summoned as witnesses my Boy Scout leader, the warden of Rhodes House, my Marine commanding officer, all the distinguished public servants and successful journalists I had ever worked for, and all the students, now at the top of their profession, I had ever taught. Then all the anonymous informants would be called to the stand and, one by one, their mediocre caliber pitilessly exposed, they would eat their words against me with expressions of humble contrition. At the end, the presiding officer—the Secretary of State—would offer his hand in apology and dictate to the file a substitute declaration of wronged innocence. For some time, I half believed such dreams of glory might come true.

My own family became caught up in the cause. Janet encouraged me, egged me on. She and Lisa said they could see a movie of the book they hoped somebody would publish with Ed Asner playing Daddy. The two persons closest to me in the world were certain my case would prevail in the end. In my unremitting battle with the State Department, hoping to persuade it to come to terms with the unfairness of its security procedures, I threw my interviews with my accusers onto the stack of continuing correspondence. I wrote to Sharon B. Kotok, Chief, Privacy Act Branch, Department of State, on May 7, 1979, and informed her that I had chatted with Otto

Fuerbringer, my real "supervisor" at *Time* in 1946, and that "Fuer-bringer said that he had never been interviewed by an FBI agent about me, and when I showed him the data in the file, he immediately picked up errors which I have mentioned in my amendments to that file."

I also forwarded the information that Gilbert Cant "categorically denied making many of the statements which were summarized by ACOPS as part of the judgment declaring me a national security risk." I argued that "under any kind of due process, I could call both Fuerbringer and Cant to testify at a hearing."

I was closing in on a position, I felt, where I would have a reasonably good chance of producing Fuerbringer and Cant at a hearing, perhaps Crawford and Wechsler in addition, to put to rest the summary court martial of 1946. But the real world was not so accommodating.

I had thought it would be instructive to try to find one of my original investigators and had come upon the name "Hipsley" in the Washington phone book. I wondered if the person might be related to Elmer R. Hipsley, the State Department special agent who had interviewed Crawford, Wechsler, Lockett and the still anonymous informants so many years before. The phone listed never answered. After months I finally reached a young Hipsley who, he explained, sold used cars wholesale and was usually on the road. Elmer, his late grandfather's brother, he informed me, had died nearly 10 years before. He had died a bitter man, forced to take early retirement during the administration of President John F. Kennedy. "Grand-father used to say, 'Elmer took a lot with him to the grave.' "

One by one all the cast of characters in The File were passing on. Whittaker Chambers, Roy Alexander, Joseph C. Green, Elmer Hipsley, long since departed. The friendly witnesses in my fantasy— Boy Scout troop leader, warden of Rhodes House, Marine command-ing officer—no longer around to be called. In *The New York Times* of August 2, 1982, I read that Gilbert Cant had died suddenly of a heart attack the day before in his East Side apartment. My own Janet was desperately ill in the hospital. We had shared so much of The File together that I told her that day about Gilbert. She reached over and touched my hand. A few weeks after Cant's there was an obituary in *The Times* for Duncan Norton-Taylor. Then another in January, 1983, for Kenneth Crawford.

The wild dream of a rehearing of my case, resulting in my belated exoneration, was not only unlikely, but the witnesses all would soon be gone.

I began to become acutely aware of my own mortality.

Not to be morbid about it, I was already older than any member of my immediate family had survived—my father, my mother, my brother, my sister and my wife were all gone at ages younger than my own. I didn't contemplate my own fate with more than normal fear. It was just that my life still contained one huge item of unfinished business.

There had been one interlude of temporary euphoria when it seemed for a moment that the government was conceding a point. In December of 1978, the privacy chief of the FBI wrote:

> We have reviewed our file information to which you have taken exception. It is our decision the information is not relevant and necessary for current purposes of this bureau. Pursuant to your request, and pending approval of the National Archives and Records Service (NARS), we will arrange to expunge our investigative file references to you from the FBI central records system.

Wow! Surrender! Total victory! Thoughts of sugar plums danced in my head. I couldn't wait to share the news with Sharon B. Kotok.

> I enclose a letter to me from the Privacy Branch of the FBI informing me that they have agreed to expunge from the FBI central records the investigative file under my name. These are the same documents being maintained and circulated by the Office of Security of the State Department.
>
> Thus one government agency is maintaining copies of material expunged at the source. . . . Don't you agree that is an interesting contradiction?

My euphoria over the FBI offer to destroy my file—even while the Department of Justice was still considering my appeals to find out everything in it—quickly deflated. If the FBI destroyed the records, all hope would be over of ever finding out their full contents. How could one ever challenge an anonymous informant whose identity had been permanently removed? There would be no evidence to place before any court, ever.

Along with my FBI file would disappear the original of that mysterious exchange between J. Edgar Hoover and Col. Sheffield Edwards, director of CIA security, in which everything had been expurgated save my own name. But what about the copy still in possession of the CIA? Who knows in how many other agencies copies and digests of the original file still exist and are still circulated unbeknownst to me? The more I thought about it the more I was disinclined to accept the offer "pursuant to your request." I said nothing.

But someone in the State Department eventually saw the logic of the argument I had since thought better of. For the second time in six months I received a proposition from my tormentors. Wrote Sharon B. Kotok on May 22, 1979:

Since you believe that the information in your security file is neither timely nor accurate, the Office of Security has agreed to destroy your file, if you so desire. Please let us know if this proposed action is acceptable to you.

Destroy the file! A letter from my old acquaintance Doug Bennet, Assistant Secretary for Congressional Relations, suggested that it might have already happened.

Dear Penn:
   I take it that the scurrilous material has now been burned or shredded. Is that right? I didn't do it, but is there anything else I can do?
                                        Best regards,

Indirectly at least, two security arms of the government seemed to be admitting to misgivings about the file they had been maintaining and circulated about me for over 30 years. No longer relevant. Neither timely nor accurate. But they refused to budge on the issue of how they had combined in the first place to condemn me in secret, with none of the rights of due process, and then through the years had invaded my privacy in ways not yet fully disclosed. No hearing on the facts. No exoneration. When the CIA file arrived, moreover, I learned that nearly everything the FBI and the State Department had offered to send to the shredders had been copied and filed by the Central Intelligence Agency. And the CIA was keeping one document it wouldn't show me at all.

The CIA has not joined the security brethren in offering to send anything to the shredders. The Freedom of Information/Privacy Branch at the CIA to the contrary has added a new hurdle to the appeals process. Since I had complained that the CIA had exceeded the legal limits in failing to reply to my request for documents filed under my name there, I was subsequently informed that my request had been reclassified as an "appeal." When I sought to appeal the expurgations I did not discover until the documents were sent to me after more than three years of waiting, I was thereupon informed that I had exhausted my right of appeal. Catch 22. As of the winter of 1983, the CIA invited me to take any appeal of their denial of appeal to a federal court.

It is hard not to become discouraged at such turns of events.

Perhaps it was this last discouragement that lifted me out of the personal, the obsessive, hope to clear my name and back to the original perspective of the significance of my file. Surely, when I die, my government can lock up The File and throw away the key. Or shred it into extinction. Probably there never will be a trial, in the State Department or in federal court. But aside from my own personal interest, my dogged determination to clear my name, how does everything that happened to me really matter to anybody else? The story of The File seems to me to be more important than the fate of a single individual. It tells us something about us all, and the society in which my child and yours should enjoy freedom with justice. If no one tells the story, nothing will ever be done about it. The File *is* an object lesson, and it can be evaluated in the court of public opinion. The court of public opinion is, after all, the most powerful court of all.

And so I combed through the tall stack of documents from which this book is drawn to find the one which might best say what purpose, beyond my injured vanity, this book serves. It is the letter I wrote on May 28, 1948, when I was only 32 years old, to Joseph C. Green of the Board of Examiners for the Foreign Service, who had been so reluctant to tell me what was going on. I was closing out, I thought at the time, a puzzling chapter of my young life. Unlike most other things one does, I feel that this last word regarding that experience has stood pretty well the test of time:

My dear Mr. Green:

I am in receipt of your letter of May 25, 1948, denying my request to be informed of the specific reasons for the disapproval of my candidacy for the Foreign Service, and refusing me either a personal hearing or a review of any kind to determine the substance of these reasons, whatever they may be.

Your letter indicates only that my appointment was disapproved "on the basis of facts ascertained in the course of the investigation subsequent to your examination." This is a remarkable statement since the alleged "facts" supposedly "ascertained" are being withheld from the person immediately concerned. I thereby stand disapproved, although previously qualified and accepted, without even knowing the charge, much less being permitted to offer evidence to refute it.

The accountability of government officials to private citizens is a principle firmly embedded in the democratic tradition. And the right of any citizen, however humble, to defend himself against official defamations has always been characteristic of democratic as opposed to authoritarian systems of government.

I cannot believe that contrary procedures, or the public officials who invoke them, can long survive the scrutiny of time. But I seem to have exhausted every avenue of approach in a vain effort to appeal to your Department's sense of fairness and propriety.

I would like to incorporate in the record, however, an unequivocal statement that I challenge the existence of any facts supported by the slightest shred of evidence that my qualifications for the U.S. Foreign Service warrant this unilateral disapproval.

I am confident that the future will vindicate my position in this case. As a citizen I can only hope that my experience will not be duplicated to the extent that appreciable numbers of young men educated and trained in international affairs will be driven off from government service by an arbitrary and indefensible attitude.

Sincerely yours,
Penn Kimball

The future is now.

INDEX

ACOPS (Appeals Committee on Personnel Security): origins and purposes, 71–74; investigation of K, 74–76, 153–62; mentioned, 99, 116, 147, 274, 341. *See also* Counsel for ACOPS

Adams, Charlotte, 105

Adjusted Service Compensation Act. *See* Bonus Bill

After Long Silence (Straight), 337

Ager, Cecelia, 105

Aikman, Duncan, 81

"Alex." *See* Alexander, Roy

Alexander, Brooke, 121

Alexander, Roy: candidate for "*Time* supervisor," 255, 258, 261; mentioned, 121, 282, 341

Allis-Chalmers: strike at, 124–25

Alsop, Joseph, 225

Amalgamated Clothing Workers, 86

America First Committee, 94–96, 218

American Assembly, 312

American Civil Liberties Union, 6, 108, 193, 198, 208

American Legion, 326

American Newspaper Guild: K's involvement with, 8–9, 21–22, 182–83, 232–35, 246–47, 323; political divisions, 13–14, 70, 100, 176, 250, 269, 280–81, 284; allegations concerning K's views while a member of, 109, 110, 143, 150–52, 176, 265, 274; 1946 negotiations at *Time*, 130–31, 137–38; importance of K's experiences in, 299–304; mentioned, 99, 108, 124, 289. *See also* American Newspaper Guild, *PM* Unit

American Newspaper Guild, *PM* Unit: history, 84–85; 1941 support for striking UAW workers, 25, 65, 68, 76, 79–80, 88–90, 97; political divisions, 85–88, 142, 149, 151

American Student Union, 108

Appeals Board. *See* Privacy Policy Appeals Board

Appeals Committee on Personnel Security. *See* ACOPS

"A-R." *See* Russell, Donald

Bailey, John, 219–24, 243, 305, 325

Baldwin, Raymond E.: involvement with K's case, 181–85, 218, 249; desire for court appointment, 223–24; K's confrontation with, 237–39

Balliol College. *See* Oxford University

Bannerman, Robert L.: conclusions from testimony about K, 24–27, 38–43, 67–68, 70, 104, 110, 141, 148–53, 254; principal antagonist toward K, 71, 77, 147, 160, 162, 192; instructions concerning K's investigation, 78, 97; mentioned, 76, 145, 146, 154, 155, 156, 214, 274, 277

"Barnaby," 105

Barnard, J. Ruggles, 335

Barnes, Robert G., 54–55

Barrett, Edward W., 312, 321, 330–31

Bell, Griffin, 203–204

Bennet, Douglas J., Jr., 199–200, 206, 219, 343

Benton, William: K as executive secretary, 224–27, 327, 331; review of K's file, 225–26, 234; K and campaign for senator, 231–32, 321, 325; mentioned, 219, 297, 312, 337

Bergman, Edward Barton, 26

Bingham, William J., 50

Bliven, Bruce, 169

Blodgett, John Quigg, 26

Boal, Sam, 105

Bonus Bill, 53–57

Bourke-White, Margaret, 82

Bowles, Chester: and the America First Committee, 94, 95, 126; head of Office of Price Administration, 125–26; K as press aide, 218–24, 227, 236, 305, 327, 331; mentioned, 81, 199, 292

Boylan, James R., 225

Bradford, Saxton E., 161–62

Bramson, Jack, 26

Brennan, Hank, 165

Brewster, Kingman, Jr., 95–96

Bridges, Harry, 139–40, 265

Brooklyn Eagle, The, 83

Brooks, John, 121

Broun, Heywood, 9

Broun, Heywood Hale, 82

Broun, Woody, 105

Buckley, William F., 250

Button, Dick, 291

Byrnes, James, 139, 168, 260

Cant, Gilbert: possible motives for testimony against K, 133–34; testimony against K, 142–45, 274–75, 285–86; K's confrontation with, 274–88; mentioned, 262, 263, 266, 267, 269, 270, 271, 341

Carlson, Lisa, 181, 222, 231, 241, 243, 324–25, 340

Carter, Hodding, II, 105

Carter, Hodding, III, 193, 194

Carter, Jimmy, 9, 102

Carter Administration: position on K's file, 14, 15

Cavanaugh, Barbara, 194

Central Intelligence Agency. See CIA

Cerf, Ed: K's friendship with, 17, 119–21, 128, 135, 145, 169, 171; joins American Newspaper Guild, 131; writer for Time's Army & Navy section, 133–34, 142, 282; career at Time-Life, Inc., 164; others' memories of, 263, 269

Chambers, Whittaker: position at Time, 139; candidate for "Time supervisor," 258, 260–61, 263, 341

Chapin, Selden, 68, 69, 70, 162, 176

CIA: K's file, 5, 7, 192, 195, 214, 217, 236; denial of information to K, 15, 240; interest in K in mid-fifties, 312–31; domestic surveillance, 339; recent additions to appeals process, 344

Civil Service Commission: rights of employees, 74

Civiletti, Benjamin, 215

Clare, Daniel H., Jr.: State Dept. investigator of K, 78, 91, 98, 117, 118, 134, 147, 264, 267, 271; conclusions about K, 87–90, 103–105, 114–15, 135–45, 149; inadequacy of investigation of K, 97, 108, 113, 135–45

Cole, Gordon H., 102, 252

Cole, Wilton D., 302

collaboration (between journalists and law enforcement agents), 5, 13–14, 109, 205, 248. See also informants

collective bargaining. See labor

unions; American Newspaper
Guild; names of specific unions
Collier's magazine, 294–304, 306,
323
Colton, Joel, 26
Columbia University Graduate
School of Journalism, 5, 239, 289,
323
Communist Party: K's lack of
involvement with, 4; investigations
into K's alleged sympathy, 9, 36,
38–43, 52–53, 63–70, 74–78,
100–17, 135–62, 329; registration
of members, 72; American
attitudes toward, 107–108
CON. *See* Controls, Office of (State
Dept.)
Conant, Howell, 297
Conant, James B., 50
Conference for Inalienable Rights,
151
"confidential informants":
description of K's, 99–117.
Controls, Office of (State Dept.):
handling of K's file, 71, 74–78;
mentioned, 25, 147
Cooke, Alistair, 290, 292
Counsel for ACOPS: instructions for
new investigation of K, 74–78,
97, 99, 109, 115, 118;
Bannerman's report to, 150–53;
conclusions about K, 137, 153–62,
246; mentioned, 104, 135, 145,
266
Crawford, Kenneth: testimony about
K, 75–76, 99–102, 149, 157–58,
250; name as informant released
to K, 204, 206, 207, 208;
mentioned, 22, 144, 252, 341, 342
Crisler, H. C. (Fritz), 47
Crowell-Collier Publishing Co.,
293–304. *See also Collier's*
magazine
Curran, Joseph, 139–40, 152–53,
159, 265, 271
Cutler, Lloyd, 198

Daily Princetonian: K's experiences
on, 45–53; mentioned, 17, 19, 94,
201

Davidson, Bill, 294
Democratic Party, 4
Department of Justice. *See* Justice
Dept.
Department of State. *See* State Dept.
DeSapio, Carmine, 307
Deutch, Albert, 105
Dickman, Irving Richard, 26
Diekos, Victor H., 194–98, 200
Dies, Martin, 108
Dodd, Thomas, 224, 243
Dodd, William E., 336
Donovan, Dick, 266
Doswell, J. William, 317
Dowd, Jack, 269
due process: denial of K's, 14, 163,
339–46
Dulles, Allen, 331
Dupre, L. J., 206

Ecole Libre des Sciences Politiques,
61
Edson, Dr., 18
Edwards, Sheffield, 312–14, 328, 343
Egan, Michael J., 215
Elmo Roper Associates, 304, 305.
See also Roper, Elmo; Harris,
Louis
Engle, William, 88
Esquire, 302

FBI: file on K, 5, 7, 192, 195, 200,
258, 312; inadequacy of
investigations of K, 9–10, 36–43,
52–57, 60–67; denial of
information to K, 15;
investigations of K, 25–28, 35–43,
51–57, 60–67, 75, 135–45, 234;
changing reputation, 35–36: K's
attempts to obtain file from,
208–14; possible surveillance of
K abroad, 240; investigations into
citizens' lives, 339; offer to destroy
K's file, 342; mentioned, 13, 69,
70, 90, 217, 258, 316; agent's
endorsement of K, 11–12, 37–38,
43. *See also* Hoover, J. Edgar;
Webster, William H.
F.D.R. *See* Roosevelt, Franklin D.

Federal Bureau of Investigation. *See* FBI
Federal Communications Commission, 242–44
Field, Marshall, III, 81, 85, 104
Fitch, Thomas J.: head of State Dept.'s security arm, 75, 77–78, 91, 144, 148, 160; summary of second State Dept. investigation of K, 145–47; refusal to disclose K's security clearance, 172–80
Flow, Mr., 241
Flynn, A. P., 316–17
Ford, Henry, 83, 94, 95. *See also* Ford Motor Co.
Ford Foundation (TV-Radio Workshop), 289–92
Ford Motor Co.: strike at, 83, 112, 124
Foreign Service: K's attempts to join, 3, 16–19, 27, 172–86; handling of K's security clearance, 67–69, 172–80, 328, 345–46; mentioned, 7, 72, 91, 97. *See also* Government employment
Fraser, Janet. *See* Kimball, Janet Fraser
Freedom of Information and Privacy Acts: rights of citizens under, 5, 6, 191–92, 197–98; handled by FBI, 208–14; decline in government favor toward, 216; mentioned, 3, 251
Freeman, Ira Henry, 308
Fuerbringer, Jonathan, 256
Fuerbringer, Otto: editor at *Time*, 131, 134, 265, 268, 283; denies being "*Time* supervisor," 135, 255–61, 340–41; mentioned, 171, 262, 263, 266, 271, 340–41
Fulbright grants: K's attempts to win, 147, 239

Gallup, George, 304
Gauss, Christian, 49–52, 155
Geesa M. G., 240
Gentile, G. Marvin, 240–41
Gleason, Roger, 43
Goodman, Warren, 121
Gorin, Lewis Jefferson, Jr., 53–57

Gottfried, Manfred, 126–27
Government employment (thwarted by file), 240–44, 251, 258, 270–71, 274–75, 314–31. *See also* Foreign Service; Fulbright grants; CIA
Government investigations of K: techniques, 10–15. *See also* CIA; FBI; State Dept.; Security, Office of
Graduate School of Journalism at Columbia University. *See* Columbia University Graduate School of Journalism
Gray, Barry, 309
Green, Joseph C., 172–79, 181–87, 193, 341, 345
Greenberg, Nat, 325
Griffith, Tom, 258
Gross, Leonard, 294
Guild. *See* American Newspaper Guild

Hale, William Harlan, 165
Hammett, Dashiell, 82
Harriman, Averell: K's work on 1958 campaign, 307–11, 321, 323, 327, 331
Harris, Louis, K's employment with, 267, 304–307, 319, 322, 336. *See also* Louis Harris & Associates
Harris Associates. *See* Louis Harris & Associates
Hartford, Huntington, 82
Havemann, Ernest, 255, 258, 263
Heald, Robert L., 63
Healey, Denis, 61
Heath, Edward R. G., 60–61
Hellman, Lillian, 81
Hemelt, G. V., 19
Henry, E. William, 243
Henry-Haye, G., 93
Hillman, Sidney, 86
Hipsley, Elmer R.: investigator of K for State Dept., 78, 91, 117, 118, 145, 147, 204, 205, 252–53; inadequacy of investigation, 97, 144; investigation of K for ACOPS, 98–102, 108–13, 248; K's attempt to locate, 341

Hirsch, Diana, 294, 302
Hiss, Alger, 260–61
Hoffman, Mr. (Office of the Chief
  Special Agent), 176
Hogan, Frank S., 321, 327, 331
Hoover, J. Edgar: memo, 7, 236,
  338; letter to CIA about K, 5,
  312–14, 328, 343; mentioned, 29,
  35, 234
Hormel, Jay, 94
Howe, Mr. (Board of Examiners,
  Foreign Service), 172
Howe, John, 231
Huberman, Leo, 140, 246–47, 265
Humphrey, Hubert, 246
Hunter, Edward, 88, 280, 281

Ickes, Harold, 125
informants, Government:
  characteristics, 12–14; description
  of K's, 99–117
Ingersoll, Ralph: editor of *PM*,
  81–84, 92, 95–96, 104, 212, 247;
  mentioned, 65, 166, 229
Internal Security Act of 1950, 72
International Ladies' Garment
  Workers' Union, 268
International Longshoreman and
  Warehouseman's Union. *See*
  Bridges, Harry
Irwin, John N., II (Jack), 60, 320

Jenkins, Roy, 61
Jones, Henry L., 51
Jones, John Paul, 56
Jossell, Len, 296–98
Journalism, Graduate School of, at
  Columbia University. *See*
  Columbia University Graduate
  School of Journalism
Jova, Joseph John, 26
Justice Department, 72, 193, 209,
  215, 340, 342

Kaiser, Philip M., 102–103, 155
Kennedy, Edward M., 198–99
Kennedy, John F., 283, 306
Kennedy, Robert, 198, 243, 249
Keogh, Jim, 259
Kiley, Richard, 292

Kimball, Arthur (author's father),
  23–24, 29–30, 34–35
Kimball, George (author's uncle),
  34, 40
Kimball, Janet Fraser: as *Time*
  researcher and Guild member,
  130–32; as author's wife, 168,
  169–72, 177, 181, 198, 219, 222,
  227, 228, 231, 237, 241, 265, 275,
  284–85, 299, 317–18, 322, 324,
  325, 326, 327, 340, 341; view of
  Whittaker Chambers, 260–61;
  alleged involvement in spy ring,
  318, 319, 330–38
Kimball Lisa (author's daughter).
  See Carlson, Lisa
Kimball, Penn Townsend (author's
  grandfather), 29–30
Kimball, Penn Townsend (author):
  childhood, 28–35; college
  memories, 44–62; as Rhodes
  Scholar, 20, 57–61; at *PM*,
  80–87, 89–90, 93–96; during World War
  II, 91–97; investigation by State
  Dept., 98–117; postwar at *Time*,
  118–34; interest in labor, 21–22,
  124–25; life 1946–1948, 163–87;
  reasons for wanting to see file,
  197–98; in politics, 1948–1950,
  218–27, 230–32; at the *New York
  Times*, 228–34; life 1954–1959,
  288–313; graduate studies, 305–
  307; attempts to see and correct
  files, 191–217; confrontations with
  informants, 244–83; employment
  at Columbia Graduate School of
  Journalism, 312–13. *See also*
  Government employment; Foreign
  Service; CIA; FBI; State Dept.;
  American Newspaper Guild
Kimball family (history), 29–35
King, James E., 60
Klaus, Mr. (State Dept. employee),
  69, 70, 71
Knight, Francis G., 316–17
Korn, Jerry, 294
Kotok, Sharon B., 340, 342, 343

labor unions: K's interest in, 21–22,
  124–25

La Follette, Robert M., Jr., 283
Lanan, Patrick, 298–303
Landers, Frary & Clark, 19, 29
Landman, Amos, 114–15
Landon, Alf, 45
Larsen, Don, 298
Larsen, Roy, 121
Lawrence, David: testimony about K, 20–25, 75, 79, 156; K's refusal to resume working for, 17, 70, 156; mentioned, 8, 63, 67, 82, 157, 229, 294, 338
Lehman, Herbert, 307
Lewis, John L., 86
Lewis, John P., 20, 250
Lewis, Kathryn, 94
Lieberman, Henry, 105
Lindberg, Charles A., 94–96, 218
Linen, James, 141, 254–55, 278
Lockett, Eddie, 205–208, 271, 341
Longworth, Alice Roosevelt, 94
Louis Harris & Associates, 306, 322, 323, 327. See also Harris, Louis
Loyalty Board, 73, 74
Luce, Clare Booth, 256
Luce, Henry: editor of *Time*, 25, 122, 254, 256; mentioned, 121, 126, 230, 259
Lyon, Fred, 26

Maas, Peter, 294
McAvoy, Eleanor, 303
McAvoy, Eleanor et al vs. Crowell-Collier, Inc., 303
McCarran, Pat, 72
McCarran rider, 72–73
McCarthy, Harry L., 51–53, 57
McCarthy, Joseph R., Jr.: K's memories of, 226–27, 283; K's *Time* article on, 227; Gilbert Cant's relationship with, 282–84; mentioned, 26, 145, 155, 238, 251, 316
McCarthy era: K's case anticipates, 15, 186–87, 249
McCorry, Joseph F., 65–67, 70, 254, 262, 263
McCreight, Allen H., 208, 210–14
McGlynn, Margaret, 333

Machak, F. M., 206
Maness, David, 294
Manning, Gordon, 294
Margolis, Sydney, 105
Marine Corps: K's service in, 3, 16–17, 76, 100, 102–104, 293; assessment of K, 20; FBI and K's associates from, 118, 152
Maritime Union. *See* Curran, Joseph
Markel, Lester, 228–30, 234
Marshall, E. G., 292
Martin, H. P., 183–86
Matthews, Thomas, 127–28, 131, 135, 171, 255, 266
Maxwell School of Public Affairs (Syracuse, New York), 306, 322
Meany, Tom, 105
Merrilat, Herb, 121
Messersmith, George E., 162
Mihailovitch, Draja, 139
Minow, Newton, 242–44
"Miss Real World." *See* "Real World, Miss"
Morros, Boris, 336–37
Morton, Sterling, 94
Murdoch, Rupert, 247
Murphy, Thomas, 233
My Ten Years as a Counterspy (Morros), 337

National Negro Congress, 108
Naval Intelligence, Office of, 7, 80, 116, 192, 195, 200, 214
Naval Investigative Service. *See* Naval Intelligence, Office of
Neville, Bob, 105
New Republic, K's employment at, 164–71, 181, 255, 337
Newspaper Guild. *See* American Newspaper Guild
New York Guild. *See* American Newspaper Guild
New York Newspaper Guild. *See* American Newspaper Guild
New York *Post*: James Wechsler an editor at, 112, 246, 247; Gilbert Cant's employment at, 280; role in 1958 Harriman-Rockefeller campaign, 247, 309–10

New York State Urban Development Corporation, 240

New York Times, The: informants on K at, 5, 13; America First ad, 94, 95; *PM* ad in FBI file, 212; K's employment at, 9, 228–34, 293, 304, 319; coverage of Harriman-Rockefeller campaign, 308; mentioned, 289, 329

Nicholson, D., 179, 180

Nixon Administration, interest in K, 240

North American Aviation strike: American Newspaper Guild's position on, 76, 151; K's position on, 79, 80, 97, 146, 157; Guild division over, 142, 149, 157; mentioned, 87, 118

Norton-Taylor, Duncan, 258, 261–63, 342

Nourse, Rebecca, 30

O'Brien, Bob, 294

O'Connor, Tom, 113–15

Office of Controls (State Dept.). *See* Controls, Office of

Office of Foreign Service. *See* Foreign Service

Office of Naval Intelligence. *See* Naval Intelligence, Office of

Office of Passport Services. *See* Passport Services, Office of

Office of Price Administration. *See* Price Administration, Office of

Office of Security (State Dept.). *See* Security, Office of (State Dept.)

"Old Tigers" (Princeton alumni), 121

"Omnibus" (TV show), 242–43, 289–92, 294, 303, 323

Osborn, Robert, 170

O'Sheel, Patrick, 103–104, 121

Oxford University, K's experiences at, 57–61

Packard, Vance, 294

Panuch, Mr., 69, 70, 71

Parker, Dorothy, 82

Passport Services, Office of, file on K, 192, 241, 316

patronage system, 222–23

Patterson, William D., 165

Petrov, 337

Peurifoy, John E., 73, 176

PM: K's employment at, 8, 39, 79–90; K's alleged political sympathies while employed at, 11, 24, 63, 67, 70, 76, 320, 329; employees' testimony about K, 20, 100–101, 105–106, 110–12, 249; FBI file (origin of K's own file) 211–13; attitude toward labor issues, 80–90; K's informants at, 246–50, 252; mentioned, 9, 13, 40, 64, 75, 92, 99, 104, 118, 140, 181, 246, 263, 265, 292, 303

Price, Raymond, 294

Price, Wes, 105

Price, William H., 194–95, 200–201, 203–204, 206, 207, 209, 214

Price Administration, Office of, K's coverage of for *Time*, 125–27

Princeton Club: informant at, 64–65; mentioned, 113, 119, 121, 167, 259, 267

Princeton University, K's experiences at, 44–57

Privacy Act, 6, 191, 192, 193, 198, 208–14, 216. *See also* Freedom of Information Act

Privacy Policy Appeals Board (State Dept.), 196, 200–208, 215, 272

Pruden, John S., 194

Pullen, Wes, 121

Quill, Mike, 308

Reagan Administration, position on citizens' files, 14, 15, 192

"Real World, Miss": description, 132–34; alleged testimony of, 136–41; K's confrontation with, 264–73; mentioned, 274, 284, 288

Reinsch, J. Leonard, 242, 244

Reserve Officer Training Corps. *See* ROTC

Reuther, Walter, 224

"Revere, Paul, II." *See* Winchell, Walter

Ribicoff, Abraham A., 198–200, 201, 206, 224

Riches, Cromwell A., 175–79

Roach, Mr. (of the FBI), 26

Rockefeller, Nelson, his campaign against Averell Harriman, 247, 307–11

Rogers, William, 87–89

Roosevelt, Eleanor, 86, 87, 224, 246, 307

Roosevelt, Franklin D.: K's family attitude toward, 23, 33–34; K's support for, 40, 45, 126; endorsed by *PM*, 82; and 1941 North American Aviation strike, 80, 146, 149, 151; mentioned, 21, 53, 65, 86, 125, 166, 168, 219, 259, 297–98, 302, 307. *See also* North American Aviation strike

Roper, Elmo, 220, 304. *See also* Elmo Roper Associates

Rose, Jonathan C., 215

Rosener, Elmer, 105

Ross, Lillian, 82, 105

Rostow, Walt, 60

ROTC, 45, 57

Rounds, Frank W., Jr., 200–22, 64, 92, 293

Rushton, Urban Joseph Peters, 53–57

Russell, Cyrus, 334

Russell, Donald ("A-R"): revocation of K's security clearance, 5, 162, 175, 176; calls for Security Committee review of K's case, 71, 75, 154; mentioned, 69, 70, 73, 147, 150, 161

Ryan, Cornelius, 294, 297

Saint, Eva Marie, 292

Salinger, Pierce, 243, 294

Salzburg Seminar in American Studies, 198, 316

Saudek, Robert, 289–90

Schiff, Dorothy (Dolly), 247, 309–11

Schiff, Jacob H., 311

Schlesinger, Arthur, Jr.: warning to Benton about K, 225; mentioned, 297, 302

Schwartz, Harry, 230

security clearance (revoked), 5, 75, 150–62. *See also* Russell, Donald

Security Committee (State Dept.): assessment of K as security risk, 67, 68, 150–62; description, 71–72; mentioned, 147

Security, Office of (State Dept.): files on K, 3, 5, 7, 328; investigation of K, 4, 38, 75, 80, 98–117; inadequacy of investigation of K, 10, 11; denial of information to K, 14–15, 200; offer to destroy K's file, 343

Shannon, James, 220

Shea, Quinlan J., Jr., 209–10

Sheils, Peter, 194–95, 206, 261

Sicre, Ricardo, 113–14, 324

Smith, Howard K., 60

Smith, Paul, 293–304

Smith, Velma T., 194

Sorensen, Theodore, 306

Soule, Henri, 229

Stalin, Joseph, K's alleged views on, 42, 43

State Dept.: classification of K as security risk, 4; file on K, 4–7, 67, 192; investigation of K, 10, 19–20, 25–26, 75–78, 217; refusal to grant K a hearing, 14; refusal to embargo K's file, 15; incompetence in investigating K, 112–13, 116; decisions about releasing K's file to him, 195–208; invitation to K to lecture in Southeast Asia, 240–41; list of subversive organizations, 268–69; offer to destroy K's file, 343; mentioned, 17, 28, 36, 52, 65, 72, 135, 286, 317, 340. *See also* Security, Office of; Controls, Office of; Security Committee

Steffans, Pete, 304

Stein, John H., 318

Stern, Alfred K. and Martha Dodd, 335–37

Stevenson, Adlai, 34, 232, 246

Stewart, Kenneth, 104, 113

Stone, I. F., 82, 105
Straight, Beatrice, 167, 337
Straight, Michael: director of *New Republic*, 165–66, 168–71; mentioned, 337
Straight family, 164
Stuart, Robert D., 94–96
Studds, Gerry E., 317

Taskar, Dana, 282
Taylor, Telford, 301–303
Thomas, John M., 202–203, 206–208
Thomas, R. J., 87
"Tigers" (Princeton alumni). See "Old Tigers"
Time magazine: K's employment at, 9, 17–18, 64, 118–34; informants at, 13, 66–67, 76, 109–10, 135–45, 158–59, 205; editorial practices, 121–23, 127–29; sexism, 129, 134, 138; K's McCarthy article for, 227; mentioned, 37, 77, 250, 293, 319. *See also* "*Time* researcher"; "*Time* supervisor"; "*Time* writer"
"*Time* researcher," K's attempts to confront, 264–73, 277. *See also* "Real World, Miss"
"*Time* supervisor": testimony of and its effects, 66–68, 75; K's attempts to confront, 254–63; mentioned, 70, 118, 141, 157, 277, 288
"*Time* writer." *See* Cant, Gilbert
Tito, Josip B., K's alleged sympathy for, 9, 138, 152, 159, 160
Transport Workers Union, 308
Trezyvant, Dick, 294
Truman, Harry S., 72, 125–26, 166, 168, 236, 305
Truman Administration: loyalty checks, 27, 73, 238; alleged harboring of Communists, 71
Turner, Stansfield, 314
TV-Radio Workshop (Ford Foundation), 289–92

UAW. *See* United Automobile Workers
United Aircraft Corporation, 96

United Automobile Workers, 25, 83, 87, 124–25, 229
United Mine Workers, 86
U.S. Department of Justice. *See* Justice Dept.
U.S. Foreign Service. *See* Foreign Service
U.S. Information Agency Advisory Commission, 242, 244
U.S. Marine Corps. *See* Marine Corps
U.S. News and World Report: K's employment at, 8, 20–25, 62, 80, 92, 124, 294; offer of job as foreign correspondent, 17. *See also* Lawrence, David
U.S. State Department. *See* State Dept.

Vance, Cyrus, 5, 193, 194, 203
Van Zandt, James E., 55
"Veterans of Future Wars," 53–57, 235
VFW. *See* "Veterans of Future Wars"

Wallace, Henry: editor-in-chief of *New Republic*, 166–70; K's roommate, 167–70, 181; K's interview with, 235–36; mentioned, 260, 337
Walton, William, 82, 105, 165, 170
Washburn, Gordon G., 335
Weaver, Pat, 307
Webster, William H., 210
Wechsler, James A.: testimony against K, 111–12, 248; as informant, 112, 157–58, 204, 206–208, 267, 271, 274, 288; K's attempted confrontation with, 246–53, 272; role in New York *Post*'s coverage of Harriman-Rockefeller campaign, 309, 311; mentioned, 83, 341
Welles, Sam, 121
Whalen, Edward R.: investigation of K, 11–12, 37–43, 113, 114; mentioned, 51

White, Byron R. ("Whizzer"), 60
White, Richard L., 19
White, Theodore H., 164, 170, 294, 300
Whitney, John Hay, 81
Winchell, Walter, 82

Winnett, G., 206
Winston, Harry, 291
Wood, Robert E., 94
Woodhouse, Chase Going, 224

Zubilin, Vassali Mikhaelivich, 337